The
SHOCK
AND AWING OF
AMERICA

Echoing Consequences
of Fear and Alienation

By
XIMENA ORTIZ

TABLE OF CONTENTS

PART III: PRESCRIPTIONS, A CLARIFICATION AND A QUIBBLE

With Special Thanks to the Society of Professional Journalists for Its Much Appreciated Grant Support

PREFACE:
A SHOCK FAR AND WIDE

America has not achieved the recovery that seems its birthright. The United States has careened into various errors domestically and abroad throughout her history, only to regain her footing. Renewal has been the recurrent theme to the nation's history. In the past ten plus years, its prospect for so long seemed a foregone conclusion. Where there is a bust, a boom must be in the offing. And so we have naturally been waiting for that pivotal moment.

That break has not come. And the reason resides in our own minds. The 9/11 attacks made a direct hit on the country's collective psyche. They delivered a shock far and wide.

The April 2013 bombings in Boston are seen through a 9/11 perspective, heightening their psychological injury. Any subsequent assaults will be regarded in the same manner, even when those attacks differ significantly in execution from the very distinctive, consecutive attacks in New York and Virginia and Pennsylvania. The 9/11 attacks carry a strong, damaging resonance.

And the impact is felt in waves. Shock at the attacks has morphed into rude surprise at our hemorrhaging abroad only to give way to anguish over an economic maelstrom that continues unabated—and has roots in the monetary aftermath of 9/11/01. The country has witnessed one calamity after another. For that reason, this crisis has delivered especially tough consequences.

And it is not only a sense of vulnerability and limitations that has descended on the American people. Revelations regarding the phenomenal scope of the National Security Administration's (NSA) phone surveillance program, for example, left many Americans feeling alienated from an increasingly secretive, intrusive state. That sense of alienation has contributed to an American cultural devolution.

What's more, the country has become dangerously polarized along economic, racial and political lines. Roughly half the country is suffering from a kind of ideology fatigue, residing in a delusional belief that the president can steer the apple cart towards prosperity—without the need for dramatic and fraught reform. Much of the other half, meanwhile, remains in the thrall of a siege mentality, subscribing to a host of hyperbolic and irrelevant fictions.

In the 2012 elections, the presidential candidates meagerly addressed the main issues facing the nation: the need for financial reform and the urgency to end America's itinerant military strikes and engagements abroad. The public seems content to keep the wars on a remote, drone-powered cruise control. And on financial reform, there is scarcely any sustained interest on any side.

America's roving crises have at times seemed to subside, only to rouse again with accrued consequences. The shockwaves of the 9/11 attacks continue to be felt for two reasons. The country continues to regress civically and culturally, and policy makers make the wrong decisions, because of the shift in the zeitgeist. In addition, the bad calls that were already made in the past, even the mistakes committed ten years or so ago, continue to create negative consequences. The people's gradual under-standing of the of the damage wrought by 9/11—more than a decade later—intensifies and prolongs the sense of vulnerabil-ity and injury, further threatening the composure that progress hinges on.

What's more, policymakers were sometimes harried, and implic-itly pressured, by their understanding of the psychological blow to the nation. They were shocked and awed by the people's shock and awe—a phenomenon that former Fed chief Alan Greenspan discusses in his memoir—albeit in different terms. Those policy actors acted in conformity with what they believed the country's state of mind was at the time, and made decisions that time has revealed to be devastating mistakes. This book looks not only at policymakers' shock and awe, the shock and awing of the American people, but also policymakers' foreboding about the public's anxi-eties and fears.

A GATEWAY BLOWN OPEN

The shock and awing of America descended swiftly after 9/11, but not immediately. Right after the attacks, the country coalesced— but was seeking answers. The W. Bush White House was first on the scene to fill out the 9/11 narrative after the attacks. Lie by lie, transgression by transgression, a new American ethos emerged.

A corrosive question mark began to take hold of the American people, threatening the national unity that proved to be fleeting. The questioning began to wear away at America's collective wisdom and consensus. All the lessons the country learned in the course of its dramatic history no longer applied. America was attacked. And the protocols of the past failed to protect her. The laws, traditions and cultural currents of before became obsolete. They were discarded with something close to panic, like some distant and inapplicable memory. The psychological impact of 9/11 has not only led to a broad-based American deterioration, it has also led to a very particular type of decline.

Shock at the attacks blew open the gates of the Third World for America. Then the United States crossed the threshold. While serial crises often keep Third World countries Third World, for

America 9/11 was a gateway crisis. And then the serial crises began.

America has suffered devastating intelligence errors, unexpected and explosive challenges and costs to the foreign wars, startling government inability to aid and protect its citizens in the face of Katrina, an economic contraction of global and fearsome proportions, ferocious divisions within the country and a deep disillusion that replaced a once hopeful attitude toward President Obama. That succession of crises not only illustrates the depth of the psychological impact, it also mirrors the problems of the Third World. In poor countries, governments often manage plodding progress, only to have it erased by the blow of the next devaluation, or military conflict, or constitutional crisis, or coup d'état.

The culture of the Third World is a temptress. It has a primordial, universal attraction. Almost all of humanity seems to have a weakness for it in the DNA. And it affects all aspects of political, judicial and social life of a country.

Before 9/11, the success of America had consisted in cordoning off the temptress. America's legal and political foundation prevents cultural inclinations from undermining the branches of government. In short, early Americans and successors worked hard to protect the country from itself.

Americans succumbed to the lure of Third Worldism after 9/11. The heavy focus on foreign threats, the disproportionate military spending, the blunt approach to warfare, the assault on digital information freedom all hint at not only a Third World country, but a Third World rouge regime. An American honor/warrior culture has risen. No president since 9/11 dares to challenge that honor culture, and both have bolstered it, to varying degrees, through props and rhetoric.

The fear and loathing related to the attacks have become bigger than Osama bin Laden and his death. Americans have begun to feel that they are threatened not by a single boogeyman or terror organization, but by an amorphous sector of humanity. Women activists who pushed back against the warrior/honor ethos have been attacked in archaic and ferocious fashion, rebuked by professional fulminators that have become engorged with influence—and money.

There is often just a thin and sparing sense of a shared, national ethos in developing nations. It is not uncommon for those countries to suffer bitter, debilitating divisions. Those traits are looking all too familiar here. They are filling America's cultural contours.

America, like other First World countries, has always had a current of traditional, honor culture running through it. Indeed, 9/11 did not give create it. But the attacks undercut the pragmatism and tolerance that have also been a prominent element of the American mindset—tempering the honor reflex.

September 11 supercharged pre-existing American tendencies—and then put them on steroids. The trauma of 9/11 became a force multiplier for America's baser instincts. The underbelly of

American culture rose into the daylight, mainstreaming animosity and militarism.

U.S. policy and culture are now reinforcing themselves mutually—and perversely. America's engagements abroad reinforce jingoism and militarism. The economic missteps have intensified an emergency and under-siege mentality. The restriction on liberties has soothed the public but also left it disaffected. While a great deal of the American public may indeed be skeptical about a host of post-9/11 changes, an ambivalence has set in—allowing cultural overlords to set the tone.

There is nothing intrinsically American about turning to violence to resolve problems, or assigning greater powers to the president, or detaining captives indefinitely without due process, or curbing rights to free speech and other liberties. But such ideas emit a strong gravitational pull. They seem to promise a short cut to results and security. And there is a popular sense that, in wake of the injury and humiliation of 9/11, America is reasserting a more elemental, stronger, less adulterated form. There is much talk of applying American power.

Such convictions contradict the Founders' principles and America's proudest traditions. And in turning to such a philosophy, Americans are indeed restoring beliefs that date back to an earlier, more elemental time—but they predate the establishment of America! There is something instinctively alluring about building up the power of a leader in the face of a perceived security threat, using force to solve problems, and patriotism or tribalism in general. The drive to champion such impulses is ancient, global.

And that may help explain why so much of the rest of the world yields to them—and, indeed, why most of the rest of the world remains poor and underdeveloped.

U.S. officialdom launched wars in a hurry after 9/11. It crafted monetary policy with a crisis mindset that was influenced by misperceived patriotism and, apparently, a panicked perception of geo-politics—rather than a clinical focus on economic realities. Those distorted monetary decisions did not cause the 2008 meltdown—but they greased the freefall. A continuing crisis mindset prevented two administrations from dealing with the root weaknesses in the financial system, which could set the stage for a subsequent crisis, or round of crises.

Those tendencies fit into a pattern. Third World countries are so often pressured into reaction mode. Policy makers are constantly facing emergencies, and lack the space and time to craft far-seeing policy. This has become America's affliction.

In making the case for America's decline, this book draws only from the official story provided by U.S. officialdom or well established newspapers and journalists and policy experts. This is not to discount the ground-breaking work of the alternative media, but rather to stress the fact that America's devolution has become so incontrovertible, that the mainstream outlets provide more than enough compelling material.

America entered a new common era (NCE) after 9/11. It has become clear—given the changes of presidents of differing political persuasions, shifts in congressional majorities, and passage of time—that America is mired in the era. The sum of the changes in the American ethos and policy mark an age of unprecedented action—and inaction. Looked at individually, they may not seem particularly alarming. But in the collective, they sweep categories and have altered America's character.

The United States is on its way to becoming the richest country in the world with, discordantly enough, retrograde attributes. It is becoming an economic superpower with Third-World proclivities. That paradox will not last forever.

America's distinction from the Third World is blurring. This is primarily due to the fact that the most significant impact related to 9/11 belongs to the invisible realm—the hearts and minds of the American people. The attacks of September 11th hang on the American psyche like the imperceptible toxicity of Ground Zero's noxious air. They have driven the country's most consequential actions. They define the zeitgeist.

SHOCK AND AWE: THE STRATEGY

Much of the media has been reticent to clinically examine the terrorists themselves, just what theories went behind their 9/11 scheme and, most importantly, what those factors mean for America. There has been healthy debate on the terrorists' geopolitical motivations in the more avante-guard and edgier forums. But even in those outlets, there has been scarce questioning about the sweeping strategy of the attackers themselves and just what the long-term psychological fallout could be for the United States.

America's attackers appear to have cribbed from cutting-edge theory. They did not just get lucky. While they had access to just a small budget, they certainly seem to have been intimately aided by a military mind, versed in theory.

And in hindsight, it appears that, in some macabre twist of irony, one of the strategies that the hijackers appear to have borrowed from is Shock and Awe—the very proposal that the W. Bush administration later attempted to apply to Iraq. This is not to say that the attackers replicated the theory down to the letter, but the parallels are dramatic. Indeed, the 9/11 attacks were distinct from any terrorist assault in world history, for a host of reasons. The attacks made a break from the traditional jihadi-attack approach.

"Death by 1,000 cuts" has long been the staple jihadi's strategy for challenging a superior power. Cut by cut by cut, the aim is to cumulatively bleed a better armed and funded country. That familiar strategy has been used against Israel, India and Russia—causing a formidable attack in the collective.

But launching a sum of assaults requires a proximity to your target. And that is all but impossible for jihadists to deploy against the United States. Jihadi camps are oceans away from America, and terrorists simply cannot follow up on attacks in any quick succession.

So those that struck America on September 11th broke with the strategy that has characterized terrorist attacks throughout history. The 9/11 attacks—which entailed a horrifying, well-planned, coordinated assault carried out on a single day—remain unprecedented. It has been the only attack to truly break from the 1,000 cut strategy.

Indeed, it is no accident that the attacks wreaked such a tremendous psychological toll. They were shock and awe on the cheap—in conformance with the limitations that attackers faced in lashing out at the greatest power the world has ever known. Of course, the terrorists did not have the power to inflict any materially significant and long standing economic or strategic harm by their own accord. But they were successful in goading America to inflict material injury upon itself.

The strategy and impact of the 9/11 attacks parallel the Shock and Awe ideas put forward by elite, U.S. strategic experts in October 1996. Washington dusted off and attempted to apply Shock and Awe in Iraq in 2003. Undoubtedly, the 9/11 attacks caused a psychological reaction that far outstrips their direct physical damage, as the theory recommends. The 9/11 attackers targeted the psychological composure not only of the public, but also U.S. policy makers at the highest, most sophisticated level, as the following pages maintain. In terms of those who hijacked the planes, the force size was miniscule, a principle of shock and awe brought to an extreme. As the strategy calls for, the hijackers struck multiple spheres of American society, injuring key civilian, military, financial and transport structures. The diversity and scale of the damage punctuated a broad sense of vulnerability. What's more, the theory calls for leveraging existing technologies of America's private sector in warfare. The hijackers did so by using commercial airliners as instruments of war—just not (of course) as the shock and awe architects had envisioned.

In laying out the Shock and Awe theory, the authors advised that, in order to unleash it effectively, the United States had to "get into the minds of the adversary far more deeply than we have in the past" and acquire a "cultural understanding" of that adversary. The 9/11 architects seem to have acquired such an understanding of the American mindset and security protocols. They put that knowledge to savage effect. In contrast, America seemed to pay little attention to cultural intelligence in executing its own attempt at Shock and Awe in Iraq. And Washington continues to project its own desires and objectives in a culturally tone deaf manner in Afghanistan and beyond.

In wake of 9/11, the U.S. architects of the shock and awe theory seem eerily prescient today. The U.S. architects of shock and awe warned, back in 1996, when they put their ideas to paper:

"...faced with American military superiority in ships, tanks, air-craft, weapons and, most importantly, in competent fighting personnel, potential adversaries may try to change the terms of future conflict and make as irrelevant as possible these U. S. advantages. We proceed at our own risk if dismiss this possibility."

The hijackers and their handlers seem to have heeded this advice. They did change the terms of the conflict, in trying to sidestep and marginalize America's conventional superiorities. America's technological prowess on the battlefield has become a tactical advantage but a strategic liability, with drone attacks killing targets, and creating new recruits with a blood score to settle with America. The people's trust in government allowed two administrations to launch wars—and continue them through scantily substantiated claims of "turning the corner." U.S. financial prowess and unmatched command of credit has allowed the government to create dangerous bubbles, moral hazards and indebt itself to stratospheric levels. What's more, that access to credit has allowed two administrations to perpetuate conflict by way of machine and mercenary. Surely, the 9/11 masterminds never dreamed a shocked America would heap such ruin onto itself, but they may have anticipated some degree of self-inflicted damage.

And therein is the key difference between shock and awe theory and the apparent intentions of the 9/11 attackers. As a theory, shock and awe is geared towards nullifying an adversary's will to resist by assuming swift and overwhelming dominance. A group like al Qaeda could never achieve such feat over a country like America. But if the conventional wisdom of most al Qaeda experts is correct, the strategy of 9/11 masterminds was to provoke America onto the battlefield of Muslims lands—not to eliminate its will to fight. And that is precisely where the terrorists' aims were more labyrinthine than the American shock and awe theory.

And, of course, the American shock and awe architects did not envision or recommend suicide attacks. No U.S. strategist would ever recommend such a thing. It is anathema to American thinking. But the suicidal element of the 9/11 attacks gave them a particularly traumatic punch. Gerald W. Thomas, who served in VT-4, described the experience of surviving a Japanese Kamikaze attack in the blog "Air Group 4; Casablanca to Tokyo":

"I know something of the fear and panic that is generated when Kamikazes approached our Navy Task Force. I saw our ships' gunners so jittery by the presence of Kamikazes that they fired on our own planes returning from strikes on Japanese targets.

…As we were returning to the States in May 1945, we were ordered not to mention the word "Kamikaze" or to mention damage caused by these suicide tactics. The Navy did not want US citizens to know the extent of damage, nor did the Navy want the Japanese to know how effective these tactics were. We have similar challenges today."

Despite those differences, the 9/11 attackers seem to have helped themselves extensively to the central concepts of Shock and Awe theory. Given the outsized impact of 9/11, the only country to have officially attempted to wreak Shock and Awe warfare appears to have been a victim of it.

This is not to exaggerate the reach and capabilities of the 9/11 attackers, which has already become a cottage industry. Indeed, the attackers could hardly have anticipated that America would invert its natural geo-political, economic, civic and cultural advantages to such a degree. And as stated before, the attackers' war chest was minimal. But their advantage was conceptual.

And America's disadvantages have been made in the mind, as well. This book illustrates the cost of a country collectively losing its composure and its vitality. It chronicles the great psychological undertow that the 9/11 attacks originated. A shock of 9/11's magnitude can certainly sow ruinous paranoia, fear and rage. It can also contribute to a wide ranging disengagement, escapism, and, therefore, the ebbing of civic enthusiasm, of the sort that once defined and distinguished America. In a roundabout way, these pages tally up America's losses—with an eventual renewal and restoration in mind. They are a call to strong-willed, sober decision making as a means of reclaiming America's natural advantages.

PART I:
GOING SOUTH
A THIRD-WORLDING AMERICA

CHAPTER 1
SUFFER THE AL-EASING
Al Qaeda-phobia at the Monetary Levers

America is trapped in an economic purgatory. Policymakers in 2008 were able to beat back the palpable financial Armageddon, but they have come far from delivering a recovery. Indeed, the country, and the global economy, has barely made headway in the past few years.

The crisis itself has had a surreal, intangible quality to it. Policy makers faced an economic vortex that emerged from the depths of the surreal, e-trading sphere–where time is measured in milliseconds and volumes are quantified in the billions. While it is true that the crisis was born in the real world, by physical bankers and homeowners signing real loans, the international financial institutions globalized and scattered the risk to phenomenal, incomprehensible levels. When that vast, global, Internet-armed community shifted psychologically, the impact was colossal.

Policymakers came face to face with, potentially, trillions in losses buffeting the system—and they punted. They threw money at the problem, staving off a complete meltdown but failing to purchase any recovery. And there will be no recovery because officialdom never dealt with the underlying financial malignancy. Amid that opacity, investor confidence has failed to return.

To understand the dimensions and origins of America's current predicament, it is necessary to take a brief look back at the recent past—and weigh just how the shock and awe of the main protagonists contributed to the errors plaguing the country, laying the ground for the stupefied and compromised decision-making that continues to this day.

PATRIOTIC MUSIC FROM THE PARAPET

A hazardous dust was just settling on Ground Zero when America's economic affliction began. Amid the very top echelon of America's corporate leadership, unnamed fear and pessimism descended and spread like a fog. The material impact of 9/11 was negligible, but it dealt an outsized psychological impact. Amid pre-existing challenges for the economy, investor confidence simply collapsed.

Policy makers looked to the obvious choice for a boost to the economy: the Fed. It executed the most drastic monetary policy to be deployed since central banks were given the monetary levers in wake of WWII. U.S. financial institutions were deluged with free cash. The amount of liquidity to hit financial institutions, virtually free of charge, is difficult to exaggerate.

And while the much-maligned Fed did not cause the greatest crisis since the Great Depression, it greased the wheels of the overleveraging that was the impetus of the meltdown. The Fed's moves unleashed a tsunami of liquidity, and the banks threw a dangerous party with it. Again, that tsunami of cash did not cause the housing bubble and the resultant trillions of dollars in uncollateralized liabilities, but it did abet the recklessness.

A look back at the mentality and state of mind surrounding those fateful decisions to incrementally switch the monetary engine to full hilt is perhaps more revealing and troubling than the monetary actions themselves. After all, something prompted Fed chief Alan Greenspan—wont to caution against irrational exuberance—to break with a tradition of relative restraint. Another member of the Fed's decision-making board exhibited even more worrisome logic after 9/11—not at all befitting a financial technocrat.

In the aftermath of the attacks, America's most sophisticated and politically insulated financial policymaking body—otherwise known as the Federal Open Market Committee—succumbed to the pull of 9/11 mentality. Although the Fed is far removed from the turbulence of American politics, it appears that political (and geopolitical) issues encroached on the board's decision making. The most powerful members of the FOMC—the board chairman,

Greenspan, and the president of the New York Federal Reserve, William McDonough—became entrenched in the 9/11 zeitgeist.

As bizarre as it may seem, at the landmark September 17th, 2001, policymaking meeting, McDonough recommended that the Fed take monetary action that not only made economic sense, but was also patriotic. He said at the meeting that he agreed with a recommendation by Greenspan to cut the federal funds rate target and the discount rate by 50 basis points. And before he broached any economic issues whatsoever, he made a revealing comment:

"It is the right thing for the Federal Reserve to show the flag at this awesome, awful moment in our country's history. The timing of the action before the major markets of the United States open this morning I think is absolutely ideal."

Presumably, what McDonough had in mind was that the Fed board members would act not just as economists, but as patriots. Needless to say, such a response was understandable in light of the horror America had just been buffeted by. But it now looks to have been a problematic posturing in economic terms. Rather than focusing on a show of economic might, the Fed should have been laying the groundwork for real and sustainable economic recovery. The Fed's monetary action that day, in combination with subsequent monetary acceleration policies, contributed to a devastating confluence of economic and deregulatory factors—not too unlike other sweeping policy decisions that were wrapped in the flag.

After the Committee discussed the weighty economic issues it faced, McDonough pronounced:

"Over time, we will be moving our people back to lower Manhattan. In the meantime we have the [New York Federal Reserve] building wrapped in bunting, we have a big flag flying, and we're playing patriotic music from the parapet."

Indeed, that comment seems completely out of place at an FOMC meeting. McDonough was addressing his fellow policy-making board members, not counterparts in a military junta. The Fed should play no part in brandishing the props of patriotism. Rather than engineering a patriotic rebound, replete with "patriotic music from the parapet," America would have been better served by empirical analysis. This is obviously easier said than done, but if the United States is going to extricate itself from its downward trend, it has to soberly consider where it erred regardless of how well intentioned the actions might have been.

But perhaps more worrisome than McDonough's curious impulse to wave the flag through monetary action were the sweeping, non-financial variables that Greenspan was weighing in the aftermath of 9/11. Two days after the 9/11 attacks, the FOMC held a conference call. According to the transcripts, Greenspan's usual laser-like focus seemed dispersed, and he began discussing seemingly random issues, like the condolences expressed by the head of the central bank of the United Arab Emirates. Greenspan's own memoir, "*The Age of Turbulence*", in conjunction with his interviews following up the book, put his comment about the UAE in context.

It turns out that in wake of 9/11, the Fed chairman harbored cataclysmic concerns about the former Saddam Hussein regime in Iraq and his potential ability to block America's access to oil. He expressed those fears to Amy Goodman in "Democracy Now!" in September 2007:

"The point I was making was that if there were no oil under the sands of Iraq, Saddam Hussein would have never been able to accumulate the resources which enabled him to threaten his neighbors, Iran, Kuwait, Saudi Arabia. And having watched him for thirty years, I was very fearful that he, if he ever achieved—and I thought he might very well be able to buy one—an atomic device, he would have essentially endeavored and perhaps succeeded in controlling the flow of oil through the Straits of Hormuz, which is the channel through which eighteen or nineteen million barrels a day of the world's eighty-five million barrel crude oil production flows. Had he decided to shut down, say, seven million barrels a day, which he could have done if he controlled, he could have essentially also shut down a significant part of economic activity throughout the world.

The size of the threat that he posed, as I saw it emerging, I thought was scary. And so, getting him out of office or getting him out of the control position he was in, I thought, was essential."

In another interview with Greg Ip of The Wall Street Journal, Greenspan reiterated his opinion about Iraq:

"My view of the second Gulf War was that getting Saddam out of there was very important, but had nothing to do with weapons of mass destruction, it had to do with oil."

Greenspan appeared to be in an almost paranoid state of mind after 9/11. He ascribed to Hussein a nuclear potential that the tyrant did not come close to possessing, as we now know. While that alarm may have been understandable in light of the W. administration's pronouncements, Greenspan's views were erroneous and harmful.

Surely, there was no one in the W. Bush administration who would have been interested in talking Greenspan down from his sweeping concerns. Politically speaking, the W. Bush administration could have only benefited from Greenspan's panic, if such a response contributed to an expansionary monetary policy. Indeed, if Greenspan did have geo-political talks with W. Bush officials, then it is only logical to assume that they would have told the Fed chief the same things they told the American people. And what they said is in the public record, including their stated certainty that Hussein had weapons of mass destruction and suggestions, by innuendo, that Hussein had ties with al Qaeda.

At any rate, we know that Greenspan talked geo-politics with Bush officials because he has acknowledged doing so. In the aforementioned interview, Ip asked the usually circumscribed Greenspan if he shared his concerns with then-Vice President Cheney and Defense Secretary of Defense Donald Rumsfeld. "Oh yeah," responded Greenspan succinctly. If the vice president and the defense minister believed a certain monetary policy should accompany a war effort, they clearly had an opportunity to discuss it with the Fed chairman.

In his own memoir, "Age of Turbulence," Greenspan gives the reader a privileged glimpse into his thoughts immediately after 9/11. He writes about his fear that America would be struck again in another attack that could dwarf 9/11, such as a nuclear assault. The Fed chairman said: "on the record I took a less pessimistic stance because if I had fully expressed what I thought the probabilities were, I'd scare the markets half to death." And while he no doubt endeavored to make rational decisions while leading FOMC meetings, Greenspan appears to have been appreciably knocked off balance by the attacks and his expectation of a devastating sequel.

Greenspan never acknowledged that his state of mind led him to make monetary errors, but he did cryptically admit: "Anticipating a second terrorist attack was probably one of the worst predictions I ever made." In light of what is now known about the state of mind of key Fed decision makers, some logical but painful questions arise out of the economic wreckage:

- Did the Fed, out of a misguided sense of patriotism, set the monetary pump at full blast to create the appearance of economic resilience, to the detriment of a real and sustainable recovery?

- Was the Fed driven in part by a desire to prevent al Qaeda from scoring points against the mightiest economy in the world? Was that the flag-waving monetary action that McDonough was referring to? Was the Fed (in conjunction with the federal government) trying to create a "decent interval" between the date of the attacks and a downturn of the economy?

- And finally, did Greenspan's concerns about oil and Saddam Hussein compel him to maintain a monetary environment conducive to the launching of the war in Iraq? Did he perceive a responsibility to prime the monetary pump in the run up to war?

If the answers are yes, then the Fed in effect allowed itself to be goaded into monetary policy that facilitated the worst crisis in post-WWII global history. And of course, the protracted financial malaise has proven to be as financially ruinous as the wars have been disastrous strategically. And like the wars, ordinary Americans have borne the brunt.

And if the answers are yes, there is another matter to think about. The Federal Reserve has always been the most respected central bank in the world, with only perhaps the German Bundesbank commanding comparable credibility. Central to that credibility has been the Fed's independence from political *sturm und drag*. That independence and credibility is a First World phenomenon. Central banks in the Third World are often more susceptible to political pressures. The Fed had established a legacy, in the eyes of much of the world, of a bedrock institution, with as much prominence as, say, U.S. courts.

And so if the space between the Fed and the executive is seen as narrowing, the Fed stands to lose more than its credibility. It is also going to forfeit some of its First World luster. Put simply, it more strikingly resembles its counterparts in the Third World, even if it retains legal autonomy. And it is therefore natural that Americans will then look to modifying the Fed in some way as part of an effort not only to restore the credibility of the monetary system, but also to reclaim the Fed's First World clout.

Although Greenspan and McDonough may not have given it much thought, non-economic variables encroached on their considerations—that is clear from the public record. From one day to another, the Fed became co-opted and began serving an agenda that should have remained well apart from monetary calculations. And that was in large part a function of 9/11 and its shock and awe impact. The Fed was compromised in the crisis.

This is not to say that the Fed was always kept wholly sterile of any political contamination before 9/11. And no Fed chairman has ever been in the running for sanctification. But the undermining of clinical decision-making at the Fed reached an extreme after 9/11—and indeed prompted the institution to take actions it has never taken before. For some reason, Greenspan broke with his more cautious and effective response to the 1994 recession.

CEOS SHOCKED AND AWED

In an October 2003 speech, Anthony M. Santomero, president of the Federal Reserve Bank of Philadelphia assessed the nature of the 9/11 damage.

Certainly, the most profound event affecting the course of the recent business cycle would have to be the attacks of September 11. It goes without saying that September 11 stands as one of the most shocking and tragic episodes in our nation's history. But I want to step back for a few moments and focus on its macroeconomic repercussions.

The supply side effects of September 11 were visible enough. We saw the great loss of life, and the horrific sights of the collapsing towers, the damaged Pentagon, and the smoldering wreckage of a jet in western Pennsylvania. But against the backdrop of our collective resources — our nation's labor force and infrastructure — the purely economic consequence of the loss of productive capacity must be assessed as relatively small.

Materially, the economic damage was fundamentally, as Santomero put it, relatively small. And yet today, it appears that the psychological impact of the attacks prompted staggering losses. Santomero in his speech points to the important element of fear. After the Fed put in motion the first wave of monetary expansion, it was not the fear of the masses that set the country on a downward spiral. It was instead the trepidation of the most sophisticated players.

America's CEOs had been shocked and awed. And despite the loose money available, they continued to sit it out. Santomero sums up the chain of events:

All things considered, consumer spending came back relatively quickly. But for businesses, it was a much different story. Already left with an overhang of equipment from the investment boom of the late 1990s, businesses confronted these new uncertainties about the future and saw new reasons to defer and delay investment spending.

The events that followed in the aftermath of September 11 — the anthrax attacks, and then the wars in Afghanistan and Iraq — only served to heighten these uncertainties. In the case of Iraq, the uncertainties were extended and indeed still remain.

In short, in an effort to lure CEOs toward capital expenditures, the Fed continued lowering rates. In the end, it helped to build a hazardous bubble. All that free money had to go somewhere. And corporate America was not a taker. So during the Great Easing, financial institutions found predatory opportunities in the white-picket, American dream: home ownership.

But the Fed is far from the only culprit in the crisis. The banks and their overleveraging were the chief agents of disaster. And the banks' culpability appears all the more rank considering the millions of dollars they spent lobbying to get regulations relaxed—the very rules that were constructed to prevent overleveraging. To those pre-existing conditions, the Fed added a phenomenal dose of monetary lubrication. Regulations had already been relaxed under the Clinton administration and money was now free.

A BAILOUT OF NECESSITY!

Emergency measures are a hallmark of Third World policy making. In the midst of an economic crisis, all manner of urgent, emergency, vital, nation-saving action must be taken immediately, now, now, now! There's no time to consider the fine print, or consequences! Action is needed immediately to prevent the indefinite punishment of global investor alienation. No time to consider moral hazards! There's a crisis. No time to think about economic blowback and the potential creation of new economic weaknesses. Didn't you hear? There's a CRISIS! And the incoming economic maelstrom could take the whole country, including your house and family, into its unforgiving vortex.

Indeed, such propensity and even penchant for under-the-gun decision making seems to be in the bloodstream of Third World countries. It rallies and awakens the country. It gives the heads of state an air of gravity and consequence. It is something of an addiction. In Latin America, a pervading culture of urgency and drama has taken root and has never been eradicated.

Taking a multi-decade view of Latin America, the political and economic pendulum has swung wildly, from experiments with statism, sometimes under military regime, as in the case of Brazil;

to democratic statism; to Marxist revolution; to military regime with laissez faire policies; to the mixed and varied status quo of today.

Very often, the crises have been real and only slightly exaggerated rhetorically. Many governments have really ridden off an economic precipice and dragged almost an entire nation into financial ruin—at least temporarily. But the policy remedies the governments peddle have often been complete and utter hyperbole. Crises would not be staved off because legislators and the executive act at that very instance, without a moment's consideration—now, now, now, now.

The crisis is usually long in the making, and after months and years of inaction in key areas, policy makers go into frenzied overdrive. It's such a familiar sequence of events. And it is a retracing of those steps that has taken Latin America and other regions all over the political and economic landscape. After the crisis has made landfall, or is narrowly averted, there is little energy left for the government's self-reflection. The stage is set for the next set of calamities—and extremes.

In this regard, few countries can offer such a colorful example as Argentina—a high velocity country of tremendous potential, that has for decades careened down its emergency rails, with no foreseeable escape. And few policies could better exemplify a Third World approach to economic policy than Argentina's Decrees of Urgency and Necessity that became a signature policy of former Argentine President Menem.

Under Menem, Argentina had not recovered economically from its past war with Britain and the profligacy of the military junta. It was facing genuine crisis. Menem became unique, even by Third World standards, for pushing through "urgent" economic and fiscal policy. He invoked 472 Decrees of Urgency and Necessity (the term is pure tragic-comedy) from 1989 to 1998, and he refined the Third World art of crony capitalism and centralizing state power. He used privatizations as form of political patronage, doling out the country's assets at below market prices, with no bidding, no vetting (sound familiar!).

America's a la carte bank bailouts, which transferred enormous risk from favored banks to the government, has some shades of Menem's Decrees of Urgency and Necessity. The general principles became America's modus operandi after the banking crisis hit. The U.S. Treasury had been depleted by the wars. The American people had already been called upon to go out and spend out of patriotic conviction. They were maxed out.

So America requested, in fine, Menemesque fashion—what else?—its own bipartisan policies of Urgency and Necessity—of the sort the American people had never seen before, but which the inhabitants of the Third World are now resigned to. After W. Bush had already instituted a first round of extraordinary bank bailouts under TARP, Larry Summers (on behalf of president elect Obama, who was soon to be inaugurated) made the appeal for the second round of TARP funds. He said, in fine Third World fashion, that the need for billions of dollars was "imminent and urgent."

The Fed's decision to take ownership of mortgage-backed securities that were once held by financial institutions—transferring the risk from the institutions right onto the U.S. taxpayer—is a first in American history. It has never been done before. In enacting that policy, the U.S. government courted considerable moral hazard, in Third World style.

In asking for the money in a hurry, Summers pledged the most elevated objectives, promising it would go toward a "sweeping effort" to save homeowners threatened with foreclosure and small banks and businesses, along with corporate giants. Obama, in turn, promised to improve TARP's transparency, but his Treasury Department later refused to do just that—particularly when Treasury attempted to reign in the independence of the congressionally mandated watchdog of TARP, run by Neil Barofsky.

But the TARP money that the big banks got from the government, after all, is only the very beginning of the bailout, and not the most significant part. Indeed, for all the murkiness surrounding TARP, it is still the most transparent element of the bailout. TARP amounts to small change when compared to the other government programs geared towards rescuing the big banks, which form an arcane array of acronyms: TLGP, TALF, PPIP, SMDIA.

Treasury's propping up of bankrupt government-sponsored entities (Freddie and Fannie Mac)—at the taxpayer's risk and expense—is also probably more significant than TARP. Since the big banks were exposed to Freddie and Fannie obligations, the bailout of those entities was, in effect, another bailout of the big banks. Ah, but the bailout does not end there. In addition, the Fed bought a hair-raising $1 trillion in mortgage-backed securities, which helps bolster the value of those securities for the big banks that hold them. The Congressional Budget Office estimates that Treasury's bailout of the GSEs will cost the taxpayers approximately $380 billion through fiscal year 2021.

The government's convoluted support of the big banks is modeled on Third World schemes. But still, there is one crucial difference. In the Third World, banks and their creditors are forced to reckon with reality. The banks are forced to restructure and they pay only part of their outstanding obligations. Their creditors must take a haircut.

But the United States can afford to court delusions for a long period of time. And that is just what Obama decided he would do, perpetuating the emergency-type policies of his predecessor. Faced with decisions of enormous importance, the president extended half-measures. And he never repositioned the policy to deal more fundamentally with the deep blow the banks' dealt to the U.S.—and indeed the world—economy. Since 9/11, the president and chief policy makers have been in reaction mode.

According to Jose Barrionuevo—who in 2004 and 2005 led the team of investment banks that restructured Argentina's $104 billion sovereign defaulted debt in what remains the largest sovereign debt restructuring in history—March 2009 was a critical moment in the U.S. and global financial crisis. At that point, the Obama administration announced that it was changing the accounting system and that it would no longer require banks to price its assets at market value. That practice, which the government (with no intended sense of irony) dubbed "fair evaluation," allowed banks to price their assets at whatever they deemed them to be worth.

"And obviously everyone prices really high, so [that on paper] you don't have losses. But that doesn't matter, because everyone knows that what you are holding is garbage," said Barrionuevo, who joined StormHarbour hedge fund in 2010.

That may seem like 2008's story. But it remains trenchant today for the plain fact that the mortgage-backed securities that the banks still hold remain worthless (more or less) because U.S. housing values have not recovered. But it is not only that the assets are essentially garbage. The main problem is that to buy those now worthless securities, the banks borrowed to the hilt. And now the banks have no collateral against that mountain of debt. It is difficult to exaggerate how overleveraged these institutions have become.

And so after all the money that has been spent on rescuing the moribund banking industry and reviving the economy through stimulus, the banks are still holding "garbage." And the "fair evaluation" that Washington sanctioned in 2009 may put gift-wrapping on the numbers, but U.S. investors still know what they are.

And why is the garbage so prevalent, years after the initial meltdown? Because the bailouts prevented U.S. banks from having to restructure. And since there has been no restructuring, the banks are still holding ribbon-wrapped, uncollateralized liabilities. As Barrionuevo put it: "what's interesting is that most people voted against [the Democrats in the November 2010 mid-term election] because they basically were voting against how Obama **solved** the crisis. Most people think the crisis has been resolved. They have yet to find out that it wasn't resolved, and that's when it's going to get worse. Because that's when [the people] are going to get really upset."

Some people already are. They are perhaps not so much upset as decidedly pessimistic. America's most sophisticated (and unsophisticated!) CEOs are still declining to hire American workers not because they don't have the funds to do it, but because their outlook for the economy stays their hand. And blame for that rests with the president. Banks may have gotten what they wanted, but the corporate sector isn't buying in to the economy, or the nation's leadership. Underlying a stagnating economy is a lack of confidence in the president.

"A lot of people, when they voted for president Obama, and actually I was one of them," Barrionuevo said, "we paid a lot of attention when he said he was prepared to make the tough choices that needed to be made. And a lot of us felt like he knew what he was talking about. And it was very evident by late March of 2009, which is when they decided to just do some artificial accounting and not solve anything, that he was not prepared to make any tough choices."

By forfeiting the touch choices and a leadership position, Obama put the American people in harm's way, financially speaking,

Barrionuevo explained. And in doing so, Obama broke with an American tradition of presidential leadership:

"The emphasis [of the Obama administration] to this day has been to preserve the interests of those that actually created the crisis. I don't know why that's been the emphasis, but that's what it's been. You go back to the Great Depression, or even the crisis of 1907 when Teddy Roosevelt was president, in every one of those instances, the presidents chose to be on the side of the American people, to try to limit their losses. Because at the end of the day, the people will always suffer, there's no way around it. You have a recession, of course, the people will always suffer. But you want to try to mitigate that and assign the cost in a more proportional way—basically assessing that cost to those that created the crisis.

It's the first time in the history of this country that you have a president that chose exactly the opposite. He assessed that cost in a disproportionate manner on the people and obviously very little on the banks."

To resolve the crisis, the United States should take its cue from the Third World, Barrionuevo said. That is not to equate U.S. problems with the more sweeping troubles of underdeveloped countries, but the magnitude is so colossal that Washington must undertake full-blown crisis management, of the sort more typically used in Third World countries.

First, consider the extent of the problem. The leverage of financial institutions was sky high in the pre-meltdown period. Lehman is believed to have used a ratio of liabilities to assets of about 45 to 1. The Bear Stearns ratio was probably about 40 to 1 and the average for the banking system was likely around 15 to 1, said Barrionuevo. And so taking the average rate of 15, for every $16 dollars the banks bought of mortgage-backed assets, they used $1 that they owned and borrowed $15. And when the value of those mortgage-backed securities was wiped out by the freefall in housing prices, the banks were left with $15 in obligations for every $1 they owned.

To put the consequences of that overleveraging into the context, Barrionuevo explains: "If you're going to use 15 to 1 [as an average leverage ratio], and we know we have seen basically about 2 trillion in mortgages [that served as collateral] go under, then you know that potentially, not definitely, but potentially, we could be talking about something close to 2 trillion times 15—about $30 trillion in compromised assets, which is twice the size of the U.S. economy. And indeed, that's a very scary number."

Apparently, the policy makers themselves were shaken by the proportions of the problem. With their backs up against an intimidating wall of financial adversity, the policymakers just didn't rise to the occasion. The crisis didn't motivate a reckoning with the circumstances, of the sort that might generate temporary grief but lays the groundwork for a sustainable recovery. Rather than taking control of the crisis, a sense of crisis claimed the policymakers.

Whether the policymakers subscribed to cynicism or delusion is unclear. But in crucial areas, they just failed to mobilize as the circumstances required. Barrionuevo believes that a First World perspective may have impaired the decision making: "There's very little experience in Europe and the US with crisis and most policy makers tend to think of them even today as liquidity crises. So their reaction is always to provide liquidity—just throw money at the problem. Because they think that if they fix the cash flow that will take care of the problem. And that is actually wrong because if you have a solvency crisis, what happens is that your entire stock of debt matters, not just what is coming due, which is the cash flow portion."

When a team led by Barrionuevo worked on Argentina's restructuring, they finally sized up the depth of the problem. They arrived at a number—a real number. And the Argentine government could begin to deal with it. That, of course, is a step yet to be taken in the United States and Europe.

The key, though, is that the limitations of the Argentine economy forced upon the government and the banking system a measure of transparency and responsibility. And so in this case, as with so many other current problems, America's preeminence has become a liability of sorts. The country's advantages morph into disadvantages. To some degree, the United States has become a victim of its own economic wherewithal.

The banks were able to leverage to such an enormous degree because they were perceived to be backed implicitly by the largest economy in the world. That overleveraging became so immense, that even the U.S. government could not assume all the liabilities.

And America could not turn to a lender of last resort, because it is the lender of last resort.

So America's vast resources have bought the banks time, but they have not bought a recovery. And so eventually, the banks will have to restructure, according to Barrionuevo and others, because the system will demand it. The country would have been better served if the restructuring had been handled earlier, in an orderly manner.

Unlike Third World countries that suffer a drop in the value of their currency in wake of a crisis, the United States cannot export its way out of trouble. The global economy has been driven in such a unipolar manner by the U.S. economic engine that the United States cannot look towards the consumption of other countries as a way out of the hole. The multipolarity—in economic and strategic terms—that was expected to emerge as a result of the waning of U.S. strength has not appeared, to the extent it was once expected to.

There are some engines of growth in the midst of the ongoing global lethargy, such as Brazil, but nothing powerful enough to compel a global recovery—not by a long shot. The crisis is here, and everywhere. The patchouli-scented youth that repeatedly hit the streets of DC in the 1990s with their towering, paper-mache effigies have been correct, after all, in highlighting the breadth of the all-encompassing vulnerabilities of the global financial system. And the shock of 9/11 helped the prophecy to come true.

Press coverage of America's ongoing financial crisis initially focused on the urgency of "saving the patient," and since then has scarcely addressed what long-term risks have been created or what remedies should now be employed. Treasury's and the Fed's post-crisis intervention has prompted financial institutions to become even bigger, and cast an even more threatening shadow. More than ever, the banks have America, and the world, by the too-big-to-fail vital organs and are offered special protection through exclusive benefits and a veil of accounting opacity. These circumstances carry echoes of Third World crises. The sacrifices demanded of America's ordinary people may not stave off a phase 2 crisis indefinitely.

GET YOUR IEBS! TREASURY'S IMPROVISED EXPLOSIVE BONDS

There is an old adage about deficits and starving the beast. But there is no bumper-sticker sound-bite about quartering the beast via a coordinated attack, deploying ticking time bombs. That is probably because the idea of amputating the beast—or rather the American federal government—may alarm the electorate a little too much. Many Americans calling for fiscal austerity still want the hungry beast to deliver Medicare and Social Security payments and to foot the bill for trillion-dollar wars. Eventually, all those expenses will detonate.

In wake of the borrowing for the wars and other new spending, America's deficit and debt begins to mirror the estimates of

Argentina and other Third World countries in times of crisis. In their book, "The Three Trillion Dollar War," Joseph Stiglitz and Linda Bilmes argue that, taking a realistic to moderate perspective through 2017, America's financing costs of Iraq war-related debt exceeds $2 trillion. That figure does not include the financing costs for Afghanistan (the book deals with the costs of Iraq war-financing alone), nor does it include the longer-term borrowing costs of covering veteran's benefits and health care.

Economists have not reached a consensus on when the U.S. debt level would reach a tipping point and foment a full blown disaster. There are numerous Third World countries that have debt levels lower than America's, and vice versa. The CIA calculates rankings based on debt-to-GDP ratios, but they are somewhat unreliable because the official data of many Third World countries is half-baked.

Importantly, though, America is in new territory now, when it comes to debt. So the country can no longer look towards past business cycles as an indication that everything will be OK going forward. According to a CBO report: "Over the past few years, U.S. government debt held by the public has grown rapidly—to the point that, compared with the total output of the economy, it is now higher than it has ever been except during the period around World War II." The report notes that while America might be able to sustain higher debt levels than other countries because of the "safe harbor" appeal of the U.S. dollar, "its private saving rate has been lower in the United States than in most developed countries, and a significant share of U.S. debt has been sold to foreign investors."

Conditions could get quite ugly if America gets hit with a sequel crisis while it is still mired in downward cycle, said the CBO. Pointing to the crises in Argentina, Ireland and Greece, the CBO suggested a confluence of economic problems could impair a recovery.

And for future crisis, there is another wild card to consider: a global commodity that trades on the international market, highly susceptible to psychological factors and geopolitical shifts.

OIL SHOCK

The same year that banks took turns imploding and threatening the global economy, oil prices ascended sharply, intensifying a contraction. In the years following 9/11, prices have been marked by phenomenal volatility. But importantly, that volatility has not been driven fundamentals. There have been no substantial changes in supply. Rather, it has been driven by psychological factors. And those shifts in perceptions have had extraordinary material consequences.

The shock and awe that drove the Iraq War led to a shock of expectations regarding oil supplies. But again, the Iraq War did not significantly affect supplies. Iraq currently produces about 2.68 million barrels a day, a little bit more than under Saddam Hussein. So the amount of Iraqi oil hitting the global market has not fallen. The war in Libya did cause oil supply disruptions after it began in February 2011, but those disruptions were temporary and cannot, of course, account for the spikes that occurred preceding that conflict.

A rise in the price of oil may be a bonanza for multinational oil companies and oil producing states, but for every other company, government and consumer, a sharp rise in oil prices constitutes a cost. In the case of the U.S. economy, the sharp rise in oil was just one more negative factor, contributing to a host of other troubles. According to "The Trillion Dollar War," by Joseph Stiglitz and Linda Bilmes, eight years of high oil prices represented an added cost of about $400 billion, according to a realistic to moderate estimate.

That oil price volatility will probably continue to resonate in the coming years and decades. If another price shock—fueled by any change in geopolitical expectations—should accompany a phase 2 of the economic crisis, the impact would be too foreboding to contemplate.

But importantly, what is at stake is not so much America's economic preeminence. America may well remain the alpha economic power because all rich countries are suffering grave economic difficulties. Still, the United States won't render the opportunity and quality of life that it was once able to deliver.

The American people have already been through considerable economic hardship. And there are indications that the worse may not yet be over. This is due to a host of complicated issues, but the ground was laid by the psychological shockwaves of 9/11. Those shockwaves have had considerable reach—penetrating all kinds of institutions—and consequences.

CHAPTER 2
THE INTELLIGENCE COMMUNITY
America's Metaphoric Ground Zero

The intelligence community was ground zero of the 9/11 attacks—psychologically speaking. You may not be able to see it, but the community is still clearing out its institutional rubble. And there are bodies trapped underneath. The wreckage carries a potent and eerie irony, because the organizations that were closest on the heels of bin Laden were the hardest hit in the aftermath of the attacks.

The community was left reeling from the political consequences of 9/11. Its glaring failure to predict and prevent the 9/11 attacks knocked the agencies off balance. That weakening set the stage for a succession of failures. And those failures continue to reverberate today.

THE DRAMATIC DEFEATS AND MISTAKES

After the attacks in 2001, the chagrined community had to very quickly produce intelligence assessments on a country (Iraq) that had it (correctly) assigned only a mid-level priority—second to North Korea and Iran. The community had very thin and uncorroborated intelligence on Iraq. And so it began to seek intelligence and prepare assessments at break-neck speed, in the most slap-dash fashion, for its top "client" (aka the W. Bush White House). That client was using all its considerable post-911 muscle to politicize the intelligence assessments from various intelligence organizations, at a time that the CIA in particular was already weakened.

And so after its failures regarding 9/11, the CIA walked off the precipice again—with considerable pushing and prodding—by failing to stress the weaknesses in its own intelligence on potential Iraqi WMDs. Indeed, the second failure was very much borne out of the first. Since the CIA seemed to have missed 9/11, it lost the institutional confidence and credibility to adhere to its own standards and protocols. Had it stuck to its standards, it might not have been able to prevent the Bush administration's inexorable march to war in Iraq, but it would have protected its own reputation.

And while it is true that the Agency remained a voice of reason regarding the dubious claims of Iraqi defectors—which the Office of Special Plans trumped up to a disgraceful degree—it made bewildering errors in interpreting the probable use of aluminum tubes that the CIA said were most likely intended for building a nuclear capability. The Department of Energy—which was the premier authority on the tubes—correctly disputed the CIA's interpretation of their suitability for centrifuge use in a nuclear program, as did the International Atomic Energy Agency. And so the CIA has borne the brunt of the intelligence failure. Ultimately, the CIA is intelligence central, and it is the organization first on the peoples' minds regarding the Iraq WMD chimera.

The CIA then suffered another blow when its aiding and abetting of the Bush administration's enhanced interrogation techniques—aka torture—became public. In contrast, the FBI came out looking institutionally more independent, effective and principled in that imbroglio. The CIA's involvement in torture looks especially damaging in light of reports that some detainees were tortured not because they were believed to have knowledge of any "ticking-time bomb" terror plots, but rather to coerce confessions regarding an Iraq-al Qaeda operational link that would bolster a pretext for war under the W. Bush administration.

And then, in Afghanistan in 2009, the Agency suffered a major embarrassment and operational setback when one of its apparent sources within the al-Qaeda network turned out to be a double agent and suicide bomber, detonating an explosion during a briefing that killed not only elite CIA operatives but also private contractors that were mysteriously present. The incident proved the Agency was failing to uphold its security safeguards and that private contractors were now present during the CIA's most sensitive, ground-breaking briefings—indicating an alarming encroachment of mercenaries into America's intelligence sphere.

And finally, the drone warfare that the CIA had been spearhead-ing in Pakistan and beyond will ultimately cause the Agency more lasting damage to its reputation. This is not only because of the moral arguments that can be made regarding the civilian casual-ties. Also, Islamic militants have widened their authority over increasing swaths of land in Pakistan despite—or because of—the dramatically escalated drone attacks. A reasonable observer is left with only two possible interpretations: either the drone attacks are ineffectual despite the phenomenal loss of life or they are actually strengthening the hand of religious militants. And in Pakistan, the latter conclusion appears more likely.

The warfare by drone relies on the illusion that final victory is just around the corner, just a few drone attacks away. It also cre-ates a dangerous impression that America's war aims can be achieved from robotic attack waged from the heavens, while the U.S. public can remain safe and detached. The decision to esca-late drone attacks is political and belongs to President Obama, rather than the CIA. But the CIA has become so politically com-promised, that it has publicly put its own imprimatur on the reli-ance on drones. Leon Panetta, in his very first news briefing as CIA director, staked the agency's reputation on the efficacy of the drone attacks, claiming they "have been successful" and pledged to continue them.

It appears the CIA has been put so on the defensive by 9/11 that it has sought short cuts to bolstering its reputation and its *raison d'être*. That defensiveness probably prompted the Agency not only to overstate the significance of its sparse WMD intelligence on Iraq and to become ensnarled in the Bush administration's *enhanced* interrogations but also to advocate for the drone attacks. While the drone attacks certainly do yield tactical victories, they have become a strategic liability.

Given its recent actions, the CIA is looking a little like the intelligence agencies of so many Third World countries, such as Pakistan's ISI, which is always looking for convoluted ways to bolster its institutional importance, at a cost to Pakistan's overarching and long term national interest. The ISI has gone so far as to collude with menacing jihadi groups that target India but ultimately pose a threat to Pakistan as well—a practice that in Pakistan is known as "riding the tiger." Of course, the ISI will argue in back rooms that the jihadi groups it protects help keep India at bay and may help Pakistan to one day recapture "strategic depth" in Afghanistan by propelling Islamic radicals to power. But that is a defeatist mentality that keeps Pakistan trapped in a rear guard posture, rather than progressing strategically and economically. Pakistan could choose to develop mutually beneficial relationships with its neighbors, but it is stymied by the ISI's stratagems.

A shocked and awed CIA has similarly advanced its own parochial and institutional advantage at a cost to America's vital long term interests. Its forfeiture of standards and protocols and ethics has prompted it to more closely resemble the intelligence services of Third World countries. But the CIA is the lesser offender when compared to the Office of Special Plans. The OSP's egregious actions have marred the reputation of the intelligence community, by association.

While it is true that behind closed doors agencies battled with the members of the Office of Special Plans to uphold higher standards in interpreting raw intelligence, the W. administration's decision to validate the unfounded conclusions of the OSP injured the image of the community as a whole. Based on the statements of the OSP leadership itself and the accounts of many insiders, the special plans office clearly fought a bare-knuckled battle to legitimize intelligence that other agencies believed was too shaky to put stock into. The rogue OSP broke dramatically with protocols by doing so and was entirely incorrect in its assertions.

The CIA can fairly claim that some of the Bush administration's false assertions on Iraq were based on the OSP's conclusions. But that is a distinction not widely appreciated. And although the OSP resorted to the flimsiest of intelligence, it is also true that the CIA validated speculative intelligence on WMDs in Iraq.

SHOCKED, AWED AND AWAKENED

THE COMMUNITY REGAINS A SPHERE OF COMPETENCE

So the shock and awing of America has taken its toll on the agencies. But there is one area that bucks the trend. In terms of human espionage, the United States seems to rousing from its somnolence. That statement may sound so very Third World, but the United States has always relied on human spying—a practice that dates back to the Revolutionary War. Surely, it would seem to reflect a Third World approach to governance by way of opacity and deception. But an effective and responsible intelligence capability gives governments the ability to deter war, dispel lies and myths, and prevent overreaction to foreign threats.

Organizations that work outside the purview of the public are always going to be the weaker link in the institutional nervous system of a democratic country. Enforcing accountability in the face of failure is always a greater challenge. Mission creep is always a challenge. Maintaining quality controls is always a challenge. Working in the shadows of a democracy, operatives functioning within an organizational echo chamber might even begin working at cross purposes to the national interest.

And for that reason, Americans should consider with much wariness NCE proposals—such as the plan Adm. William H. McRaven, head of Special Operations Command, floated in February 2012—calling for a streamlined and expanded approach to deploying the special-forces that work with the intelligence community. Those elite forces should only be deployed in the most select missions and should never be employed with a global whack-a-mole mentality.

What's more, such a streamlined approach to launching secret missions has other hazards. The U.S. government has a demonstrated penchant for secrecy, particularly in this era. And it has been shown to get lazy and sloppy and dangerous under the protection of that secrecy, as U.S. detention and interrogation practices have shown in numerous ways.

Of course, an important task for the U.S. intelligence community is to detect any plot to attack the United States. That does not entail action against individuals who are not fond of America or say mean things about Washington or even those who inspire jihad through their sermons. Those kinds of individuals will always exist. The community must pursue those with operational plans to attack or those who have participated in attacks in the past. Period.

All the same, bolstering the competence and professionalism of the intelligence corps seems the surest route to preventing mistakes, corruption and abuse. It is true that the intelligence errors on Iraq's WMD loom over the community, but those failures were driven in large part by an executive that bore down on America's intelligence community—not the other way around. Had the intelligence corps deployed more effectively around the world, it would surely have more assertively pushed back against the executive.

America must take effective and responsible overt and covert action to prevent another devastating terrorist attack on the homeland. Although it is true that America has rallied many of its enemies through provocative foreign policies, it is also true that, even if it corrected those policies tomorrow, those enemies have now been roused and mobilized. Those Americans that want to see their country move beyond 9/11 must be mindful of just how much effort and resources must be invested in preventing a sequel to those attacks. Given how counterproductive U.S. actions were after 9/11, it is painful to imagine just what scale of injury the United States could inflict on itself (and the world) should it become shock and awed by a sequel attack of similar magnitude.

America must be willing to expend extraordinary efforts and resources to prevent such a scenario.

Fortunately, America's ability to conduct such human intelligence operations has improved since 9/11, said W. Patrick Lang, former head of human intelligence collection and Middle East intelligence at the Defense Intelligence Agency and recipient of the Presidential Rank of Distinguished Executive award. Before the attacks, Lang said, "the managers at the CIA, DIA had a profound case of timidity" about conducting clandestine human espionage. Most those managers "had never done that kind of work, most of them were bureaucratic managers, politically appointed in one way or another, and they were really frightened."

And given that fear, the community never had a real chance of forecasting 9/11, Lang believes. "The diagnosis of why the 9/11 attacks were undetected in advance was mostly wrong and continues to be largely wrong—in that people are always talking about the inability of analytical community to connect the dots. ... But I don't think that was the problem really. The problem was that there weren't enough dots," said Lang. That diagnosis indicates that the intelligence community failed in regards to 9/11 due to political paralysis, rather than chronic institutional incompetence. The sharpening audacity of the intelligence community demonstrates that its professionals are as good, and only as good, as the political leadership.

The political timidity is lifting. The intelligence community's role in finding bin Laden and cooperating with Special Forces helped to boost morale. The groups that deal with foreign agents have "rediscovered the challenge that they had once had but they had lost by atrophy," said Lang.

What's more, the agency can lay claim to another sphere of competence that remained intact even during the lead up to the Iraq War. Although the CIA did get wrong crucial technical interpretations of intelligence on WMD issues, its more qualitative analysis and assertions have been borne out by the realities that the United States has encountered. In terms of the guerilla tactics U.S. forces would be facing in Iraq and the depth of the hostility between the Sunnis and Shia, the CIA got it right. But the CIA's "customers" simply shrugged off that analysis.

The events of the early NCE demonstrate that the community has few institutional defenses against a political "cooking" of intelligence. And that is because the agencies and analysts cannot speak in declarative terms, for the most part, while the president and his subordinates can. The agency cannot categorically refute claims that have been obviously trumped up because it cannot disprove a negative.

In other words, if an administration uses suggestive terms that would falsely and cynically lead American citizens to draw conclusions, the community cannot respond. If, for example, a U.S. president says that it doesn't want Iraq's "smoking gun" to be a "mushroom cloud," the community has no ability to refute the statement, because it's a vague, hypothetical declaration— indeed, it was intentionally so. While the imagery laden warning would understandably alarm the American people, it does not specify a robust nuclear program, or its level of maturity. While the statement strongly suggests the potential for an imminent attack, the word imminent is never used. The W. White House engaged in a dangerous and virtually unassailable semantic game.

There are few institutional protections against the leveraging of intelligence material for ulterior motives. Ultimately, a democracy's best institutional protections are elections, if they offer the people real choices. In crisis laden times, when the American people are angry and disorientated, unfortunate presidential decisions can have an avalanche of consequences.

If a president chooses to rely disproportionately on drone attacks, the intelligence community will execute them, as it has done. If an administration decides to employ enhanced interrogation, then agents will comply, as they have done. But if a president decides to carry out a brazen operation to mete out justice, the community is given license to get creative—as indeed it did.

Like with so many other examples of 9/11 related damage, the attacks compounded pre-existing problems and then unleashed a fury of new challenges that continue to consume the community. The intelligence community has bolstered its ability and license to conduct human espionage since 9/11, but it is also facing stiffening challenges in that regard, also due to NCE policy mistakes.

Indeed, errors seem to beget errors—and violations. All the sectors involved in national security are on a continuous threat treadmill and many have instituted run-away policies of questionable effectiveness. Those moves have marred the government's image abroad and with the American public.

CHAPTER 3
TAKING LIBERTIES

In June 2013 Edward Snowden dragged out into public view the NSA's phone-surveillance program, which is alarming not only for its audacious intrusiveness, but also its unimaginable capability. Given America's post-9/11 trends, what remains surprising is not that the government would choose to snoop on its citizens in such a sweeping manner, but rather that it can. Such a program was the bureaucracy's natural destination, in light of the secrecy and zeitgeist of the NCE.

The granting of rights tends to gather a momentum of its own, based on enlightened logic—as evidenced by the arduous but incremental erection of liberties in America. So does the denial of rights. That also begins to gain momentum, given a certain psychological backdrop.

America is losing its liberties based on such a predictable cliché, in the same worn manner that so many Third World countries have lost theirs: with a pretense amid an under-siege atmosphere. What an unoriginal narrative. In so many developing countries, governments have taken away liberties, brandishing a boogeyman, amid a crisis. And while it may be difficult to believe, America—the vanguard of democracy and liberties, with all its checks and balances—continues to lose liberties based on that story.

Many countries in the Third World had once established robust constitutional rights. Then they were scared into giving them up. The developing world is now synonymous with flawed democracies and limited liberties. In Latin America, for example, the suspension of civil liberties by way of military juntas in the 1970s and 1980s caused long lasting damage. Part of the fallout was cultural, part institutional, and part economic. Argentina never rebounded in terms of morale and civil society, and it has never sustained an economic recovery.

To many Americans, a loss of liberties pales in significance to the prospect of another, 9/11-style attack. And to a large degree, that mindset is rational. In terms of the pyramid of human priorities, protection of life and limb comes ahead of the right of speech or privacy or due process.

But a suppression of rights will not guarantee security. A host of U.S. policies are putting Americans at risk by unnecessarily provoking foreign enemies. And so the yoke on freedoms is not only a costly violation in and of itself, it also diverts America's attention from the actions and rhetoric that stokes violent attack on the homeland. Threats to American citizens do exist, but U.S. policies are by and large motivating those threats. The focus should be on correcting those policies—rather than subverting rights.

It's true that most of the sacrificed liberties do not seem to affect ordinary Americans minding their own business. But the government's "persons of interests" are not only terrorists. They often include the individuals on the ideological fringe: activists, protesters, radicals. And if the fringe is silenced through intimidation, mainstream America will pay a price.

FRINGE BENEFITS

The American people have a full right to be aware of—and reject if they so chose—the ideas of the fringe. Increasingly, that privilege is being precluded. The first innocent victims of America's expanded government powers have been the very individuals that produce not only some wayward theories, but also pioneer cutting-edge insights and detection of wrongdoing and abuse. They are the ones who can be bothered to take to the streets when the government or corporations (or government with corporations) trespass the red-lines of rights and rectitude.

A report by the American Civil Liberties Union surveyed news accounts and studies of questionable snooping and arrests in 33 states and the District of Columbia over the past decade. It concluded:

" 'Our review of these practices has found that Americans have been put under surveillance or harassed by the police just for deciding to organize, march, protest, espouse unusual viewpoints and engage in normal, innocuous behaviors such as writing notes or taking photographs in public,' " Michael German, an ACLU attorney and former Federal Bureau of Investigation agent, said in a statement.

The ACLU detected a heavy-handedness with anti-war organizations. Such a tendency threatens America's democratic and cultural vitality. The activists and demonstrators that belong to the ideological fringe have been correct on many issues, such as the folly of the Iraq War, an impending financial crisis, the extent of U.S. abuses of detainees, etc.

The global economic catastrophe that began in America, buffeted the world, and is still voraciously claiming financial victims illustrates the importance of freedom of speech, assembly, privacy and thought. After all, the puppet-bearing activists that took to Washington streets during IMF meetings and other summits had been warning for years about some great, looming risks and dysfunction in the global financial system. The intelligentsia laughed off those protesters in part because their clothes weren't starched (to say the least!) and their paper-mache props were amateurish.

But primarily, they were dismissed because their warnings and forecasts seemed at the time to be so all encompassing, imprecise and sweeping. They used terms that seemed vastly general, such as the global financial architecture. And so it was difficult to digest warnings of such dramatic proportions. The great unwashed and their fantastical, apocalyptic predictions were felicitously shrugged off. But those demonstrators were by and large on target, in the sense that the lack of transparency of a whole host of financial instruments and liabilities posed a potential crisis. That lack of transparency was the handmaiden of the collapse. And certainly, the antiwar marchers have been vindicated.

A decision to ignore the fringe must be made by the American people, not the government's ability to tie it up. The curbing of the civil liberties of fringe activists could cost you your job, if underlying threats to the economy are not recognized. Perhaps it already has. Or it could cost you your child, deployed and allowed to die in a backwater of the world, as a result of war based on fraudulent premises. Perhaps it already has.

The targeting of the fringe is a national past-time for many Third World governments. Inequities, corruption, unjustified wars and other abuses are common in so many poor countries that the fringe is always looking for ways to mobilize. And the governments are always looking for ways to put it down.

So the actions that U.S. officials are resorting to (including the poorly justified searches of houses) resemble the policies of many Third

World countries. Americans should ask why its government has so much to fear from the fringe. And why is it so afraid of the Internet?

POLICING AMERICA'S VIRTUAL SUPER HIGHWAYS

Censorship is in the eye of the beholder. In the world according to the now deceased but still notorious Venezuelan President Hugo Chavez, the rash of media gagging laws he had spearheaded were geared towards civility and national stability. And indeed, civility and national stability are such nice things to have. But they should be attained as a result of social and economic progress, not infringements on speech rights. If American revolutionaries put civility and stability ahead of individual rights, there would be no United States.

According to the Obama administration, efforts to silence WikiLeaks are fashioned to protect national security—a very popular pretext these days. But really, the Venezuelan and U.S. governments have simply attempted to hamper an adversarial media presence. At stake is not national security—but rather the security of the governments' image. They are fending off a challenge not to the country, but to their legacy.

Freedoms of speech and of the press are the most delicate organisms in the civil liberties ecosystem. Electoral rights are, by comparison, much hardier. Take Venezuela, for example. The people of that country have been allowed to participate in elections and a variety of referendums. But civil liberties of all sorts are under real threat there. Latin America has well established electoral rights.

But even in the region, freedoms of speech and of the press are spotty. In the U.S., officials' repressive maneuvering resembles that of Latin America demagogues.

The 2010 Democracy Index report sums up the problems in Latin America:

"Electoral democracy, for the most part, remains firmly entrenched in Latin America, but media freedoms have been eroded significantly in several countries. Most visibly, there have been a number of attempts by governments to intimidate or block certain private media outlets since 2008. Aside from Cuba (the only state in the region without any independent media), Venezuela is the worst offender. Alongside a crackdown on the traditional media (including efforts to revoke the license of the only remaining television channel that is critical of the administration), there are rising concerns about a crackdown on non-traditional web media."

Those actions should ring a bell to Americans. Apologists of censorship will often enshrine repressive actions with catchy, attractive principles. But a free press isn't necessary civil or conducive to the stability and security of a particular administration or political party in power. Consider this rationalization of Chavez's internet censorship in Venezuela, compliments of "journalist" Eva Golinger in her "Postcards from the Revolution" dispatch:

"Recently, the Venezuelan legislature passed a law called the Law of Social Responsibility in Radio, Television and Digital Media. The law does not censor internet or any other form of media. What it does do is disallow calls to assassinate the president or other individuals, as well as prohibit incitement to crime, hate or violence on websites operated from Venezuela. This is a standard in most democracies and is a sign of civility. The law also instills on media a responsibility to contribute to the education of citizens. Media have a huge power over society today. Why shouldn't they be responsible for their actions?"

The lauding of civility, once again—Golinger apparently received her e-mail of talking points! This kind of sophistry is a well-turned assault on press freedoms, because it clearly put the longevity of a Chavez administration above fundamental rights and freedoms. There are substantive flaws in this circular argument defending censorship. Who is to decide what constitutes an incitement to crime or what contributes to the "education of citizens"?

People around the world have particularly protective feelings about the Internet and the information freedom it provides us. It has sparked revolutions, not only through social networking but also by bringing sensitive, regime-altering information to the masses. In an age of redundant secrecy and covert operations, the Internet is the last, technological frontier of freedom. And we are mesmerized by the multiplicity of possibilities that it holds.

Unhindered access to the virtual world is seen as a hallmark of democracy, Western values and the industrialized world. But when information freedom via the Internet becomes inconvenient to the world's superpower, officials crack down with every instrument at their disposal. The U.S. government has launched its own an attack on WikiLeaks—and web freedom in general.

U.S. law, fortunately, is strong enough to repel the government's direct retaliation against the web publisher. But U.S. officials have coordinated an assault on WikiLeaks by private-sector proxy. Visa and MasterCard and PayPal blocked donations to WikiLeaks in December 2010. Amazon, at the urging of Sen. Lieberman, kicked WikiLeaks off its server. Visa hired Norway-based financial services company Teller AS to conduct an investigation of WikiLeaks, and it determined that the Website had not broken any laws, according to documents obtained by the Associated Press. All the same, Visa did not lift the block on donations, and then vaguely added that it would conduct its own internal review regarding the legality of Wiki's actions, and gave no date on when that might be concluded.

Not content with the proxy attack on WikiLeaks, U.S. officials have also vilified WikiLeaks from the bully pulpit. Secretary of State Hillary Clinton lambasted the site for launching "an attack on America." Lawmakers have also been condemned the site and its founder, Julian Assange. "I think the man is a high-tech terrorist," said Sen. Republican Leader Mitch McConnell. Vice President Biden echoed that sentiment.

Most important has been the Justice Department's reaction. In November 2010, Eric Holder made no attempt to downplay his zeal for prosecution, making it abundantly clear that he had already decided on Assange's culpability. He also intimated that Justice would go on a fishing expedition in an effort to pin blame on Assange, which foreshadowed actions that were soon to come:

"Along with other members of the administration, I condemn the action that WikiLeaks has taken... We have an active, ongoing, criminal investigation with regard to this matter. Let me be very clear: this is not saber rattling. This is, as I said, an active ongoing investigation. To the extent that we can find anybody who was involved in the breaking of American law and who has put at risk the assets and the people that I have described, they will be held responsible, they will be held accountable."

Holder unabashedly grandstanded the administration's prosecutorial bias, which was based not on any specified legal merit of the case, but rather on a pre-existing decision to pursue Assange. The Justice Department was clearly attempting to retrofit U.S. law around a pretext for prosecuting the Wikileaks founder, rather than considering in an impartial manner whether the website substantively broke U.S. law.

Justice then launched its fishing expedition, with its subpoena of Twitter accounts and other information, in search of a relationship between Assange and the imprisoned Army Pfc. Bradley Manning. They failed to find any such relationship. In its haste, Justice appears to have also trampled on civil liberties, by requesting private communications that, according to many legal experts, should be protected from government intrusion.

U.S. freedom of expression laws have protected WikiLeaks and Assange from a legal strike by the administration. No publisher or journalist has ever been convicted of espionage for publishing government secrets in the United States. There is no legal precedent for it in U.S. history. The Justice Department has never tried to prosecute a journalist or journalistic organization for publishing a leak, even under President Nixon.

Those that leak information, particularly if they are government employees, have faced prosecution and whistleblower laws have been too flimsy to protect them. Indeed, whistleblowers face pronounced peril since 9/11. And the Obama administration has set a record in pursuing them.

The administration's accusations about national security are trumped up. When asked whether WikiLeaks disclosures had hampered the war effort in Afghanistan, Defense Secretary Robert Gates said such accusations were "significantly overwrought." He added the while the disclosures might be "embarrassing," they would have only "modest consequences."

Indeed, the raison d'être of WikiLeaks is based on a standing assumption of the public's right to know the secret dealings of governments and other actors. All the same, the website has been more than just a virtual data dump. It has collaborated with newspaper partners in deciding which State Department cables to leak and which redactions to make.

Whatever embarrassment WikiLeaks might have posed to the U.S. government is dwarfed by the administration's embarrassment to itself. Indeed, the administration's vilification of the web publisher was just as "overwrought"—to borrow a term—as Chavez's characterization of his own political opponents.

But the assault on WikiLeaks is by no means the only attack on digital freedom. Although the U.S. government has gained unprecedented snooping authority since 9/11, officials continue to press for more and more, encroaching on freedoms inch by inch. The most dramatic encroachment on Americans' phone privacy would not be known, were it not for Snowden's dramatic revelations. Once the yoke on the state is loosened, powers are easily abused. And that is not only theoretical.

CIRCULAR JUSTICE AND THE BLACK LIST

In the NCE, the U.S. government can put any organization on a terrorism black list at whim, with no kind of overview from a judge or court whatsoever. It can then seize the assets of such an organization. What's more, any person that speaks to that group in a purely peaceful manner can face 15 years in prison if it is somehow deemed "expert advice." This is a sharp reversal of the rights U.S. citizens used to hold, which protected even types of non-peaceful speech.

In the Holder v. Humanitarian Law Project, the Obama administration pursued an aggressive interpretation of the Patriot Act, arguing that a provision barring material assistance to terrorist organizations should bar U.S. citizens from exercising their speech rights in certain ways. In that case, then-Solicitor General Elena Kagan (who was soon to be awarded Justice Stevens' spot on the Supreme Court) argued the case for the administration, and maintained that lawyers could be sent to prison for filing friend-of-the-court briefs on behalf of groups on the black list. In June 2010, the court regretfully decided in the executive's favor.

The law leaves entirely unclear just what "expert advice" might be. It could incriminate American citizens who try to broker peace deals involving groups on the blacklist or who urge those groups on the list to shift from armed insurgency to political engagement. And consider that the executive places groups on the terrorism black list arbitrarily, and with no checks and balances.

For example, an Iranian group that has been trying for many years to weaken and overthrow the mullahs ruling their country is on the list—a fact that some members of Congress are trying to change. And that Iranian group does use violence, but does not target civilians. Meanwhile, the Libyans who labored to overthrow Qadaffi—also through violence—got U.S. air support, not to mention soaring accolades from the U.S. president. They are, of course, not on the blacklist.

So the making of the list has proved to have its problems. But more importantly, there are fundamental problems with the structure of the law, because it requires U.S. courts to penalize American citizens for peacefully exercising their rights of speech with groups that have not been deemed by U.S. courts of any wrongdoing. It is a circular justice that circumvents due process.

David Cole, a lawyer for the plaintiffs in the case from the Center for Constitutional Rights, delivered a stinging rebuke of the law and put it into historical context:

"In the past, the Supreme Court has ruled that the First Amendment protected the right to advocate even criminal activity, including overthrow of the government, so long as one's advocacy was not intended or likely to produce an imminent crime. In the Humanitarian Law Project case, however, the Court ruled—for the first time in its history—that speech advocating only lawful, non-violent activity can be subject to criminal penalty, even where the speakers' intent is to discourage resort to violence."

There have already been pragmatic problems with how the law is being applied. The FBI has made use of the law's broad scope to launch what appears to be harassment of peaceful U.S. citizens. In September of 2010, the FBI said it had searched the homes of anti-war activists who had recently announced at a news conference that they would stage anti-war rallies at the 2012 Democratic National Convention, if it was held in Minneapolis. The individuals targeted by the FBI had previously organized an anti-war protest at the Republican National Convention in St. Louis that rallied tens of thousands participants. The FBI acknowledged they were applying the "material support of terrorism" law to justify searching the homes of the activists.

"These were search warrants only," FBI spokesman Steve Warfield told The Associated Press. "We're not anticipating any arrests at this time. They're seeking evidence relating to activities concerning the material support of terrorism." Certainly, the law is so vague that it could be used often for "search warrants only."

And if the pragmatic implications of the law are not alarming, the law's affront to due process and attorney-client privileges approximates the United States to the Third World. The Third World often targets attorneys in politically sensitive cases, making an end run around the judicial process through official thuggery. This practice was illustrated by Dr. Mohammed Younas Sheikh, a professor at a medical college, in a letter from his Death Cell to author Akbar Ahmed, as Ahmed recounts in his book "Islam Under Seige." In the letter he said that the Pakistani court had "succumbed to threats" and "after dubious ... proceedings sentenced me to the death penalty under the said Blasphemy Law 295/C PPC without good evidence...even my solicitors were harassed with a fatwa of apostasy and they were threatened with the lives of their children."

U.S. attorneys may not be threatened with the lives of their children, but 15 years in prison is a potent enough threat to ensure lawyers stay clear of anyone or any organization on the government's black list. This provision of the Patriot Act, as upheld by the courts, look an awful lot like the blasphemy and libel laws of the Third World—which, in effect, block legal representation and muzzle speech.

THE DISAPPEARED, THE HIT LIST AND THE TRIBUNAL

Obama and his subordinates don't much like to execute U.S. citizens extra-officially. But they will. And in February 2013, NBC News released the 16 pages of obfuscation that the Department of Justice utilizes to justify those executions. A numb and disaffected public scarcely reacted to the rationalized, methodical elimination of due process, made official and perpetual in black-and- white, legalistic improvisation. The presidential overreach was in large part justified by the crisis and a so-called imminence of threat, though the authors of the memo also acknowledge they are redefining key terms, allowing for "a broader concept of imminence." Indeed.

Since the execution of Anwar al-Awlaki and others in September 2011, the U.S. president now holds the power of judge, jury and executioner of U.S. citizens. Indeed, even the deeply flawed due process that detainees received in Guantanamo is superior to Awlaki's adjudication, which involved the president signing a piece of paper and a U.S. drone carrying out the hit robotically.

In America in the NCE, U.S. officials have also assigned themselves the power to detain human beings indefinitely and incommunicado, without recourse to a lawyer or any kind of due process—relegating them to the netherworld of human warehousing. Like the dirty war prisoners of Latin America, detainees held by the U.S. military face the white terror of uncertainty and invisibility.

The AP reported in April 2011, that at Joint Special Operations Command sites, detainees are still being interrogated for weeks without charge in secret, military-run jails across Afghanistan, according to U.S. officials. Human rights groups added that the detainees at those sites are forced to strip naked, then kept in solitary confinement in windowless, cold cells with lights on 24 hours a day and are told by interrogators they could be held indefinitely.

The AP report corroborates similar accounts by the New York Times and the Washington Post. Those newspapers have also reported that U.S. Special Forces operate black-site prisons, where detainees are abused and hidden from view. The reports reveal that prisoners give consistent stories regarding what kind of treatment and conditions they were subjected to.

And while Guantanamo detainees certainly benefit from better oversight than the more wretched prisoners held at sites abroad, the military commissions at Guantanamo have still combined judge, jury and prosecutor in a single branch, representing a shoddier pretense of justice than what prevails in many Third World countries. The American public is too shaken to clamor for applying the full credibility of U.S. courts to the landmark trials of suspected 9/11 conspirators. And that is a shame. Such a spectacle would have granted America a commanding lead in the global ideological battle. Instead, it forfeited that natural advantage.

In the NCE, the state now intersects with citizens in new ways, and in every sphere. The government has given itself the power to order the killing of American citizens without any due process whatsoever, even the procedural scrutiny of a military court. It can relegate detainees to an "indefinite detention" lasting as long, and at whatever justification, the state chooses. It can check your e-mail, police content on the Internet, and eavesdrop on telephone communications—also at will. It can also put U.S. citizens (and non-citizens) on a no-fly list, without having to explain why the individuals are on the list or give the individuals any meaningful recourse to rebut the government's allegations, which are kept secret anyway and are not reviewed by any court.

For all its checks and balances, America is not immune from an affront to its democratic principles and laws, by way not only of the executive, but also a deteriorating culture. America is the longest-established democracy in the world, but liberties are perhaps impossible to sustain by a shocked and awed citizenry. When a crisis throws those policies off the rails, the culture that emerges—in tandem with the security apparatus—is no longer hospitable to democratic freedoms. If current trends continue, the laws and customs and oppression of the Third World might not look so foreign to Americans. But one tenuous bulwark remains.

THE GAVEL VS. IRON FIST

Around the world, students are often the instigators and pioneers of revolutions and your run-of-the-mill street protests. But lawyers and judges have also played a key and courageous role in driving reform. Around the world, they have demonstrated sterling courage in staring down despotism and corruption in defense of the laws of their lands.

Perhaps the most dramatic activism ever mounted by lawyers and judges took place in Pakistan in 2007. In the Spring of that year, Pakistani lawyers launched one of the best-dressed and most consequential protests of modern history. The next day, pictures of the Pakistani police billy-clubbing the gabardine-clad demonstrators graced the New York Times and other publications. Many of those Pakistani lawyers who took to the streets—facing down a despotic government that was backed by the world's only superpower—later languished in prison.

But their bravery and activism was not in vain. They managed not only to re-install the country's Chief Justice Iftikhar Muhammad Chaudhry—a powerful, respected Pakistani judge of unfailing credibility and legitimacy that then-President Gen. Pervez Musharraf tried to dismiss—but also, in so doing they blocked the general from extending his rule. When Musharraf later that year declared emergency rule and dissolved the courts of Pakistan, the lawyers took to the streets again and stormed the High Court, congregating on the building's roof. Again, the police responded aggressively. But the lawyers' activism helped put Pakistan back on a shaky return to democracy.

In Argentina, after the Dirty War ended, the lawyers and judges also rose up, in protest of then-President Alfonsin's attempts to limit the scope of investigations of those involved in the torture and murder of their fellow Argentines. And while they did not achieve all the accountability they sought, their aggressive, unceasing activism drove the establishment of a truth commission. That commission, which would only document the abuses and crimes of the formerly governing *junta,* began to look like the lesser of two evils for the generals and subordinates, in light of the zeal for justice that the attorneys were demonstrating. Those lawyers were able to document the disgraces of the criminal syndicate that ran Argentina into the ground, in moral, economic and political terms.

Interestingly, America's enduring strength also parallels that of many poor countries. The branch of government that in America has remained most resistant to an erosion of standards is the same sector that has been defiant in the Third World. For all the "kill the lawyers" jokes, the American courts have demonstrated the most integrity to law and tradition in the NCE when it comes to habeas corpus issues.

When the court has faced questions on the scope of the U.S. president's authority to imprison human beings on his say so alone, it has scaled back the executive's blatant and sloppy abuse. In that regard, the courts have been the only party slowing the runaway excesses of the executive, because Congress appears to be caught in the headlights of the ongoing crisis. The fourth estate has also been willingly ineffectual.

And the judges who have served as a bulwark of rectitude amid the petulant abuses of the executive branch come, after all, from the ranks of lawyers across the country. Also, many lawyers have been willing to take personal and professional risk—potentially undermining a lucrative career that would otherwise come after an expensive education—to defend the U.S. constitutional order.

U.S. courts have also provided the most penetrating window into the abuses of America's NCE government. The findings of the court have been more revealing, in some regards, then the extensive disclosures of WikiLeaks.

Consider this astonishing fact and just what it reflects about the U.S. government—even when run ostensibly by the no-torture president. Between October 2008 and July 2010, 38 out of 52 prisoners won their habeas corpus petitions, because the government could not present even credible evidence (the lowest evidentiary burden that exists in U.S. jurisprudence) that it had sound reasons for imprisoning them. Since July 2010, the U.S. government has had a better record on its efforts to suspend the habeas rights of individuals not because it has put forward more reliable evidence but because a handful of Circuit Court judges have in effect ordered the lower courts to weaken the government's already low burden of proof, according to some legal experts.

If that analysis is correct—and the U.S. government was broadly unable to meet a low evidentiary standard and then was granted by activist judges some diluted standards—then a host of officials have pursued a haphazard, apathetic and brutal approach to security. There may not be videos or pictures to illustrate that breach of justice and judgment, but it should be remembered every time the executive insists it will behave judiciously if only it is given a free hand in dealing with security matters. U.S. policy makers appear prepared to warehouse human beings (who don't even have a credible reason to be incarcerated) until their decomposition—if not challenged by the courts.

The Supreme Court's 2008 Boumediene decision constituted a firm challenge to the president's power grab, establishing habeas corpus rights to Guantanamo detainees, against the executive's wishes. That decision was preceded by landmark Supreme Court decisions in 2004 and 2006 that reined in the military tribunals and bolstered standards for treatment of detainees.

This is not to say that U.S. courts function perfectly. Indeed the courts have made some alarming judgments that bolster the government's surveillance of citizens, curtail speech rights and grant the government a level of impunity in wake of wrongdoing. But the more enlightened decisions indicate that, of all the branches of government, the courts have been the first to recover from NCE shock and awe, and regain some measure reason and sobriety.

And in many cases, the long arm of the law has been handicapped not by judges, but by administrations. In this regard, torture in America remains a painfully open chapter.

CHAPTER 4
THE SLACKER TORTURER

Torture is a live debate in America. The killing and capture of Osama bin Laden resurrected the discourse. Just as soon as the team of Navy Seals dispatched the al Qaeda leader, advocates for abusive interrogations vied for the trophy corpse to advance their agenda. They claimed their methods helped to pinpoint the al Qaeda leader. The future of America in terms of torture hangs in balance, with the bin Laden's body and his neutralized threat on one side of the scale and the lingering revulsion at the Abu Ghraib abuse on the other. Over the course of the decade, events could decisively tip the scales.

The Obama Justice Department closed the prospect of accountability for detainee abuse. As the New York Times put it, a September 2012 decision by the department "eliminates the last possibility that any criminal charges will be brought as a result of the brutal interrogations carried out by the CIA." With that possibility shut down, the chances that detainee abuses could return improves.

After all, perception is reality. It is highly questionable that the abuse of detainees ultimately netted bin Laden. In an email interview, former CIA agent Robert Baer put those claims in question. "I've seen claims enhanced interrogation helped. But frankly I'd be skeptical of it at least until something solid comes out," he said. So far, that solid piece of evidence has not been seen, but advocates of "harsh interrogations" can always take cover behind "classified" information in making those assertions.

Even before bin Laden's killing, polls indicated that only a minority of Americans believed that torture can *never* be justified. A shocked and awed America remains, perhaps grudgingly, supportive of torture. Much of America has converged around this sentiment on torture: "it's a dirty job, but someone's gotta do it."

One of the distinguishing features of the Third World is the degree to which many ordinary people (to say nothing of the so-called elite) believe that those kinds of "dirty jobs" are the ultimate, unavoidable solution—resorted to with a shrug of the shoulders, in the name of security. And that conviction infects like a cancer. It is a contagion that takes hold of a national psyche and generates institutional decay.

Americans might be put off by the idea of inflicting physical torment onto a captive individual, applied in a premeditated, official fashion. The government's sterilizing terminology to justify the actions—such as enhanced interrogation techniques (EITs), stress positions, etc.—may not even obscure the issue for them. Many remember the ghoulish images of Abu Ghraib.

But torture may well make a comeback in America, largely because U.S. administrations have guarded the secrets. Washington has not even had a Third World-style truth commission on the topic. And victims have not been able to ventilate and address their grievances in court. As a July 2010 report by the American Civil Liberties Union puts it:

> "The truth is that the Obama administration has gradually become an obstacle to accountability for torture. It is not simply that ... the [Obama] administration has fought to keep secret some of the documents that would allow the public to better understand how the program was conceived, developed, and implemented. It has also sought to extinguish lawsuits brought by torture survivors— denying them recognition as victims, compensation for their injuries, and even the opportunity to present their cases."

Former directors of the CIA hold definitively open the prospect of "harsh" interrogation returning in America, as Gen. Hayden made clear when he castigated Obama for allowing the techniques to be made public. Should there be another attack on America, the country could swiftly return to torture like it's 2001.

And it turns out that America doesn't have "precision guided" interrogators, capable of hitting just the right pressure points only on the highest value detainees who hold the most time sensitive information. America's "rough" interrogations pretty much resembled the approach of poor and developing countries around the world. That reality is crucial to the torture debate. Many Americans seem to believe that the United States tortured "differently," but all evidence points to the fact that it fell into common, Third World tendencies.

The most brutal treatment was not reserved only for those captives who were so high ranking that they might hold the secrets of orchestrated, time-ticking plots. The idea that only select high-value detainees were subjected to "enhanced interrogation" by disciplined interrogators makes a nice story but conflicts with declassified information. America's torturers behaved with little more restraint than their counterparts in Latin America, or the rest of the Third World. The numbers belie the mythology around the practice. Torturers were not precise and they were not selective.

"Government documents show that hundreds of prisoners were tortured in US-run detention facilities, and that more than one hundred were killed, many in the course of interrogations," said a July 2010 report by the American Civil Liberties Union.

Not only did America torture, not only did it torture often, the profile of the American torturer also bears similarities to his counterpart in the Third World.

POOR, UNDERPRIVILEGED TORTURER

The left wing of rich countries has traditionally been associated with denouncing the military regimes of the 1980s, in Latin America, Asia and Africa. In particular, they have singled out torturers for special disdain. But that was so 20th century.

In the cutting-edge world of political correctness, the torturer of the past becomes the "violence worker" of today. Under such a perspective, the torturer himself is a victim of the system. And really, the poor torturer! Surely, getting some good shut-eye can be rudely interrupted if you have those rude flashbacks of blood-curdling screams and broken, anguished human cries. Putting aside extraneous sympathies for the torturers, this bit of politically correct retrospective has been useful in clarifying just who did the torturing in Latin America and other countries. According to "Torture, Terrorism and the State," by Vittorio Bufacchi and Jean Maria Arrigo:

"Military training programs have been studied through interviews with former torturers in Greece, Argentina, Brazil, Chile, Uruguay, Nicaragua, and Israel. Often the young, the poor, or the uneducated are recruited. Brutal training at the outset desensitizes trainees to their own pain, suffering, and humiliation. Confinement and initiation rites isolate them from prior relationships. They usually experience moral tension in their new roles and variously resort to denial, psychological compartmentalization, alcohol, or drugs. The efficacy of shame tactics in disorienting subjects tends to lead to sexual tortures that in turn contribute to stigmatization and corruption of torturers. Haritos-Fatouros, who has deeply researched the training of torturers, observed that 'the perpetrators of evil in the Abu Ghraib prison have also become its victims who will suffer disgrace, imprisonment, and mental disorders in the years to come'. 'Who is responsible for so many ruined lives?' she asks. A study of 'violence workers' in Brazil's suppression of 'communist insurgents' showed that torturers experienced even greater job-related stress than members of death squads." (Journal of Applied Philosophy, Vol. 23, No. 3, 2006)

This kind of analysis shows that the poor and uneducated were recruited to do the "manual labor" of the military regimes. Now the U.S. government did not troll the fringes of society to find torturers, as Latin American regimes seem to have done. But it did crawl down the hierarchical totem pole, recruiting outside contractors of questionable expertise to conduct the rough interrogations, according to information now declassified. It did not involve its elite interrogators with years of experience and knowledge in dealing with detainees, sometimes because those agents balked at implementing the EITs. Many were not even present during those kinds of abusive interrogations.

The American interrogator was often hired and paid to conduct the abusive interrogations. Often, they were not the regular staff of the CIA or any other government institution. Many were employees of Mitchell Jessen & Associates, a publicly traded company that (as all public companies are organized to do) was geared towards making a profit, in this particular instance as a result of detainee abuse.

And importantly, those contractors did not have training on how to interrogate detainees. Instead, most came from a military school that trains service men and women to **resist** the torture techniques of the Third World. And so what they knew, quite specifically, were Third World, abusive interrogation methods.

In America, those two different kinds of expertise had been kept distinct. You have the elite interrogators, on one side, doing the interrogating. In another camp are the folks who help U.S. personnel resist the kind of torture they might be subjected to in the Third World. In the NCE, those two backgrounds were conflated. After all, standards and protocols were being thrown to the wayside, like so much quibbling nit-picking of a bygone era.

And so the U.S. government tapped contractors who knew a thing or two about Third World-style torture. And that methodology, according to many knowledgeable sources, is commonly geared to breaking down a captive in order to coerce false confessions for propaganda purposes, rather than extract accurate information. The U.S. contractors were familiar with, and used on detainees, Third World techniques, as conducted by Chinese communist interrogators on US soldiers during the Korean War. The abuse was geared to making American captives "confess" to war crimes.

Colonel Steve Kleinman, the former head of the Air Force's strategic interrogation program, said of the EITs: "People who defend this say 'we can make them talk.' Yes, but what are they saying? The key is that most of the training is to try to resist the attempts to make you comply and do things such as create propaganda, to make these statements in either written or videotaped form. But to get people to comply, to do what you want them to do, even though it's not the truth—that is a whole different dynamic than getting people to produce accurate, useful intelligence."

Kleinman said that the EIT-type interrogations used on U.S. servicemen during the Korean War "actually compelled some of our pilots to admit to dropping chemical weapons on cities and so forth, when in fact that didn't happen." He adds that such treatment is not just physically harsh, it is also geared towards inducing debility, depression and dread through emotional and psychological techniques. Those techniques, he said, "profoundly altered somebody's ability to answer questions truthfully even if they wanted to. It truly undermined their ability to recall, so therefore it would call into question its efficacy in an intelligence-based interrogation." He said such an approach "stands in stark contrast to intelligence interrogation, where the overriding objective is provide timely, accurate, reliable, comprehensive intelligence."

So not only did the U.S. government mimic Third World practices by failing to deploy its most talented and qualified interrogators in questioning the most highly prized captives, it also borrowed directly from the Third World playbook, utilizing communist, Chinese strategies, that date back to the Korean War. In doing so, the United States regressed. American military and civilian institutions that are involved in conducting interrogations have put considerable research, thought and ingenuity into strategies to extract information from recalcitrant, violent detainees. Some of those tactics are not pretty. But they conformed to norms of decency. And according to many authoritative sources, they work.

The NCE seemed to demand a break with the past. In making that break, the United States tortured like Third World countries, using torturers of similar characteristics. Importantly, it has also suffered comparable institutional consequences.

TORTURED INSTITUTIONS

After all, the introduction of a practice as controversial as torture is bound to divide institutions. Though much of the world sees members of the Third World military elite as uniformly responsible for torture especially in the '70s and '80s, armed forces of developing countries can be ideologically diverse. The exile and later assassination of Chilean Gen. Carlos Prats, an adversary of Gen. Augusto Pinochet, is a salient example, but similar divisions abound in the Third World. Consider the following, also from the Bufacchi, Arrigo study:

"Torture programs have been very disruptive of military organization. To save itself as an institution, the Brazilian military gradually eliminated torture practices between 1975 and 1986, under the leadership of several generals.

Divisions revolving around torture also arose between and within U.S. institutions. While many CIA interrogators opposed the abuse of detainees, the CIA top-brass supported the practice. The FBI, under the leadership of Robert Mueller, meanwhile, decided against the use of EITs. And so the FBI, which is geared towards extracting information from criminals, could not cooperate with the CIA on interrogations. Former FBI agent Ali Soufan in 2009 broke with his earlier silence on the issue of enhanced interrogation techniques and said in May of that year in Senate testimony:

"Another disastrous consequence of the use of the harsh techniques was that it reintroduced the 'Chinese Wall' between the CIA and FBI – similar to the wall that prevented us from working together to stop 9/11. In addition, the FBI and the CIA officers on the ground during the Abu Zubaydah interrogation were working together closely and effectively, until the contractors' interferences. Because we in the FBI would not be a part of the harsh techniques, the agents who knew the most about the terrorists could have no part in the investigation. An FBI colleague of mine, for example, who had tracked KSM and knew more about him than anyone in the government, was not allowed to speak to him."

What's more, in the Third World the torturing of captives tends to corrupt supporting professionals, such as doctors and psychologists. The Rehabilitation and Research Centre for Torture Victims (RCT) of Copenhagen, Denmark claims that, according to documents, "many hundreds of doctors have participated in torture" in Uruguay, Chile and Argentina.

In the United States, the EITs also compromised medical professionals, causing institutional harm in that regard. Steven H. Miles, MD states in a study ("Abu Ghraib: Its Legacy for Military Medicine) that: "Government documents show that the US military medical system ... sometimes collaborated with interrogators or abusive guards, and failed to properly report injuries or deaths caused by beatings."

Indeed, two retired military psychologists Bruce Jessen and Jim Mitchell played a key role in devising and experimenting with Chinese, WWll-era torture techniques that were used on Abu Zubaydah and others. Some medical professionals opted out. As Soufan states in testimony, while Abu Zubaydah was being tormented by CIA contractors, "an operational psychologist for the CIA had left the location because he objected to what was being done."

So not only have America's abuses resembled those of the Third World, the consequences have also been similar. But the Third World has made some stabs at accountability, regarding torture and the medical profession. According to Dr. Miles, in a separate article for medical journal BMJ: "In Greece, Dimitrios Kofas, a doctor stationed at the persecution section of a prison in Athens, was sentenced to prison within a year of the military junta being deposed. The Chilean Medical Society actively investigated complaints against doctors and expelled six doctors for overseeing torture during Pinochet's rule. Three years after Argentina's junta fell, Dr. Jorge Berges was sentenced to prison for carrying out torture. A South African medical board tabled complaints against police doctors who failed to report or treat the fatal head injury inflicted by police on civil rights leader Steven Biko; two doctors were punished eight years after his death."

Where is the comparable accountability in America?

COALITION OF WILLING TORTURERS

Even a cursory look at techniques being used in the Third World to torment detainees illustrates similarities with the EITs conducted in America. Apart from cribbing from communist Chinese torture techniques, the United States' EITs resemble those of most any Third World country that treats its captives "roughly." Throw a dart at a map of the world's torturing regions and there you will find policies similar to EITs.

A State Department human rights report on Jordan, for example, states: "The most frequently alleged methods of torture include sleep deprivation, beatings on the soles of the feet, prolonged suspension with ropes in contorted positions, and extended solitary confinement." That sounds alarmingly similar to American EITs. The U.S. government, either through contractors or U.S. officials, subjected detainees to stress positions (which included being shackled naked to a floor), waterboarding (a regular dousing of cold water while in a cell of about 50 degrees Fahrenheit), sleep deprivation, etc.

And that similarity has apparently led to another troubling development. America's decision to deploy EITs has put it in league, at least circumstantially, with Third World countries and at odds with other rich and industrialized countries of the world. After a decade of negotiations, the UN General Assembly in 2004 approved the Optional Protocol to the Convention on Torture. The protocol is geared towards bolstering enforcement of the convention on torture by establishing a system of regular visits to prison facilities. It was adopted with 127 votes in favor and 4 against (and 42 abstentions). The four states that opposed the treaty were: Nigeria, Marshall Islands, Palau and, yes, the world's only superpower, the United States of America. Israel, one of the states that voted in favor, later said it had cast that vote by mistake, due to "human technical error."

Prior to 9/11, the country's decision to refrain from torturing its captives was more vital than a commitment to a treaty or convention. It was intrinsic to the American ethos. It was upheld consistently and—more often than not—unilaterally, even in the absence of any treaty. America, in its continued shock and awed state, seems liable to dust-off the EITs and general lack of standards and safeguards that led to detainee abuse. Surely, the supporters of such policies are waiting for their opportunity to launch their techniques again.

It is difficult to prove conclusively that torture isn't useful. The Obama administration has given credence to much of the mythology and romanticism surrounding torture by refusing to make public crucial information that could change people's minds. Given the suppression of that information, advocates for torture control its image.

What remains clear, though, is that torture is a Third World phenomenon. And by submitting to fear and corruption, the United States used the same kind of techniques, similar kind of torturers, and suffered comparable consequences to Third World torturing countries. When the debate on torture resuscitates in response to some global event, the American people should remember those troubling parallels and decide just what direction they want their country to go. Indeed, the similarities with the Third World have become broad, varied and difficult to foresee.

CHAPTER 5

IF DISASTER HITS, BYOR (BRING YOUR OWN RAFT)

Paranoia Stupefies the Government

The National Hurricane Center in Miami has determined that the Atlantic is in a cycle of heightened hurricane activity, due in part to higher sea-surface temperatures. The cycle could last 40 years. So Americans should stock up on duck tape!

All sarcasm aside, the American people seem to have a sense that their government is somehow impaired in its ability to respond to disaster, or even impart helpful guidance on preparation. This is problematic, because super storms could increasingly make land-fall on the homeland. And American preparedness is vulnerable now not only to physical and logistical shortfalls, but also to psychological impairment—as Katrina so gruesomely illustrated.

The American people know their government failed the victims of Katrina. And perhaps they have a sense that the government could fail them, too, should they be caught in the eye of a storm. But there have been lame attempts to explain why. A look into that recent history indicates that the government could bungle another emergency response and that the instruments of the battlefield are apt to surface in the homeland.

AL-KATRINA

In this book "Blackwater," Jeremy Scahill hits on a lingering, ominous factor that could resonate well into the future in America. Put simply, America was trapped in an overly offensive mentality in the face of Hurricane Katrina, which caused officials to conjure threats that simply did not exist, and to lose focus on the overwhelming and urgent need for help. America sent guns—lots and lots of guns—for crowd control purposes at a cost to its humanitarian response. And it could all happen again—next time with drones flying overhead.

The U.S. government seemed so intent on pacifying, rather than helping, the victims of Katrina that it even sent mercenary forces, armed to the teeth, into New Orleans. As Scahill points out, Blackwater won a major (and, of course, no-bid) security contract from the Department of Homeland Security's Federal Protective Service to participate in the "rescue" mission. Its employees operated with minimal oversight as they exercised their will not in Iraq, but in America, among U.S. citizens that are still protected by considerable Constitutional rights.

According to Scahill, documents show that the government paid Blackwater $950 a day for each of its guards in the area—or about $600 more per man than the company was allegedly paying its men. By the end of 2005, in just three months, the government had paid Blackwater at least $33.3 million for its Katrina work for DHS.

Importantly, the effort to fly in guns and mercenaries apparently did not suffer from the disgraceful logistical inadequacies that marred other Katrina-related emergency endeavors. Frank Borelli, a former military policeman who worked for Blackwater, told Scahill, " 'The logistics operation to support the operation is awesome, and I *know* ammo was just flown in on Monday. More came in on Wednesday. It is a comment on the spirit of the American cop/warrior that Blackwater can put so many men on the ground so fast. Supporting them is a daunting challenge."

A daunting challenge, no doubt, but achievable nevertheless. But to overcome the difficulties, Blackwater had to set certain logistical goals. And it certainly appears, in the aftermath of Katrina, that the U.S. government set ambitious security goals but more modest humanitarian and emergency-response objectives.

And with Katrina, U.S. authorities demonstrated how cavalier they can be in transferring its war tactics and approaches to homeland challenges. And that should raise some alarms. Contractors have generated considerable controversy in U.S.-led foreign wars, causing considerable civilian casualties under highly questionable circumstances—with no accountability. Just what rules of engagement those contractors should follow when operating within America is a dangerously open question.

As Michael Ratner, president of the Center for Constitutional Rights told Scahill, " 'This vigilantism demonstrates the utter breakdown of the government.' " He added, " 'These private security forces have behaved brutally, with impunity, in Iraq. To have them now on the streets of New Orleans is frightening and possibly illegal.' "

None of the issues that Ratner brought up to Scahill have been resolved. And America remains injuriously shocked, awed, and fearful of security threats. What's more, America is on precarious financial footing, which augurs badly for future emergency responses. And if disaster hits your neighborhood, you could see well-armed mercenaries and patrolling drones before you see an emergency response team. Don't ask them for water.

What's more, there is another foreboding aspect to America's longer term-reaction to the Katrina catastrophe. In 1953, war-ravaged Holland, much of which is under sea level, suffered a catastrophic storm that caused a breach in its own levee system. The resource-strapped country was not prepared to deal with the disaster, due to the wreckage of WWII and an inadequate radio system to warn people of the approaching flood. The Dutch's rescue operation was underwhelming, although the 2,000 U.S. service men who responded to Holland's call for help saved innumerable lives. The death toll was almost identical to Katrina's in New Orleans, around 1,800.

Importantly, though, immediately following the disaster, the Dutch immediately embarked on a multi-decade endeavor to erect the most sophisticated and durable system of levees and dikes and dams the world over. The project was sustained through various administrations and was finally completed, to remarkable effect, in 1997. The system is built to withstand all storms, except the kind that is so catastrophic, that it rises only every 10,000 years, or so. So although the rescue operation of the war-ravaged Dutch may have been Third World, the long-term response was phenomenally industrialized.

Where is the parallel U.S. response? There hasn't been one, despite sizable stimulus funds that were promoted as a means to rejuvenate not only America's economy, but also its sagging infra-structure. There has been some reinforcement of levees here and there, but nothing that comes anywhere close to the unrelenting, super high-tech Dutch effort.

That Katrina saga is worrisome not only because of the potential human toll that storms could cause in the future, but also because of what it signals about the amnesia of the American electorate and body politic. Much of the dead from Katrina's wrath lay anony-mously face down in the putrid flood waters of New Orleans. That spectacle, along with the chaos that prevailed in the officially desig-nated evacuation centers (Superdome and Convention Center) traveled the country and the world, projecting an unfortunate image of impotence, negligence, and callousness. But the United States and the world has still has not awakened to the tremendous impact that paranoia and overreaction had on the rescue opera-tion—and on so many other policy errors of the U.S. government in the NCE.

Nor has the American public really asked questions about how the practices of the battlefield can be brought to the homeland—to worrisome effect. The American people remain somewhat apa-thetic about U.S. actions in foreign wars because it is all happen-ing "over there." But the deployment of Blackwater demonstrates that, once the U.S. government begins taking a certain problem solving tact, it is sometimes difficult for it to change gears, and apply different standards in America, for the American people.

This issue remains trenchant given some other foreboding trends along those lines. Congress is looking at ways to mandate the FAA to open up U.S. skies to drones by September 2015. And the American people might have little to say about such a worrisome expansion of the government's surveillance apparatus. Polls indicate that Americans widely support the U.S. drone policy in foreign lands, and they have presumably become desensitized to their use alongside passenger aircraft at home.

The errors of the Third World are sometimes driven as much by state of mind as physical shortfalls. In the case of Katrina, the United States suffered both logistical shortages—due to the ongoing wars—and a skewed mentality. A shocked and awed America overreacted, and under reacted, to the crisis at hand. It launched an over-militarized response to a humanitarian crisis. It brought the strategies of war to a rescue mission on the home front. And that is because America has already undergone a cultural shift.

Americans have tolerated an expansion of the surveillance megastate, in exchange for the promise of greater security. But the economic and cultural decline of the country imperils public safety in unpredictable ways. The United States has assumed a Third World, overly offensive mindset. America and the world have perhaps not fully grasped the magnitude and consequence of that shift—even as the spectacle of the Superdome traveled the airways across time zones.

EMERGENCY RESPONSE, A LA PUTIN

There is a crucial difference between Third World countries and wealthy ones. And that is exhibited in how their governments respond to natural disasters and other crises. Rich countries have a leg up, culturally.

Developing countries with a strong honor culture and sense of fatalism are intractable in their unwillingness to seek expertise and help from the outside. A tendency to hide inadequacies and mistakes can undermine rescue efforts and cost lives. A retrograde sense of honor and pride has been on display not only the poorest backwaters of the Third World, but also in Eastern Europe, as memorialized dramatically with the grisly drowning of 118 Russian marines caught in the death trap of their Kursk submarine, back in August 2000. Vladimir Putin demonstrated little effort in saving the lives of the marines and rebuffed offers of help from Norwegian and British teams.

The same life-threatening attitudes were on display in October 2002, when the Russian government bungled another crisis. But in that case, another Third World, cultural impediment went on display. That year, terrorists took hostage innocent civilians at a theatre in Moscow. Authorities snatched defeat from the jaws of victory, after they had successfully incapacitated the terrorists by deploying a gas into the theatre. The Russians then successfully separated terrorists from civilians—in what appeared to be a game changer in crisis. And then authorities let their fellow citizens die an avoidable death, by declining to identify to doctors the gas that was used, due to the off-chance that a rescue worker would reveal the details.

The Russian's took an overly offensive posturing in the crisis. They exhibited First World bio-technology meets Third World over-drive. The Russian authorities were focused so singularly on the terrorist threat that they neglected their crucial, defensive responsibilities towards their citizens held hostage. And that overly offensive approach to crisis resolution is not uncommon with Third World governments that are eager to show off their law-and-order (and repressive) might, while allowing emergency-response abilities to atrophy.

Chile, in turn, joined the ranks of the First World in 2010 in one important regard, after it successfully saved trapped miners in what has been billed the most challenging rescue in human history. Unlike Putin, Chilean President Pinera sought and received outside help. He didn't attempt to conceal the shortcomings of Chilean capabilities and infrastructure. The rescue was not only a procedural success, it also marked a cultural leap forward for Chile. The government declined to become immobilized by Third World honor or pride or fatalism, and successfully saved its citizens—all of them. When the miners emerged, Chile ascended. And a spellbound world cheered.

A shocked and awed America has taken a *Putinesque,* overly offensive posture since 9/11, which marred the post-Katrina rescue effort. To top it all off, Americans have become dangerously distracted from pervasive vulnerabilities in infrastructure, which could lead to another fatal calamity and further damage the citizens' trust and confidence in their government.

HOMELAND DEFENSELESS

There is no meteorological divide between First and Third Worlds. Hurricanes, tornados, heavy rains and droughts affect poor and rich countries alike. But there is an unmistakable difference in the way natural disasters affect industrialized countries, in contrast to the developing world.

There is an unspoken understanding in rich countries that any single natural disaster will take only a limited death toll. There can be no such expectation in the Third World. When have Americans and Europeans last died in large numbers due to a mere heavy rainfall and subsequent mudslides? That simply does not happen in wealthy nations, but it is a regular occurrence just miles south of America's border in Central America, due to shoddier structures and a lack of erosion-prevention measures. Even earthquakes, the most unpredictable and deadly of all disasters, take a more limited toll in the lands of plenty, due to stronger construction. And there is no comparison between the logistical evacuation potential and response capabilities of First and Third World countries—all of which reduce fatalities.

A study by the Belgium-based Centre for Research on the Epidemiology of Disasters looked at a recent 30-year period comparing natural disasters in the world's 10 richest countries to those in the 10 poorest countries. The center found that the average annual number of victims per 100,000 population per rich country was 36; for the poor countries it was 2,879, even though rich countries experience the same amount of disasters.

Hurricane Katrina shook America because, in a single day, it tore down our First-World assumptions about our superior safety and security. More than 1,800 people died from Katrina. Many Americans died as helplessly as Central Americans when no one was there to heed their plea for help. And a careful analysis that parses so much slanted reporting suggests that conceptual errors handicapped America's preparedness.

First, a caveat. It is important to recognize that the Katrina disaster would never have unfolded as fatally as it did, had there not been Third-World style political corruption in New Orleans, which was unrelated to 9/11. A confidential and independent report (which was leaked) commissioned by the Pentagon concluded that "corruption and mismanagement within the New Orleans city government" had "diverted money earmarked for improving flood protection to other, more vote-getting, projects. Past mayors and governors gambled that the long-expected Big Killer hurricane would never happen. That bet was lost with Hurricane Katrina." So residents of New Orleans were living in the richest country in the world, in a city administered by a Third-World style political body that maintained a Third-World style levee system. After all, the National Hurricane Center concluded in December 2005 that Katrina was a mere category 3 when it slammed ashore the Gulf Coast, incapable of wreaking such catastrophic damage had it not been for the failure of levees.

That same independent report that pointed to New Orleans' corruption—which was compiled by Stephen Henthorne, a former professor of the US Army's War College, and reported on by The Independent—also found: "Another major factor in the delayed response to the hurricane aftermath was that the bulk of the Louisiana and Mississippi National Guard was deployed in Iraq. Even though all the states have 'compacts' with each other, pledging to come to the aid of other states, it takes time, money and effort to activate and deploy National Guard troops from other states to fill in." That unambiguous conclusion, which has been echoed by many involved in the relief effort, was obscured in press coverage due to a host of partisan, ideological, and logistical issues.

In terms of sheer numbers, the Katrina response was impressive. The nation deployed the most massive relief operation in its history. Over 35,000 guardsmen and active-duty troops were deployed to assist with relief operations. Those widely reported numbers would seem, on their face, to deflect any theory that the foreign wars diverted human resources from needed rescue operations.

But importantly, most of those troops did not arrive on the scene until the fourth day after Katrina had passed. At that point, the Guard could have deployed twice as many troops without saving a significant number of lives. And while the force size was impressive, it also presented considerable coordination challenges. It was too much, too late.

Because at the time the hurricane hit, the Louisiana National Guard was just 5,700-strong, with only 4,000 on duty. And 3,200

Louisiana guardsmen had been deployed to Iraq. And if there is a clear consensus among disaster experts, it is that local forces—who know the area and, just as importantly, know each other—are the lynchpin of the response.

Lt. Gen. Steven Blum, chief of the National Guard Bureau, said that 'arguably' a day or so of response time was lost due to the absence of the Mississippi National Guard's 155th Brigade Combat Team and Louisiana's 256th Infantry Brigade, each with thousands of troops in Iraq. "Had that brigade been at home and not in Iraq, their expertise and capabilities could have been brought to bear," said Blum. Blum also said communications systems were scarce during the rescue, adding that he could have used more of almost everything. Blum later backtracked from those comments, claiming Iraq was not a factor in terms of manpower. But his initial comments remain a fact of public record.

So during the most critical stage of the crisis, it is no exaggeration that in much of New Orleans, it was every man for himself. The available force was challenged in reckoning with a disaster of that size. And to further tax an already overwhelmed guards' force, the equipment they needed had also been sent off to Iraq and Afghanistan. In total, the National Guard estimates that it has only 34 percent of its equipment available in the United States.

John Goheen, of the National Guard Association, made a similar claim: "The need in Iraq is obvious, but when our units come home, they have a mission" and when they "return home without their equipment ... they are unable to respond quickly." When asked by The New York Times whether the 3,200 soldiers deployed to Iraq could have made a difference, Lt. Col. Pete Schneider, a spokesman for the Louisiana Guard, replied: "Well, of course. We would have used them if we'd had them. We've always known in the event of a catastrophic storm in New Orleans that we'd use our resources up pretty fast."

Undoubtedly, there was a multiplicity of failures. But in particular, there was a tragic need for more equipment and local forces. The two brigades that were in Iraq were needed at home. Those short-falls are not identical to the limitations of a Third World response capability, but they narrow the difference. And they combined with an offensive mindset that undercut methodical rescue planning.

Indeed, America's shock and awe has made landfall at many institutions, needlessly undermining the safety and sanctity of many, including those already in harm's way.

CHAPTER 6
FESTOONED FODDER

In the immediate aftermath of the 2012 elections, the American public caught a glimpse of a resplendent world: the realm of the military glitterati. The sphere is replete with dodgy affirmations of influence, mistresses and, most importantly, sycophant-scholar groupies surrounding the elite brass. Among this crowd, the harsh edges of reality have been smoothed by flattery, flute-clinking splendor, and surgically implanted enhancements. All is easy on the eyes and body.

If the Petraeus/mistress scandal that captivated the American imagination in November 2012 seemed stranger than fiction to the American people, it is a reflection of the corps past dignity and professionalism. In many parts of the world, such tawdry *tele-novelas* involving high-ranking military officials are standard fare. But much has changed in the American corps since the days of

2001 and 2002, when the joint-chiefs-of-staff vigorously argued against an invasion of Iraq. Today, the military elite reside in an insulated world apart, apparently believing in the mythologies built around them.

What's more, there is more military elite to go around. According to a November 2012 report issued by Oklahoma Republican Tom Coburn, the corps is now top-heavy with generals and admirals—which increase defense spending by hundreds of thousands of dollars, in part because of the large retinue of aides assigned to each elite position. The current proportion is seven general officers for every 10,000 troops, two more than during the high-stakes Cold War.

Surely, much of the now-expanded top brass has a sense of the horrors and futility of America's military exertions. But if some of those generals seem to lack a solid understanding of the sacrifice and folly of the wars and strikes, it is in part because the phalanx of aides and highly compensated scholars and other hangers-on surrounding them. The military-industrial complex involves not only the manufacturers of weaponry—it also includes an industry of thought that advocates for the use of force.

A Washington Posts article, published shortly after the Petraeus affair became public, provides an illustrative description of the general's world while in uniform:

"In Afghanistan, the retinue grew as people drawn to his fame and eager to launch their own careers took up positions for him in Kabul. 'He didn't seek out these people, but he also didn't turn them away,' said an officer who spent 40 months working for Petraeus in Iraq and Afghanistan.

Prominent members of conservative, Washington-based defense think tanks were given permanent office space at his headquarters and access to military aircraft to tour the battlefield. They provided advice to field commanders that sometimes conflicted with orders the commanders were getting from their immediate bosses.

Some of Petraeus's staff officers said he and the American mission in Afghanistan benefited from the broader array of viewpoints, but others complained that the outsiders were a distraction, the price of his growing fame.

If Petraeus began to feel unassailable, the American zeitgeist and the entourage surrounding him certainly encouraged that conceit. And though the extra-marital affairs were mostly significant to the generals themselves, the flattery and artifice that protected the generals from the realities in the combat zone probably had far-reaching consequences.

A close look at those realities demonstrates that U.S. service men and women have been put at severe risk not only by the enemy, but also by American self-indulgence, negligence and callousness. The primary culprits of that negligence are the civilian policy makers that mandated the military action. But the fawning over generals helped to create a more insular world for the elite corps to reside in—thus obscuring the realities of the battlefield.

The campaigns in Afghanistan and Iraq always promised to be arduous and inconclusive—a slog, if you will. But given the state of mind of the American citizenry and policymakers, soldiers would come to bear a burden that was unexpected, and seemed incongruous to our modern age. They were deployed more or less like the soldiery of the Third World, with a bring-your-own-armor carelessness that many of us remember well. And with that precedent set, the treatment of those in harm's way just never reached the reasonable standards.

The public seems to have suffered a kind of sensory overload, and failed to advocate for the fighting men and women. Officialdom, in turn, seemed wracked with a kind of panic, corruption and apathy. As a result, America's soldiers became so much festooned fodder.

As the American martial spirit rose, the American soldier became an abstract and therefore expendable hero, lauded in celestial terms—particularly during sporting events. But individual lives are less important. The American soldier lost a crucial source of protection, becoming more symbol than human being in the NCE.

The expected watchdogs, capable of improving conditions for soldiers by raising awareness, opted out. Due to mistaken notions of patriotism and partisanship, media coverage of negligence has been marginalized. And so the suffering and victimization of service men and women, by way not of combat but corruption and incompetence, has passed unnoticed by many Americans.

Trouncing a military foe can be challenging enough. But trouncing a foe while also endeavoring simultaneously (not subsequently!) to transform the country of that foe puts U.S. military men and women in a particularly troubling position. For a host of reasons, the U.S. soldier was just not safeguarded, relative to America's ability to do so. Mercenaries were relied on to an extraordinary extent—posing serious problems for the service men and women of the armed services.

In many Third Worldish countries, such as Russia, the military tends to enjoy considerable clout and resources but only in the upper tiers, which in turn deploys foot soldiers with little planning or consideration of risk. Put simply, those foot soldiers are cannon fodder. And in 1996, during Russia's war with Chechnya, the country's then-national security adviser, Alexander Lebed, described the Russian soldiers fighting in Chechnya in exactly those terms, adding that the servicemen he saw at checkpoints were "hungry, lice-infested and underclothed."

Despite the pomp and ceremony surrounding U.S. service men and women, they also face shortfalls, disgracefully caused by sheer negligence. With respect to the American soldier, Gen. Zinni echoed some of Lebed's concerns when he stated: "In the lead-up to the Iraq war and its later conduct, I saw, at a minimum, true dereliction, negligence, and irresponsibility; at worst, lying, incompetence, and corruption."

It is true that the most blatant, bring-your-own-armor negligence that occurred in the early phase of the Iraq War has ended. But fatal, institutional failure has been persistent.

KILLERS IN THE MIND, KILLERS IN THE AIR

Throughout 2012, suicides among U.S. military members soared, with an average of one suicide a day — the highest rate so far during a decade of war in Iraq and Afghanistan. Even more disconcertingly, death by suicide outpaced the killing of troops by insurgent fighters. While 154 soldiers committed suicide in the first 155 days of the year, 139 soldiers died in battle. Though there were ample signs that post-traumatic stress disorder was becoming an epidemic amid multiple and grisly tours of duty, the military has had little choice but to admit it has been caught flat-footed by the suicide mill, claiming so many soldiers' lives.

Troops have also been put at risk with silent killers in the air, in the showers and electricity sockets. That underlying negligence continues to threaten the life and health of U.S. military men and women. And the wheels of accountability have moved startling slow by U.S. standards. The death of America's military men and women in the field of combat is undoubtedly tragic. But death or injury as a result of electrocution, burn pits or other exposure perpetrated by the military or its contractors represents an injustice and disgrace on another level.

Data collected from more than 7,000 veterans who served between 2004 and 2010—thought to be the largest study of its kind to date—show that some 14.5% of the 1,816 of the veterans who had served in Iraq or Afghanistan had respiratory illnesses, including bronchitis and asthma. That compares with 1.8% of the 5,335 veterans deployed anywhere else, according to researchers in New York State who conducted the study.

" 'We're confident we are detecting airway obstruction,' " said Anthony Szema, a professor of medicine and surgery at the State University of New York at Stony Brook School of Medicine, told

The Wall Street Journal. Dr. Szema, who also serves as chief of the allergy section at the Veterans Affairs Medical Center in Northport, N.Y., conducted the research under the authorization of that VA Medical Center.

The cause of such maladies has not been determined. But the use of burn pits, which the U.S. military has said are safe, is believed to pose a serious health risk, according to many medical experts. As of May 2011, the Defense Department said there were 78 burn pits in Afghanistan.

Other data suggests that the use of such pits (which contractors often employed), along with other types of exposure, appears to be the cause of a more serious condition that cannot be treated medically. Dr. Robert Miller, a pulmonary and critical-care medicine professor at Vanderbilt University, has conducted biopsies on more than 50 Army soldiers from Fort Campbell, KY who have served in Iraq or Afghanistan. Those biopsies proved that the soldiers suffer from an irreversible scarring of the airways—a rare condition.

" 'We believe they're deployed to some pretty toxic environments. They're exposed to burning solid waste, burning human waste (particularly in Iraq), and consistently exposed to fine particulate matter that's easily inhaled deep into the lungs at a level that's above what's desirable,' " Miller told Reuters Health in July 2011.

Although the condition, called constrictive bronchiolitis, cannot be treated, a medical diagnosis opens the door to health benefits for members of the military, which would not be otherwise available. The condition can only be detected by biopsy, a procedure that requires more than a month of recovery time and costs $50,000 to $60,000.

Despite Dr. Miller's groundbreaking work—or perhaps because of it—he was told that Brooke Army Medical Center in San Antonio would be handling his patients in the future. "I think this is a way to get control of an issue," Miller told VeteransToday.com in August 2010. "They can control the discussion by keeping it internal." Miller noted that he is only 30 miles from Fort Campbell—much closer than San Antonio, where Brooke is located.

Miller also told VeteransToday.com that he became concerned after the Veterans Affairs Department published a 32-page training letter detailing environmental concerns—with his findings of constrictive bronchiolitis removed from the original draft after it was reviewed by military officials. "That didn't sit too well with me," he told the Website. "I thought that was a problem."

Military men and women face many other threats caused by inexcusable negligence. Shoddy wiring, often completed by contractors, has long been a killer in Iraq and probably Afghanistan. Back in March 2009, an electrical expert for the Army Corps of Engineers, Jim Childs, testified that roughly 90 percent of KBR's new construction buildings in Iraq were not properly wired. He said he expected KBR to conform to U.S. standards but that its work "was some of the most hazardous, worst quality work I have every inspected." KBR has yet to be held accountable for electro-cution deaths in Iraq. And it was paid more than $80 million in bonuses for its electrical work there.

A July 2009 report by the Department of Defense inspector gen-eral found that the buildings occupied by U.S. troops in Afghanistan had dangerous electrical conditions similar to those found previ-ously in Iraq.

Some unexplained fires (such as a May 2011 fire in Camp Lawton in Heart, Afghanistan that killed three Marines and their K-9) are potentially caused by shoddy wiring or overloaded electrical equip-ment. A Central Command review of electrical malfunctions docu-mented more than 3,700 fires at contractor-controlled facilities from May 2007 to August 2008. That total dwarfs the 483 fires at contractor-maintained facilities reported to Congress at a July 30, 2011 hearing. The causes of the vast majority of the documented fires were found to be "undetermined." About 820 were defini-tively characterized as electrical fires, with about 275 of those resulting from "fluorescent light ballast" malfunctions, according to the review.

In September 2009, a former air force staff sergeant who had served three tours in Iraq and had been working for a private contractor in Iraq was found dead in a shower in the Green Zone. A military medical examiner concluded that Adam Vernon Hermanson was killed by low-voltage electrocution. There have been 18 Americans killed in Iraq from electrocu-tion since 2003 (16 U.S. soldiers and 2 contractors). Despite

KBR's fatally hazardous electrical work, the company in February 2009 was awarded a $35 million contract to design and build a convoy support center involving substantial electrical work and other sensitive jobs, including the building of a power plant, electrical distribution center, water purification and distribution systems, wastewater and information systems and road paving.

And to this day, KBR has yet to be held accountable for the injury and death of troops that guarded a toxin-infested facility that provided treated water to oil infrastructure. KBR won a no-bid contract to repair that facility in 2003 and U.S. troops, mostly from the National Guard, were tasked with providing security to the Qarmat Ali plant and KBR workers. According to KBR whistleblowers and memos, the company knew sodium dichromate (which is linked to cancer) was prevalent at the facility well before it took any action to inform U.S. officials. Nearly 1,200 troops were reportedly exposed to sodium dichromate and the Army is still refusing to provide most of the injured veterans with needed service-related health benefits, dishonorably denying the clear cause of injuries. KBR was paid bonuses for its Qarmat Ali work.

Today, KBR remains the U.S. government's largest contractor in Iraq and Afghanistan. In Iraq, there is one KBR worker for every three U.S. soldiers. And according to an investigation by the Boston Globe, KBR has avoided paying hundreds of millions of dollars in federal Medicare and Social Security taxes by hiring workers through Cayman Islands shell companies.

In Afghanistan, contractors currently outnumber U.S. troops, with 68,197 contractors in the theater, or 67% of the total U.S. force—more than any other war in U.S. history. And in the NCE, contractors have not only put U.S. soldiers' lives in danger through negligence, they have also threatened soldier's lives through subterfuge and underhanded dealings. An inquiry published in September 28, 2010, by the Senate Committee on Armed Services reported that U.S. contractors are bribing warlords in Afghanistan that target U.S. troops.

"The Committee's inquiry uncovered evidence of private security contractors funneling U.S. taxpayers dollars to Afghan warlords and strongmen linked to murder, kidnapping, bribery as well as Taliban and other anti-Coalition activities. It revealed squandered resources and dangerous failures in contractor performance, including untrained guards, insufficient and unserviceable weapons, unmanned posts, and other shortcomings that directly affect the safety of U.S. Military personnel. The Committee also identified serious gaps in government oversight that allowed such failures to persist."

In effect, the contractors are enriching some of the very groups killing U.S. soldiers. In a February 2010 essay for The Politic, Peter Singer, an expert on private military contractors for the Brookings Institute, itemizes some of the pitfalls of the U.S. government's unflagging dependence on contractors:

"The Pentagon estimates that as much as $10 billion dollars have gone missing or been misspent by private military contractors in Iraq. Literally thousands of weapons have similarly disappeared in Iraq and Afghanistan, with some even ending up in the hands of local insurgents or transnational terrorist groups. As many as 15 or more U.S. troops have died inside U.S. bases as a result of shoddy electrical work performed or improperly supervised by logistics contractors."

And finally, the U.S. military, in coping with its civilian directives, has also abused service men and women with "stop loss" orders that compel serial deployments above and beyond any reasonable requirement for a professional soldier. The U.S. military has exercised an institutional sleight of hand with those consecutive deployments. The practice, while not illegal, is equivalent to an " 'I'm sorry, didn't you read the fine print in your contract?' situation," said distinguished author, Boston University professor and former U.S. Army colonel Andrew Bacevich in an interview. The orders constitute one more reversal of respect and regard for the wellbeing of American military men and women.

That disregard belies the pageantry surrounding the sacrifice of America's military personnel. While it is true that American soldiers, airmen, and marines have been forced to reckon with subpar equipment in past wars, today's derelictions conflict with modern know-how. The negligence towards the service men is obscured by the militarism and disaffection of the moment. It is one more aspect of the Third Worlding of America, with clear victims but unknowable long-term effect.

FODDER FOR SALE. CUT-RATE POLITICAL SAVINGS!

All the same, the injustices and abuse directed at U.S. service men and women are less severe when compared to threats faced by a second-class of military personnel. Members of the U.S. military are, after all, protected by some bureaucratic standards, a degree of Congressional oversight, and a legacy of modus operandi and rules of engagement.

And while contracting companies have indeed put the lives of U.S. service men and women in danger, their employees are also the victims of their fatal negligence and cynicism. Employees of contractors have none of the special protections afforded members of the U.S. military. And the fact is, the firms that deploy them have proved to operate outside the reach of U.S. law, with inexorable impunity. To this day, the family members of contractors killed in Iraq or Afghanistan have been wholly unable to win even civil suits in U.S. courts. Those contractors provide true Third World-style cannon fodder—bereft of any effective American legal or institutional purview.

And then, there is a third-class of military personnel. They are the employees of large American contract companies that are sent to Iraq and Afghanistan and literally come from the Third

World. Sometimes, they are the military veterans of death squads or apartheid rule of their foreign governments. They bring "combat" skills and a modus operandi that differs from the U.S. military approach to war. And they have been abused and taken advantage of in the most extreme fashion, as Jeremy Scahill chronicles in his book "*Blackwater.*" That book illustrates the case of Colombian soldiers hired by Blackwater, who found themselves in Iraq earning considerably less than they were originally promised, trapped in modern-day, indentured servitude in a warzone.

In April 2009, the U.S. government confirmed that it had tapped Triple Canopy to take over Blackwater's contract in Iraq. That company looked to the Third World for bargain labor rates. In an interview with Amy Goodman, Scahill said, "...Triple Canopy was also known for being the company that brought in the largest number of so-called third country nationals, non-Iraqis, non-Americans. They hired, for instance, former Salvadoran commandos who were veterans of the bloody counterinsurgency war in El Salvador that took the lives of 75,000 Salvadorans, minimum. Chileans, they used the same recruiter—Jose Miguel Pizarro Ovalle—that Blackwater used when they hired Chileans. This was a former Pinochet military officer."

Many other firms have used the same cost cutting strategies as Triple Canopy, hiring mercenaries from the Third World that, in turn, have their own impact on the battlefield, at a cost to America's image. Singer noted in the February 2010 essay for "The Politic":

The personnel in this "coalition of the billing" come from over 30 countries, with about a quarter American and the rest divided among third country nationals and local citizens. As many as a quarter are in armed roles in the battlespace, sometimes described as "private security" (but "security" clearly takes on a different meaning than private security at facilities not in active combat zones). The others handle roles that range from logistics to Unmanned Aerial Vehicle (UAV) services to staffing out military advisory teams. It is important to note, however, that these numbers and roles remain in great dispute. For example, while one study reported that there were as few as 10,300 total contractors in armed security roles in Iraq, the Ugandan Ministry of Labor reported in 2008 that there were 9,000 Ugandans alone working in that role in Iraq.

America's use of contractors has remained seamlessly unchanged since 9/11. Scahill told Goodman that by phasing out Xe Services, formerly called Blackwater, the Obama administration attempted to falsely project the start of a new era of political accountability. "Well, I'm starting to call a series of pieces I'm doing 'Operation Rebranded,' " he said, "because what we're seeing unfold with the Obama administration's foreign policy is basically continuing many of the worst parts of Bush's foreign policy and sort of repackaging these policies."

Not only has Triple Canopy used many of the same tactics and personnel as Blackwater, the U.S. government's relationship with

Blackwater continues unabated, despite the trumped up cancelling of the contract in Iraq, noted Scahill. "Obama, though, is keeping Blackwater on, and the State Department has not ruled out that they're going to stay on for much longer, the aviation division of Blackwater in Iraq, and also Blackwater is on the US government payroll in Afghanistan, also working for the Drug Enforcement Agency," he said.

In June 2010, the Obama administration awarded $220 million in new contracts to Xe Services and an array of other shell companies. Under the new contracts, Xe provides security to U.S. bases and to diplomatic premises. During his tenure as CIA director, Leon Panetta leveraged the agency's reputation in promoting Xe Services, claiming the company had "shaped up its act." He then added that, anyway, America needed the security that the company provided—suggesting, presumably, that the government tapped the company because it had no alternatives. And then Panetta offered another contradictory rationalization, in case the others didn't pass muster, noting that Xe's bid for the job was lower than that of other companies.

Incidentally, the decision to hire Xe came some months after the Senate Armed Services Committee published an excoriating report based on an investigation into a unit of Xe, called Paravant. In a statement the committee chairman, Sen. Carl Levin, said the investigation into Paravant, which is still under contract to train Afghan National Army personnel, revealed "reckless use of weapons by Blackwater/Paravant personnel, sloppy vetting by Paravant/Blackwater of their personnel, violation of the rules by

Blackwater/Paravant personnel relative to obtaining weapons and carrying weapons in Afghanistan."

In the NCE, not only have employees and other victims been unable to find justice and accountability in U.S. courts, the U.S. government continues to hire the same abusive contractor companies over and over. And since contractors are now playing a role in covert operations, their rules of engagement are shrouded under another level of obscurity. Singer maintains that "as much as 75 percent of the field support to the Air Force's Predators is outsourced, while the Army has a unit of drones that is opaquely described as 'government owned-contractor operated.' "

Despite the righteous gestures and semantics of the Obama administration, the U.S. government remains unable to sever its dishonorable dependence on contractors. And the use of a rank and file mercenary force, assuming a combat role, in such overwhelming numbers is without precedent in U.S. history. It is another of so many malign American "firsts" of the NCE.

And so the level of dependence on mercenaries, particularly those coming from the Third World, is outside the American tradition. But it is commonplace in so many parts of the Third World. In the African continent, mercenaries (many also coming from other countries and continents) have been used in significant numbers and in highly controversial roles. When they have been used, they are often employed in missions that are sharply at odds with the will of the people.

Perhaps the most eye-catching, tabloid-friendly anecdote featuring foreign mercenaries in Africa involved Mark Thatcher, the notorious son of former British Prime Minister Margaret Thatcher, and British mercenary Simon Mann in a coup attempt in Equatorial Guinea. Thatcher was given a four-year suspended sentence and fined about $500,000 due to his alleged involvement in that plot. But there are many other examples involving African governments and mercenaries, often foreign mercenaries.

America's reliance on mercenaries represents more than just a passing and coincidental resemblance to a common Third World practice. In America, such an underhanded approach to war allows for a break with standards and accountability. Washington's reliance on mercenaries also allows it to maintain an unpopular military presence, indefinitely. Mercenaries have provided U.S. presidents with political insulation from the realities of the battlefield. But they have caused life-and-death troubles for American military men and women, civilian carnage, and a persistent image problem for America abroad.

And there is one other indignity involving the mercenary companies aligned with Washington. Those companies have challenged and sidestepped the rule of law and democratic will of Third World countries, in their search for willing, able bodied, cheap personnel. For all of Washington's lip service regarding democracy, the contractors intricately involved in the U.S. war effort have staged insult and affront to the legal institutions of foreign countries.

In order to stymie the recruitment zeal of mercenary companies, the South African National Assembly in 2006 was forced to pass the Prohibition of Mercenary Activities Act, which bars its citizens from becoming mercenaries, or aiding the use of mercenaries. In doing so, the South African government has taken an enlightened lead on the issue and America is not even playing catch up. It remains too entrenched in NCE thinking to take decisive control over the haphazard activities of the contractors it is allied with.

Blackwater's recruitment of Chilean military personnel that were involved in Pinochet-era operations also caused civil and political convulsions in that country, where the government and its citizens overwhelmingly opposed the war in Iraq. Under Chilean law, only the Chilean Defense Department can legally select peacekeeping forces for Iraq. But of course, mercenary companies have circumvented Chile's democratic rule of law, by hiring Chilean mercenaries on their own. So much for aiding democracy around the world!

The United States appears to be unwilling to control the mercenary companies that have been involved in Iraq and Afghanistan. Indeed, mercenary extraordinaire Erik Prince (founder of Blackwater) has been tapped by Bahrain for security purposes that probably conform with that country's despotism—in one way or another.

So while the United States has been lauding the spread of democracy and rule of law abroad, the actions of the mercenary companies aiding the U.S.-led wars have challenged those principles. In the NCE, U.S. foreign policy is supported by layer upon layer of artifice. Unlike Third World countries that are endeavouring to control the traffic of mercenaries, Washington seems to have forfeited that effort. By luck of circumstance and a lack of will, Washington may have less control over its contractors than do some Third World countries that have overcome a violent past.

Contractors and drones have become something of an addiction to the U.S. government. These elements, on top of the mindset of the country, have made war easy to wage. In this era, a U.S. president could open a new front at any moment.

CHAPTER 7
WAR ON JUST ONE-HUNDRED-MILLION DOLLARS A DAY!
Obama's Own Little War

The killing of the U.S. ambassador and others in Libya in September 2012 serves as a tragic rebuke to Washington's hastily laid war plans. The fatal and dramatic attack heightened America's pain, humiliation and rage, further entrenching the country in the ethos of the new common era (NCE). Although, the White House never said it was launching a war—"kinetic military action" rolls right off the tongue!—the American people know the unparsed meaning of the word. The government's inability to foster stability in Libya or even protect its high-ranking official was an affront to U.S. power and competency. Months later, the administration's obfuscation in wake of the killing of the Americans intensified the public's alienation from its government.

The American people originally greeted the news that America was launching a new war in Libya with an odd mix of apathy and militarism. America now seems so stupefied by alleged threats that adding another front to the roster was humdrum. While some policy wonks were seen wringing their hands, uttering halting admonitions, the opposition to the campaign was remarkably insipid.

American militarism has changed in tone and theme, but continues unscathed by the dire U.S. fiscal predicament and ongoing consequences of Iraq and Afghanistan. Obama was able to launch the war despite the fact that he didn't have Congressional authorization (which he didn't bother requesting), the support of the U.S. military, the approval of the majority of the American people or a coherent rationale.

Obama in effect justified the war with the slender pretext that it would be just a little war, and that America was coming to the rescue of the helpless, reflecting sunbeams on its glinting, white F-16s. The bombing-to-the-rescue, humanitarian campaign killed about 50,000 Libyans, according to rebels' own estimates.

Just like Iraq, Libya was apparently hoped to be just one war to support and rationalize others, as part of a sweeping ideology. What's more, Libya, like Iraq, was expected to be quick and clean, delivering clear results—a kinetic cakewalk, if you will. As Andrew Bacevich (distinguished author, Boston University professor and former U.S. Army colonel) put it in an interview:

"My impression is that there were some very articulate advocates of intervention who saw it as a way to validate the whole responsibility-to-protect concept. And that if the US and its allies could successfully implement the concept in Libya, that they would be setting a precedent that would see the concept taking on some substance, rather than simply being theoretical.

So my guess is that that was the thinking in the White House, although you could probably put thinking in quotes because it doesn't seem they thought through this enterprise in any great detail," Bacevich said.

So the Libyan ethos has echoes of 2003. According to the neoconservative vision in Iraq, the war there was widely seen as a precursor to further U.S. military intervention in the Greater Middle East. And it is perhaps due to that striking similarity that a group of neoconservatives (including Liz Cheney, Robert Kagan, William Kristol and Paul Wolfowitz) sent an open letter to Republicans in Congress, imploring them to refrain from cutting off funds to the Libyan campaign. While many neoconservatives in the NCE have been discredited and delegitimized as individuals in wake of Iraq, the compulsion to rationalize military force based on vaulted principles continues to live on with different ideological trappings. The similarities seem to have dawned on the neoconservatives themselves.

Obama failed to request Congressional authorization for military action despite the fact that America was not under any threat from Libya. Under the War Powers Act of 1973, Obama was required to seek approval of continuing military action after 60 days of having started it. Barring such approval, the president was required to halt military action after an additional 30 days. Needless to say, Obama blew through all those deadlines.

In justifying his decision to continue the campaign, Obama went against the counsel of the White House's official arbiter of legal questions: the Office of Legal Counsel. Caroline D. Krass, the acting head of the office, told Obama he had to act in accordance with the act's requirements. And so Obama instead concocted a coalition-of-willing lawyers to offer token approval of the war.

Obama acted with some supreme presidential authority that seems to be a construct of his own creative interpretation of U.S. law, and that of some hand-selected lawyers. Constitutionally speaking, his actions on Libya are even dodgier than some of W. Bush's dubious decisions. Indeed, leaders of a Third World military junta sometimes comply with greater checks and balances. They at least have to observe the consensus of other junta members.

What's more, Obama did not even need to have the military onboard philosophically, in launching the Libyan adventure. For all the facile talk of the generals running Obama, the Libyan saga demonstrates that the president, not the generals, is calling the shots. As Bacevich put it: "I mean, I don't know of any admirals or generals that were advocating" for the campaign in Libya.

Indeed, why would they? Surely, the Libyan enterprise pleases the chair-bound, Microsoft-Office hawks who have long gravitated towards Obama and the idea of liberal intervention. But in substance, there is no coherence to the war in Libya. Nearby, in Bahrain and Saudi Arabia, despotic regimes brutalize their people, with no U.S. or NATO fighter jets bombing to the rescue.

Indeed, Obama was able to act without the majority support of Americans. According to a Gallup poll conducted in late March 2011, 47% of Americans said they approved of the action against Libya, the lowest approval rating Americans have given to any U.S. military operation that Gallup has asked about over the past four decades.

Given the remarkable ease with which Obama was able to carry out his will and whim on Libya, U.S. presidents can be expected to continue to wield such de facto, Third-World style authority. The dubious Libyan opposition, NATO's less-than-desired contributions, and Washington's inability to leverage the Libyan campaign for greater soft power will pass by largely unnoticed.

During his last month in office, in June 2011, Secretary Gates described, with unique bluntness, NATO's failure to follow through in Libya—delivering the following indictment:

"The mightiest military alliance in history is only 11 weeks into an operation against a poorly armed regime in a sparsely populated country—yet many allies are beginning to run short of munitions, requiring the U.S., once more, to make up the difference."

What's more, launching the Libyan campaign did not bolster U.S. clout in Greater Middle East. U.S. popularity barely inched forward in Egypt, for example. According to a Pew Research Poll conducted between March 24 and April 7, 2011 (the United States launched its first airstrikes in Libya on March 19th), only 20% of Egyptians hold a favorable opinion of the United States, which is nearly identical to the 17% who rated it favorably in 2010.

Those realities will barely encroach on the American consciousness. The American public has become so shocked and awed by the foreign threats, the power of the presidency, the state of the economy, etc. that the executive has garnered a kind of carte blanche power. The American people have been buffeted psychologically and as a result, standards and protocols that impede the march to war have been weakened. The country seems divided between those who favor flexing military muscles and those that are too detached to register their opposition. Undoubtedly, the erosion of checks and balances does not rise to the level of, say, authoritarian rule, but it does undercut America's institutional integrity.

Of course, that fall in stature is accompanied by America's continued economic preeminence and unparalleled ability to borrow money. And so America can continue funding its militarism. Unlike, say, Argentina's military junta, economic constraints will not halt U.S. wars, little or big, kinetic or frenetic.

CHAPTER 8
A MILITARY BUDGET, FIT FOR A DICTATOR
A Tin Pot of Money for Disproportionate Spending

The empires of yore capture the imagination with their heady and disproportionate military spending. Today, this is a characteristic of Third World countries—and America. Many Americans know that their country spends a great deal of money on the military. Indeed, wealthy countries have much to spend. But many may not be aware of just how, and in what proportions, the U.S. spends on national defense. A close look reveals that a shocked and awed America allocates its defense cash not only like a Third World country but, more precisely, like a Third World rogue country.

President Obama has said he would like to reverse this trend and has tabled some modest proposals in this regard. Indeed, Obama's plans wouldn't bring down military outlays as a percentage of GDP to the 2000 level until 2018—kicking the bulk of the reduction affair down the road, and probably off a cliff! But many lawmakers have lambasted a reduction in spending anyway—and the American people are heeding those alarmist calls to continue spending like its 2001.

According to a March 2013 poll, Americans favor cutting U.S. expenditure in general—but not defense spending. The public by nearly 2-1 supports cutting the overall budget along the lines of the sequester that took effect March 1, 2013. But by nearly an identical margin, Americans oppose an eight percent across-the-board cut in military spending, according to an ABC News/Washington Post poll.

That support for defense spending has been intractable. According to the German Marshall Fund's 2011 Trans-Atlantic Trends poll, 64% of Americans wanted to either increase or maintain defense spending. So the fiscal damage that the disproportionate spending has already had could be compounded, if the will and perceptions of the American people prevail. This is unfortunate, because on this matter, America is not in good global company.

In data released by the CIA that ranks military spending by countries around the world as a percentage of GDP (based mostly on 2009 figures), Third World countries, particularly from the Middle East and Africa, dominate the first 50-plus slots. The U.S. comes in at number 24 according to CIA data, flanked by China (number 23) and Qadaffi-ruled Libya (number 25). This is not a flattering association.

Needless to say, China and Libya are not the United States. But their problems provide living, concrete examples of the dangers of disproportionate military expenditures—and the kinds of governments that resort to it. Despite Libya's considerable oil revenues, it has long suffered from a so-called infrastructure deficit, even when compared to many Third-World peers—not to mention considerable political dysfunction! Clearly, the Qadaffi-led Libyan government should have invested less on arms and more on worthwhile endeavors while it still could.

The scale of U.S. military spending is often chalked up to the overarching size of the American economy. And surely, when military budgets are looked at in terms of total spending, the United States is flanked by other rich countries. But what some Americans may not fully appreciate is that America dramatically outspends other rich countries on defense even when measured as a percentage of their wealth. Hawks who have argued in favor of the stratospherically large U.S. defense budget have in the past cited America's spending as a percentage of GDP as a way to defend their position. Before 9/11, that was a tenable argument, since America's defense spending—measured against the overall size of the U.S. economy—had been in a freefall since 1987. But that changed dramatically after September 11th, 2001. In 2011, defense spending was about 4.7% of GDP. In contrast, in 2001 the level was about 3%, given that year-to-year decline since 1987.

Like other NCE phenomenon, military spending (proportionally speaking), did not shoot up in the heat of the aftermath of the attacks only to later taper off as cooler heads prevailed. Nor has that spending been driven by the costs of the wars alone. Rather, spending has continued rising and expenditures unrelated to the wars have also surged. This kind of fiscal hemorrhaging is debilitating even for the world's largest economy and only superpower.

Since 9/11, the rise of a shadowy network of enemies figures prominently in the American imagination—justifying the colossal budget. Obama himself seems to envision indefinite conflict. He said in May 2009:

"Unlike the Civil War or World War II, we cannot count on a surrender ceremony to bring this journey to an end. Right now, in distant training camps and in crowded cities, there are people plotting to take American lives. That will be the case a year from now, five years from now, and—in all probability—10 years from now."

It is no wonder the American people want the military mill running full steam. And that yields a variety of implications, and misadventures. American policy and culture seem to be caught in a feedback loop.

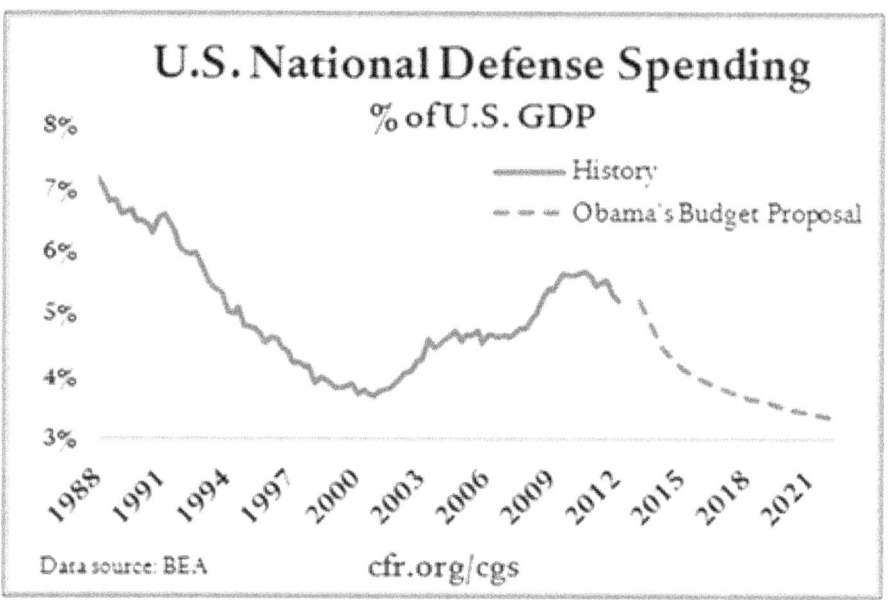

CHAPTER 9
HONOR KILLINGS

"Honor ate up the mountains and taxes ate up the plains." Pashtun Proverb

America's honor/warrior culture rose organically from the human wreckage of 9/11. Once stirred, the culture warriors are ever vigilant and prepared to engage. A drive to restore honor now courses through the American bloodstream. To many Americans, patriotism is militarism. And as a result of that shift in the American ethos, the United States is approximating the Third World.

The complete lockdown of a major American city, replete with the patrolling of tanks, is without precedent in U.S. history, despite the dramatic events of the past. But even city police now respond military-style to threats with an Islamic nature. And so it went after the Boston marathon bombings of April 2013, dramatically eclipsing the response to the much more fatal Oklahoma City bombing of 1995.

Whether or not such a lockdown is necessary or justified is open to fair debate, but the fact that it departs from the norms of the past is not. The honor crowd often plays lip service to small government but seems unmolested by a muscular security apparatus, given the safety that it seems to promise. But that constituency should also consider how definitive that security can be in a free society and a globalized world, in the face of civilian casualties claimed abroad.

America in the second decade of the NCE has settled on an unviable consensus. It has tired of war and its expense but it wants to continue to war robotically, via the bluntest of martial instruments—the drone. According to a Washington Post-ABC News poll conducted in February 2012, 83 percent of Americans approve of Obama's drone policy. The drone policy was even approved by 77 percent of self-identified "liberal Democrats." Killing foreigners (and a smattering of U.S. citizens) by way of drone remains popular.

In Afghanistan, view of man and a barely perceptible predator drone overhead. Visible only as a black dot in the sky.

But the same poll found that 78 percent of the public supports Obama's drawdown plan in Afghanistan. The American people have not accepted that the use of drones, and the fury and collateral damage they cause, entrenches America in conflict with the Muslim world—by whatever politically feasible means the U.S. president has available.

America's ultimate militaristic cakewalk has come into favor. The cakewalk hinges on a murky, detached approach to warfare. It has an obvious appeal but unknown long-term consequences. The promised security benefits could vanish like a desert mirage. Even though the United States can kill via drone from the air, it remains highly unlikely America will continue indefinitely being the only party doing the killing, in this globalized world.

The ultimate cakewalk also hinges on the American zeitgeist. Americans will support the strategy only if they view the drone victims as the "other." Central to that perception is an antipathy for Muslims, a sentiment that has had remarkable staying power.

While polls indicate the Tea Party does harbor much stronger anti-Islamic feeling than the rest of the country, the American people in general are becoming increasingly contemptuous of Islam and Muslims. Perhaps most interestingly, that sentiment has come in waves. A Pew poll shows that in 2010, 40 percent of Americans linked Islam with violence; while in 2002, just 25 percent of Americans made that link. Granted, the upward trend peaked in August 2009, when 45 percent said they believed Islam fomented violence. Then that percentage number started to go down, only to start rising again.

This data is revealing. Anti-Muslim sentiment is not steadily decreasing. But more encouragingly, it is also not set in stone. The individuals that subscribe to it are not committed to such prejudice. The antipathy is cyclical. And it seems to correlate with the economic cycle, which is has been caused by, and reinforces, the shock and awe effect. The data on the American zeitgeist suggests that just as there is a broad ideological competition in the country, there is also a narrower ideological contest within people themselves.

In the NCE, though, hostility towards Muslims often gets the megaphone, and it helps to reinforce various types of militarism. An in-depth, field-based investigation on drone strikes by the Bureau of Investigative Journalism (on behalf of the Sunday Times) found that "since Obama took office three years ago, between 282 and 535 civilians have been credibly reported as killed including more than 60 children." The Bureau notes that the drone attacks were started under the Bush administration in 2004 and have been stepped up significantly under Obama. There have been 260 attacks by unmanned Predators or Reapers in Pakistan by Obama's administration—averaging one every four days. But the collateral damage was not the most alarming aspect of the Bureau's studies.

It also documents a U.S. practice that appears to be more damaging and worrisome than the Abu Ghraib polemic. The Bureau found that U.S. drones had killed dozens of civilians who had gone to rescue victims or were attending funerals. A three month investigation including eye witness reports have found evidence that at least 50 civilians were killed in follow-up strikes when they had gone to help victims. More than 20 civilians have also been attacked in strikes on funerals and mourners.

During his first two years in office, Obama authorized nearly four times as many drone strikes in Afghanistan as Bush did during his entire two terms. And by October 2011, the number of U.S. troops killed in Afghanistan during Obama's presidency was more than twice the amount killed during W. Bush's prosecution of the war over seven years—even though Obama had been in office less than three years. What's more, America's covert activity has multiplied in the later years of the NCE. "Since 9/11, we have doubled in size, our budget has tripled, and the number of deployed special operations forces has quadrupled," U.S. Special Operations Command (SOCOM) commander Adm. William McRaven said in Senate testimony in March 2012. SOCOM has forces in 78 countries, compared to 60 countries in the Bush years.

Obama has at times tried to temper America's honor culture the way a person backs away from a predator—slowly, carefully, no sudden moves. But the president has also pandered to it. He appears conflicted, wanting to pacify America's honor reflex, but not confront it, and sometimes direct it. Obama will appeal to America's "honor constituency" when he wants to exert military force, but he has also pleaded with the American people to put their martial spirit aside—as he attempted, tepidly, during his June 2011 speech, calling for a reversal of the Afghan war surge that he himself had earlier ordered.

Obama puts his own flourish on bolstering American militarism. He goes beyond discussing America's security or talking tough or even promoting democracy around the world. In defending the Afghanistan campaign he portrayed America as the defender of all humanity—a tone he takes with the Libyan intervention as well: "The safety of people around the world is at stake."

In doing so, Obama boosts America's warrior or "honor" culture, which before 9/11 was a more latent force. When Obama appears in a leather bomber jacket adorned with an American Eagle and the words "Air Force One," he is accomplishing the same thing through props—and is adopting a slightly more subtle version of the couture preferences of Third World strongmen. Obama's halfwill to lead America towards a more rational, temperate mindset precludes his ability to do so. America's honor culture has had ten years' momentum. Even a determined president would face challenges in wresting America from its accumulated fear and rage. A surge-withdraw, ambivalent president simply has no chance of doing so.

A belief in coercion as a first resort—a standby of the Third World—has a proven tenacity in America in the NCE. It outlives Osama bin Laden. It is larger than any one president. It never rests.

THE RISE OF THE SHOCKOCRACY

A ruinous concern over honor—particularly male honor—sweeps continents in the Third World. An emphasis on nationalism (or tribalism) and honor is an integral part of life, driving the social and political direction of many countries. Men and governments alike must swiftly rectify any humiliation or victimization of themselves or their charges to uphold street *cred*. This cultural strain affects even educated elites—who dress and often sound much like their American counterparts but harbor and act upon ingrained "machismo" and ideas about honor.

For al Qaeda, the Taliban and their many off shoots, the pursuit of honor has been a crucial driver in jihadi enrollment. As Akbar Ahmed puts it in "Islam under Siege," in much of the Muslim world, a hyped-up sense of honor (or asabiyya) is being expressed. But even "those societies that economists call 'developed' fall back to notions of honor and revenge in times of crisis," he said. America entered in crisis on 9/11, and indulged such inclinations. This "asabiyya" has infected the American collective-consciousness.

On 9/11, America felt it had been attacked, humiliated, and robbed of its native honor. And according to Ahmed, it is the *loss of honor* that triggers such steroidal asabiyya. Much of the American public has grown war weary. But the public also wants the security that, according to the policymakers, only military muscle can guarantee. While the president and the public equivocate, those individuals who see the world through their strident, manufactured certainties set the tone. They form America's honor constituency and they remain a formidable cultural and political force.

Due to their activism, upholding American honor has become a prominent American ideology. It is adhered to dogmatically by a large and mobilized sector of the citizenry—with much of the ambivalent and alienated majority paralyzed on the sidelines. Honor in the NCE is as much a compulsion as it is an ideology— and it does not coexist peacefully with the cultural tendencies that elevate and distinguish the United States.

When the use of force comes into favor, it takes over a countries decision-making process. The belief in force is no longer limited to the battlefield. It is applied to detainees, whether or not they have been found guilty by a court of any sort. It overshadows Washington's approach to international problems that pose no national security threat—as evidenced with the Libyan campaign, which had only the elegantly versed pretext of a president (and no Congressional authorization) to justify it. It becomes a threat to America's formidable body of rights, liberties and protocols, as evidenced by a variety of transgressions.

The three cultural furies of the NCE (rage, fear, vengeance) are no match for the power of the president. The honor constituency will successfully challenge the executive, even when the president picks his issues with relative temerity. After all, Obama never said he would adjudicate all terrorist suspects in civilian courts—just some of them. And he never said America would stop warehousing human beings indefinitely, only that he didn't want to do so in Guantanamo.

The foundations for freedom and due process may not be able to stand up to a broad-based, culturally driven assault from the American people themselves. If much of the public, compelled by their own version of asabiyya, wants to erode Constitutional safeguards through their elected representatives, they just might be successful in doing so—indeed, they already have been.

According to the Economist Intelligence Unit, only 12.3% of the world's population lives in a full democracy. The vast majority of the world dwells in flawed democracies or authoritarian or hybrid regimes. America's democratic traditions and institutions are still a global exception.

To a large degree, the Third World's problems boil down to a single, ruinous sentiment: when trouble arises, it is time to knock heads. There is a reflexive tendency to resort to force to solve a wide array of problems. And behind that inclination is a faith in violence.

Americans are subscribing to that faith. According a German Marshall Fund's 2011 Trans-Atlantic Trends poll, 75 % of the U.S. public believes that war is sometimes necessary to obtain justice, while only 33% percent of the European public agrees with that sentiment. Unfortunately, data is not available to see how Americans' belief in the utility of violence has changed since 9/11, but compared to other wealthy countries it is notably high.

American asabiyya is not a casual faith-system. It is a vehement, uncompromising belief that can only be deeply divisive. There will always be large parts of the citizenry that don't subscribe to it. And to those that do, the doubters are public enemies—putting the country's survival at risk with lily-livered sensibilities. To the true believers, the public enemies from within are more dangerous than the terrorists without.

Amid this honor constituency, influential mouthpieces have emerged. The more outlandish their rhetorical assaults, the more heaping their pay and accolades become. They are halfway between shock-jock and pundit—a very well compensated *shockocracy*, if you will. They don't bother substantiating their arguments, relying instead on an "Oh no he didn't!" sensationalism and "Bring it on!" bravado.

MIND SLUTS

Anti-war female activists largely receded to the sidelines after Obama become president. And that reflects an unflattering reality of the liberal establishment. Protesters so often shelve their activism in favor of partisanship. Apparently, the Democrats know how to drone attack more gently than Republicans!

But back when women were in full protest mode, they displayed unflinching persistence in the face of ferocious attacks on their character. Indeed, the *shockocracy* seemed most inspired when descending on those women, and introduced unparalleled coarseness to the lexicon. Never before—not during the Vietnam War, not during the Cold War, not during the culture wars of the '60s, '70s and '80s—have Americans witnessed such base rhetorical blows. The *shockocracy* introduced the most rabid slurs to ever intrude on the discourse—and they were gender-laden attacks.

Indeed, the *shockocracy* has attempted to discredit female advocates—along with women who have attempted to give Americans the whole story on the wars—in highly personal, emotive terms. And that approach makes abundant sense. The alternative would be to argue in defense of militarism, based on facts and logic—not the most attractive option.

Some of the women activists have lost sons and daughters in the wars, and they dare to call for an end to conflict just the same, rather than advocate for continuing combat to rationalize and dignify the death of their loved ones. They are therefore a particularly difficult group to challenge morally. And the smears must therefore be all the more malignant.

The *shockocracy* has not innovated a new brand of gender-based attacks. They are drawing from generic approaches. In deploying these immemorial smears, they engage in what is probably one of the world's oldest professions.

Those kinds of rhetorical assaults have largely receded in the industrialized world. In the Third World, though, they remain an indispensable tool for repressing women's advocacy and participation. The reason for that is very simple.

If logic dictates that women should have a vital role in society and enjoy equal rights, then cultural coercion must be used to counter that logic. In America, logic dictates that the use of force should be ended responsibly but swiftly. And the women who have somehow defended such logic have been the victims of cultural coercion.

In his book "Islam Under Siege," Akbar Ahmed writes: "Honor and revenge; this is the male interpretation of social action." And if that is true even in America in the NCE, then perhaps that is why women in particular have taken exception to that form of social action. And it is also unsurprising that some of the men that agitate for militaristic revenge would put those women in their rhetorical sights.

The stand-by formula for undercutting a women's credibility, authority or rights has long been to brand her hysterical; question her sexual propriety; or characterize her as an emasculator of male will and honor. Those kinds of attacks on a woman's credibility remain rampant even in those parts of the Third World where, in legal terms, women have broad rights, such as Latin America.

In America, the cultural crackdown has been vicious and seemingly effective. Michael Savage perhaps uttered the most revealing bit of NCE ferocity, in describing Ashley Banfield. The former MSNBC correspondent reported extensively from Iraq and Afghanistan and in a 2003 speech gave a frank assessment of the media's war coverage—after which she was relegated to the journalistic wilderness. Savage said Banfield was "the mind-slut with a big pair of glasses" who "looks like she went from porno into reporting." Indeed, little needs to be said in regards to such bared-teeth vulgarity, since the aptly named Savage succinctly undermines himself when he opens his mouth—in the eyes of level-headed Americans.

And surely, Savage is an extreme even in the NCE. But consider a stealthier blow delivered via innuendo, in a May 2003 New York Times article, which was clearly geared towards downplaying the near certain prospect that Banfield was retaliated against at MSNBC for her unflinching analysis of war coverage. The article by Jim Rutenberg said Banfield "was also known in the city's gossip pages for singing in a rock band and for holding late-night parties at her loft apartment." The article made an oblique stab at Banfield's credibility. And while the former war journalists of Vietnam were rewarded the elite positions of TV journalism, Banfield was swiftly demoted by MSNBC to cable backwaters after she questioned the nature of Iraq-War coverage.

But again, all that is nothing new. Women in the Victorian age who were rash enough to demonstrate independent thought were routinely deemed hysterical, and their debility was traced back to their very female organs, which were believed to be the cause and origin of their hysteria. In other words, their own vaginas were believed to be causing the problem, which certainly made it easy for self-empowered women to be summarily dismissed.

This was no accident. Society had to defend the indefensible: denying women their right to vote. In order to keep any self-empowered women in line, society had to develop a way to usher them swiftly to the fringe, before women's reasoned arguments for equality and justice would be addressed. The violation of rights, after all, is not the province of reason, but of brute coercion in its many guises. The more a society strays from the standards reason would dictate, the more it must rely upon the smear—or worse.

Examples of such slurs abound, including one on Code Pink claiming—in fine Victorian style—that the women have "sand in their vaginas." Far from elevating the debate, those apologists for the wars have contributed to the cultural regression.

Activist Cindy Sheehan has been subjected to worse. In August 2005, David Horowitz accused her of emasculating her dead son's valor posthumously, characterizing her as some sort of craven mother out to wring personal benefit from her son's tragic death. Perhaps Horowitz was following the lead of Glen Beck, who two days earlier had referred to Sheehan as a "tragedy slut." In the NCE, no assault on a woman's character is off the table. It's hard to conceive of a similarly malign attack on any man, for any reason—including, perhaps, a murderous pedophile.

And again, what did Sheehan do to deserve such a venomous, no-holds-barred attack? She advocated an end to the war that took (or rather robbed) her son's life and never generated any substantive benefit to U.S. national interests, particularly in proportion to the staggering economic, cultural and strategic costs. But of course, the *shockocracy* does not address those issues of substance. Why should it when it can instead launch a personal attack?

The tendency to undercut women's credibility via ancient prejudices is far more common and rancid in the Third World than America, even in the NCE. Indeed, Third World examples are not an indication of what occurs today in America, but offer a glimpse of the old-world origins of an ascendant U.S. trend. The Third World examples also illustrate where such dangerous mentalities can ultimately lead, even in the First World.

Surely, the Iranians mullahs and their proxies are well-versed in such a technique. After France's First Lady, Carla Bruni-Sarkozy, said that an Iranian woman accused of adultery should not be stoned to death, a state-run Iranian newspaper trotted out the most ancient attack on a woman, accusing her of engagement in the most ancient profession. In August 2010, the Kayhan daily called Bruni-Sarkozy "a prostitute," said she led a "perverted lifestyle" and that "she herself deserves death." The editorial then went on to chronicle Bruni's pre-marital love life (which, according to the item, including Kevin Costner, Donald Trump and Mick Jagger!), revealing the editors to be avid readers of Western gossip tabloids.

Such an approach towards repressing women echoes in Egypt. The Egyptian women who courageously took to the streets to contribute their voices and vitality to their country's democratic reform movement were subsequently seized by the military-backed government and subjected to virginity exams, reported Nicholas Kristof in a column on March 30, 2011. In much of the Third World, questioning a woman's sexual purity is the stand-by for delegitimizing and intimidating her—and thereby silencing her advocacy and activism.

The *shockocracy's* attacks are more temperate in comparison, but the similarities in theme and accusation are there. The rise of such an American cultural current will have unpredictable consequences. In the NCE women have played a prominent role in whistle-blowing and truth-telling, on everything from corporate malfeasance to craven foreign policy. The loss of that activism will hamper American transparency. And if it returns, expect to see the ferocity to rebound.

THE BIRTH OF AN ERA, THE KILLING OF AMERICAN REASON

A movement has been borne that is animated by unsubstantiated opinions. The more a pundit's opinions are emotively driven, the better. This group favors opinions that rest on gut instincts, some key rhyming words, exclusive conversations with God, or (when in doubt) a tough-sounding stance with crude, jingoistic or misogynistic implications. Backing up an argument with facts is highly suspect to this crowd, given the insidious, elitist traditions of such a practice.

As part of this honor movement, intellectuals are roundly detested. Academics are derided. And the few non-corporatized, free thinking, *untrademarked* journalists that remain in America are traitorous scum.

The honor constituency in America has, to a large extent, self-inflicted a cultural crackdown on informed thought. Just as America has most needed expert guidance, a cultural bankruptcy of Third World proportions has been enveloping the country—often reinforced by flag waving and self-righteous declarations of patriotism.

In the Third World, intellectuals, academics, journalists and other purveyors of facts, theory and common sense often do not fare well. Should they dare to do a little too much informing, or theorizing, or employing basic logic, a dank cell could swiftly become their contemplation chamber. Perhaps a fellow "expert" on the intricacies of stress positions could become their only audience. Or a worse fate could await. Often, they are quieted by a culture of fear and intolerance before they dare utter a subversive word.

Naturally, it is not only democracy and liberties that an authoritarian regime represses. All sorts of free thinking and fact-finding are cordoned off. And there is no question that such intervention limits the cultural development of a society—although it certainly is conducive to a great many slogans!

In his book "Islam Under Siege," Akbar S. Ahmed notes the cultural vacuum that heavy handed governments have created in some Muslim countries:

"The Prophet's saying (hadith), 'The death of a scholar is the death of knowledge,' emphasizes the importance of scholarship. Unfortunately, in the contemporary Muslim world scholars are silenced, humiliated, or chased out of their homes. The ramifications for society are far-reaching. In the place of scholars advising, guiding, and criticizing the rulers of the day, we have the sycophants and the secret services. The wisdom, compassion, and learning of the former risk being replaced by the paranoia and neurosis of the latter."

America's cultural poverty has overtones of the paranoia and neurosis that Ahmed describes. That cultural void remains ominous today and continues in tandem with a military/security complex that is also reaching Third World proportions.

This honor, fact-averse crowd is an amorphous force that was largely identified as the Tea Party for some years but has dispersed into a nameless entity. The constituency still exists. W. Bush was one of the pioneers of the cultural movement—for all the Tea Party's distancing itself from that U.S. president. Bush, as many Americans recognize, jettisoned the overwhelming caution raised by the most serious and distinguished experts on the Middle East and non-proliferation, and instead took his cue from the ideologically deviant neo-conservatives. He justified the invasion on "intelligence" that often came not from the old-hands at the CIA, but rather a "special" office installed at the Pentagon to reinterpret uncorroborated reports that were deemed flimsy by the rest of the intelligence community. And Bush seemed to reject reasoned arguments and calls for caution by publicly claiming to confer with God. Such a claim indeed crowds out any response based on reason or logic.

The American public has long harbored antipathy for intellectuals, a phenomenon that has been analyzed and written about for decades. But again, it is not only intellectuals that are loathed today. Any individual that points out facts or bases their opinions on actual historical events or even cognitive coherence is suspect. Indeed, critical thinking is distrusted. It is as if America is self-inflicting the kind of mental handicap that is so often a byproduct of being educated in, say, a madrassa.

Before 9/11, it seemed like America had reached the end of history on "yahoo" political and social movements. It is true that some reflexive, xenophobic forces have always kept a pilot light on in

America. But in terms of a national movement, they were largely dormant before the attacks and the launching of the wars. Now, they have been roused.

Today, delivering non sequitur harangues laced with prideful denunciations of the fact-based community is a highly profitable racket for the *shockocracy*. The greater the errors of fact and suggestion, the higher the peddler's paycheck seem to be. Perhaps more worrisome, though, is the degree to which the lines between the *shockocracy* and mainstream political candidates has been blurring.

In his book "A Simple Government," former presidential candidate Mike Huckabee derides academic achievement, describing Obama as "the kid in school who waves his A test score in front of the entire class but never gets picked to play baseball. He's an arrogant nerd, and no matter how smart he is, he can't hit, he can't throw and he can't run."

In his bid for the 2012 election, Mitch Romney took a similar tone, arguing against a cut in defense spending, claiming that a decision to do so "flows from the conviction that if we are weak, tyrants will choose to be weak as well; that if we could just talk more, engage more, pass more U.N. resolutions, that peace will break out. That may be what they think in that Harvard faculty lounge, but it's not what they know on the battlefield!" While Romney did not win the election, he still garnered close to half the popular votes and reflected the will of an influential and wealthy segment.

If there was once a hope that the 9/11 attacks had triggered just a passing celebration of ignorance, current realities should dispel it. Romney never addressed the nuts and bolts of defense spending. Why should he, when he can instead take a random shot at Harvard and give a nod to some unspecified certainties on battlefield? In Romney's world, the sources of American weakness become its strength. And that too sounds terribly familiar.

DOUBLING DOWN ON DESTRUCTION

War creates a perversion of logic. The policies bleeding the country are willfully transformed into sources of strength by the honor crowd. If reason would typically prompt us to recognize both the law of diminishing marginal returns and a sunk cost, war obscures such logic. If 100 Americans (or Muslims) have died in combat, then more lives must be thrown into the inglorious pit, in order to dignify and legitimize those deaths (or martyrs). The parties involved so often refuse to believe that their fighters have died in vain, that their deaths are a sunk cost, and that escalation will create nothing more than a corpse-ridden stalemate.

The honor constituency often uses its contorted logic to uphold the sources of America's inexorable weaknesses as strengths. The phenomenal defense budget that the profiteers gorge on is strength. Logic-based dialogue with foreign governments is weakness. Simply put, that confusion is the natural, cognitive destination of honor and unreason.

There are corners of the Third World where the honor reflex is intense and delusions are dangerous. As long as America is willing to continue fighting, there seems to be no end to the jihadis ready to enter the battle and fundamentalists willing to fund it. The belief system of the American honor constituency is beginning to look like the contorted beliefs of the jihadi and his financial backer. In the jihadi, the world can observe the same confusion of weakness for strength.

Muslims are undoubtedly under brutal attack in many parts of the world. They have thus become captivated with the idea that Muslims must violently rescue their brethren from the yoke of non-Muslim oppressors. And while that notion may be compelling, it is also misbegotten. The jihadi liberator ideology has become fantastical, escapist, and boundless.

Surely, the violent reaction in 2005 to the Dutch cartoon depicting the prophet Mohammed with a missiled turban was a manifestation of such delusions. The message of the cartoon was that Islam is an inherently violent religion, a charge which a handful of Islamic extremists saw fit to counter with additional violence. Those extremists failed to acknowledge that they descended into a self-defeatist rage at the hand of a cynical Western bigot.

But Malaysian Prime Minister Mahathir Mohamad, who is much admired all over the Muslim world, characterized the phenomenon best. "I try very hard to be optimistic about the Muslims in the 21rst century of the third millennium of the Christian Era. But I must admit that I find it is very difficult for me to be optimistic. I find few Muslims understand reality. They live in a make believe world where weakness is regarded as strength, where failures are regarded as successes."

This phenomenon appeared to surface in Boston in April 2013. A young man of Chechen background failed to vindicate his ambitions as a boxer in America and turned to extremist Islam ideology—and then carnage. The bombs he set off at a Boston marathon look like, among other things, a compensation for powerlessness.

While jihadi elders might have other, self-aggrandizing schemes in mind, many young jihadis seem to believe any and all persecution of Muslims provides a pretext for violence. In that regard, the jihadis seem to be missing a pragmatic point, which Mahathir summed up so well: "Even if the enemies of Islam are at the gates, the Muslims must first attend to the conflicts within their community, conflicts which they could never resolve."

Again, that argument does not in any way excuse the violence against Muslims perpetrated by non-Muslims. Rather, it highlights the fact that Muslims are still facing the inequities, indignities and repression imposed by other Muslims—despite the dramatic political mobilization that began in late 2010.

The jihadi also seems to naively believe in the nobility of violence. It is as if the Islamic warrior is convinced of a standing justification to resort to it if anything short of a perfect justice is seen around the world. Such an ideology ignores human fallibility and is violently utopic. Since such perfection can never exist, at what point does the jihadi cede to forbearance, negotiation or accommodation? Presumably, the jihad may continue until all Muslims are delivered a celestial kind of justice. As Mahatir put it:

"Muslims are forever looking for an excuse to fight holy wars or jihad. They are and they never have been too particular about the religious legitimacy of their jihad and the weakening of Muslim countries. The main thing is to fight and to be willing to die, to become a syahid, a martyr who had sacrificed his life for Islam and will gain a place for himself in heaven. That his self-service has contributed nothing to the struggle of the Muslims does not matter. That their actions have set back the struggle of the Muslim umma by decades and centuries even, does not matter. It is the quest for martyrdom that is important."

Indeed, Islam is the lexicon of jihad, and jihadis subscribe to it *a la carte*. Talk of establishing a caliphate seems often to be just the rhetorical flourish of jihad. Importantly, jihadis have never come even close to obtaining their "constructive" goals of establishing Sunni caliphates even in the most modest sense, except when the U.S. aided the Afghan mujahedeen in Afghanistan. In general, jihadis appear to be satisfied with mere destructive goals, if the creation of a Caliphate seems out of reach. Indeed, destruction is not a means to an end. It is an end—with revenge serving as a worthy achievement in and of itself.

Needless to say, America's honor constituency does not subscribe to ideas that extreme. But it does appear to be similarly unmindful of constructive goals, upholding revenge and military action as an ends in and of themselves.

GOD, GUNS, GOVERNMENT

"Religious hatred has a mimetic quality: The opposed groups mirror the hatred, rhetoric, and fears of each other." Akbar Ahmed, "Islam Under Siege"

W. Bush was America's first honor culture president. He fed a desire to get even. He festooned himself with the props of patriotism. But most importantly, God talked to him. And apparently, God has an incorrigibly martial spirit.

It is unsurprising that the crisis and shock surrounding 9/11 prompted many Americans to put God, government and the military in the same mental and emotional category. That reflex is understandable, and patently dangerous. The 9/11 attackers used a provocatively religious rationale to legitimate a brutal attack on civilians. And that phenomenon has supercharged Americans' religiosity, and perhaps residual Puritanical beliefs.

In the NCE America, political candidates often have a direct line to God or are apt in divining his will and preferences. During the 2008 presidential campaign, God's global street cred. was on the line. At a rally for Sen. John McCain in Iowa in October, 2008, Rev. Arnold Conrad told his audience:

"There are millions of people around this world praying to their god — whether it's Hindu, Buddha, Allah — that his [McCain's] opponent wins, for a variety of reasons …And Lord, I pray that you would guard your own reputation because they're going to think that their god is bigger than you if that happens. So I pray that you will step forward and honor your own name in all that happens between now and Election Day."

That God Hindu or Buddha may have won that one battle—if ever there was a God named Hindu or Buddha! The reverend may have gotten confused about some basic theological tenets, but in doing so he gave voice to a predominant view of the NCE: a tendency to see America's predicament as a global religious battle.

Surely, he is not the only one to do so. Romney gave voice to a similar sentiment when he said at The Citadel, a military college, in October 2011: "God did not create this country to be a nation of followers. America is not destined to be one of several equally balanced global powers. America must lead the world, or someone else will." Importantly, Romney's definition of leading was to continue bleeding and dying and throwing good money after bad in foreign battlefields.

The instincts of the Third World often mangle together church and state and army. There is often a compulsion in the Third World to use religion as a pretext for force. Pakistan offers an extreme example of such a comingling of realms—particularly in the intelligence service. The tendency is also seen in parts of Africa, one of the few remaining battlegrounds for religion and an area where Christianity is gaining converts, amid a world that has otherwise decided upon its faiths.

It is true that in some select Third World countries, the armed forces have been a bulwark of secular (and sometimes authoritarian) modernity. In Turkey, Syria, Egypt and other places, the military is secular institution, keeping at bay religious fundamentalism by force or threat of force. But that phenomenon is more exception than rule. Indeed, even secular despotic regimes keep the religion card in the back pocket. Authoritarian regimes often cultivate religiosity in the corps, particularly in times of crisis.

In the United States after 9/11, the rise of the honor culture has given way to the resurrection of the Christian soldier and a convergence of religion and the military and mainstream politics. This has not been an officially orchestrated, institution-wide phenomenon. Indeed, U.S. presidents have stressed to the American people repeatedly that the United States is not at war with Muslims.

And at no moment has a surge of religiosity in the U.S. military driven U.S. military action in Muslim countries. To the contrary, U.S. civilian leadership drove the invasion of Iraq—against the wishes of the joint-chiefs-of-staff. The same was true of the Libyan campaign.

But there has been a grassroots tendency to see the wars in predominantly Muslim countries in religious terms. That conviction is taking a life of its own. And it is not a welcomed phenomenon.

America's success is in no small part due to the daylight between church and state and military. That kind of institutional independence may be more vital than election rights as a guarantee of modernity and social harmony. In the NCE, the cultural tendencies conflating those realms have taken institutional significance.

Religious military elites, allied with secular, hawkish groups that champion aggressive American interventionism, have become a cultural force. The confederacy has been advocating for an American agenda that borders on Islamophobia. In September 2010, such a confederacy published the hair-raising report "Sharia: The Threat to America." The authors include "team leaders" Lt. Gen. William "Jerry" Boykin, Lt. Gen. Harry Edward Soyster and former CIA Director R. James Woolsey, Jr. According to a summary of the report:

"For nearly a decade since 9/11, America's national security establishment's understanding of the threat of Islamic terrorism and its approach to contending with that danger flow directly from a conviction that they have nothing to do with Islam, except to the extent al Qaeda 'perverts' or 'hijacks' that religion. But what if this characterization of the problem we continue to face is simply and utterly wrong? What if there actually is a direct tie between what recognized, mainstream authorities of Islam call 'shariah' and the jihad (or holy war) it demands of adherents, some of which is manifested as terrifying violence?"

These ideas are dominant among the honor crowd. The propaganda is part Hallmark-card patriotism and part Terry Jones proselytizing—that would be the pastor of Koran-burning fame.

A full 67 percent of Tea Partiers believe that Islam is more likely to encourage violence among its believers, according to a poll conducted in March 2010 by the Pew Research Center. That compares to just 40 percent of the American public that links Islam with violence.

So the Tea Party and those that sympathize with it hold much more strident views than the American population at large regarding Islam. But it does not command a monopoly on that sentiment. Consider that even in eclectic and tolerant New York, most respondents opposed plans to build a mosque and Muslim cultural center near Ground Zero. According to a Quinnipiac University Poll released in August 2010, 52% of those polled said they did not want the mosque to be built at all, while 31% were in favor of it and 17% remained undecided.

Of course, America has always had elements of traditional society that groups God, guns and government in its own collective mind, and demands that the rest of the country do the same. But those impulses have in the past been balanced with competing American cultural forces. And the straight-up Tea Partiers of today are more vehement. They, like so much of the rest of the world, are deflecting the brunt of emasculating financial loss and military hardships. They are justifiably outraged at the 9/11 attacks, like the many people from around the Third World who have endured violent wrongs.

And like in so many traditional societies, the restoration of honor promises an antidote to the nation's grievances. Consider the following quote, filling in the first two blanks with the word Christian and the last with the word God:

"It is important in our _____Society, that the ____principles, morals and values are upheld with the fullest conviction, honor and austerity, in obedience to ____, exalted be He."

That quote is taken from the website of the Muslim Brotherhood, so the words Islamic were in the first two blank spaces and Allah in the last. But with those identifying words left out, such staple passages could be ripped from the August 2010 "Rally to Restore Honor," hosted by Glen Beck. Apart from paying homage to himself at the rally, Beck implored Americans to honor warriors and to summon God, with no reminder that those sentiments belong to different realms.

At the rally, Palin also put fighting—and dying in particular—in celestial terms, striking a rhetorical resemblance to the al-Aqsa Matyrs Brigade. This American constituency and Islamic parties often hit on many of the same principles, stressing the importance of turning back to an earlier, more pious era and restoring honor.

The Tea Party's penchant for linking the Islamic deity to violence seems like some kind of perverse joke. After all, when the Partiers get down to the business of voicing their hopes and dreams (and rage!) they pathologically merge the sword, God and the flag. And that could be mistaken for the political strategy of, take your pick, the slogans of so many Islamic groups (to say nothing of Al-Qaeda type groups) vying for political power in the Greater Middle East.

Many Tea Partiers say they to want to reduce the size and role of government but they see government as the solution on matters of faith. If America is indeed spiritually impaired, do the partiers really believe that public schools, or state governments, or any official body, could spearhead a solution of faith? Isn't that akin to a spiritual handout?

And if the partiers really want to rekindle the country's self-reliant, can-do vitality, then shouldn't the churches be the grass-roots agents of renewal? If that is the case, why are Tea Partiers convening a political—rather than a religious—movement?

Keeping church, state and the military on separate plains is a triumph over raw human nature. There appears to be a current of engrained human impulses longing to put all those elements in the same category. While many democracies have managed to keep realms from commingling, authoritarian regimes often have not. Certainly, countries like Pakistan would be much better off without such an intersection—which may serve parochial interests but undercuts the country's fundamental progress.

In America, such a trend has polarized the populace. Immediately after 9/11, the country had seemed poised to unify. American heroes emerged as demigods. First responders made colossal, life-threatening efforts to move boulder-sized rubble—rescuing victims buried alive underneath and capturing the world's imagination. But since those early days of the era, an ascendant honor culture and strident *shockocracy* has sown deep, debilitating divisions.

CHAPTER 10
CRY, MY DIVIDED COUNTRY

In mid-November 2012, immediately following the elections, Maine Republican Party chairman Charlie Webster said: "In some parts of rural Maine, there were dozens, dozens of black people who came in and voted on Election Day." In a televised interview, he added, "Everybody has a right to vote, but nobody in [these] towns knows anyone who's black," adding, "How did that happen? I don't know. We're going to find out."

Webster's racially charged comments followed on Romney's leaked characterization of 47% of Americans as people who "pay no taxes" and are essentially freeloaders. And Romney's divisive comments were concurrent with Mike Huckabee's factually challenged assertion that Obamacare forces churches to buy insurance that cover abortion and that voters therefore face going to hell if they vote for the Democratic incumbent.

Clearly, the racial, religious and political tone in America has changed dramatically since 9/11. Politics have always gotten dirty, but the discourse has reached a new trough. This may in part be opposition to the first black president, but it seems intricately linked to the shock and awing of America and what is widely regarded as higher stakes in America's survival. A mistrust of Muslims, in terms of the "other" in our midst, seems to be spilling over to other kinds of broader prejudice.

As the Blue Team and Red Team and their associates vie with each other, much of the country seems to be suffering from a kind of spaced-out ideology fatigue. The ideological excesses of the Bush administration seem to have left much of the country detached and disaffected. Amid this complacency and ideological sterility, new brands of radicalism are filling the void, or least projecting the loudest voice.

Many on the hard right see America under mortal attack not only by Islam, but also by their government and the Obama administration in particular. And the more snarling the extremism becomes, the more strenuously American urbanites from the Blue states want the government to take control, even if that entails using murky methods. Indeed, the growing anger of Red State America has unmistakably put Blue Staters on the defensive. The economically powerful Blue Staters readily consent and loftily legitimize a larger role for the state, even if it means an erosion of constitutional rights, particularly rights to privacy. And that inclination to control the rabble further incenses the Reds. So the two trends feed off each other, creating a cycle of polarization. And these divisions are dangerous for a rich democracy.

In the Third World, countries are often held together precariously. After *WWII*, the British and other empires deliberately constructed countries to remain weak and off balance. Ethnic groups were divided and pit against each other. That stroke of post-war dim wittedness has proved to have been a costly, cruel miscalculation, creating a kind of money pit of Western aid to alleviate the strife and poverty it has helped engender.

Today, divided countries remain weak countries. They have weak governments, weak institutions, weak economies. Shi'ite, Kurdish and Sunni factions have become household names in America since the start of the Iraq War. But the ethnic rivalries of Iraq are not uncommon. Similar divisions enervate much of the Greater Middle East and Africa and parts of Asia.

Rich countries have had the advantage of developing more organically, with people sharing a linguistic and ethnic heritage often living within the same national borders. There are exceptions— such as the Basque, the Catalan, etc.—but Europeans countries enjoy a cohesion that eludes much of the Third World, sometimes because, again, the latter were often deliberately created to include competing groups.

Indeed, the *Third Worldish* countries of ethnically diverse Eastern Europe have been beset with much graver divisions than prevail in the rest of the continent. In Latin American, where countries were not carved up to create such fissures, geographical tensions are not as intense.

Polarized countries are filled with distrust. And societal trust in government, in fellow man, in government, in a judicial system is a vital foundation of prosperity and democracy. As Lawrence Harrison put it in his essay "*The End of Multiculturalism*," from the January/February 2008 issue of The National Interest:

"A key component of a successful democratic transition is trust. Trust is a particularly important cultural factor for social justice and prosperity. Trust in others reduces the cost of economic transactions, and democratic stability depends on it."

According to the U.S. government funded World Values Survey, which has been conducted in waves over the past decade by a global network of social scientists, the countries with the highest levels of societal trust are generally the wealthiest on a per capital basis, while those with the lowest are on the bottom. There are some exceptions, such as China, which enjoys very high levels of trust but has not achieved solid wealth on a per capital basis. But for the most part, a correlation between wealth and trust prevails. And so America not only stands to more deeply resemble Third World countries culturally if trust continues to dissolve, a loss of trust could also come to impair America's ability to prosper.

Discontent and jingoism have pervaded the American consciousness. Many Americans believe their voices are not being heard
on the issues central to the country's survival. They subscribe to
a hair-trigger, extreme ideology. That popular sense of powerlessness, mixed with a readiness to use violence, is a combustible
mix. America is in a cold culture war with itself. And most dis-
turbingly, that cultural undertow has been gaining momentum
in the NCE.

Before 9/11, the United States had been able to remain relatively
unified in the face of its diversity by way of a national American
identity and an intense melting pot. The opportunities, freedom
and goodwill of America have encouraged immigrants to assimi-
late. But that American welcome is becoming reticent. And animosity could grow as economic troubles continue to exact
hardship.

According to a Spring 2010 report by the Southern Poverty Law
Center, the number of hate groups in America rose 54% between
2000 and 2008. That number rose again slightly in 2009 (from 926
in 2008 to 932 in 2009). The report also said: "Already there are
signs of similar violence emanating from the radical right. Since
the installation of Barack Obama, right-wing extremists have mur-
dered six law enforcement officers. Racist skinheads and others
have been arrested in alleged plots to assassinate the nation's first
black president. One man from Brockton, Mass. — who told police
he had learned on white supremacist websites that a genocide was
under way against whites — is charged with murdering two black
people and planning to kill as many Jews as possible on the day

after Obama's inauguration. Most recently, a rash of individuals with antigovernment, survivalist or racist views have been arrested in a series of bomb cases."

Since the end of slavery and state-sanctioned discrimination, the United States had maintained the kind of trust and unity that most other rich countries have enjoyed—which is to say, not flawless, but functional. There has long been a North-South rivalry, but for the most part, a working relationship has endured. Even during the tumultuous civil rights era, there was at least grudging resignation regarding which direction the country was going, except in some radical corners of the country, where individuals fought unity and equality through savagery.

Fast track now to America, in the NCE. Most middle-aged Americans saw, for the first time in their lives, a profoundly divided America sometime in wake of 9/11—after the first pangs of solidarity dissipated—with the advent of the Red and Blue states and the "real" vs. not-real America. The high priests and priestesses of the *shockocracy* have been adept at engendering divisive alarm among their followers. And the 2012 elections highlighted the durability of the divide.

According to a March 2011 Pew Research poll, 69 percent of Tea Partiers favor officials who stick to their positions, rather than make compromises with people they disagree with. So the Tea Party members do not want their elected officials to work constructively in Washington.

With the recession persisting, and more and more people joining the ranks of the unemployed, the Tea Party, the *shockocracy* and some former officials will continue to polarize the country. They are some of the most unseemly protagonists in America's cultural degradation and Third Worlding. But they are not the only players.

CHAPTER 11
THE WAR ON TV

The Justice Department hit a nerve when it claimed that it had probable cause to believe that Fox News reporter James Rosen violated the Espionage Act of 1917 by disclosing classified information, as the Washington Post revealed in May 2013. While Justice didn't indict Rosen, the administration set a dangerous precedent when it laid a legal argument for charging a journalist as a spy for publishing leaks. Whether or not Rosen erred in publishing the information to begin with does not diminish the procedural and legal significance of the Justice Department's actions. Time will tell whether that precedent will resonate into the future.

But the press corps should not have been caught unawares. The government has been giving the public ample cause for concern, in regards to press freedom and independence. In mid-2012, Americans saw a warzone tactic brought home—without a shot being fired. That tactic involved some unorthodox PR stratagems, involving an award-winning U.S. journalist working for America's largest newspaper. After publishing a series of articles calling into question the soundness of a military contractor's PR strategy in Afghanistan, that same reporter found himself a victim of an under-handed smear campaign from that same Pentagon contractor. The fact that the contractor would launch such an attack against a reporter for USA Today demonstrates the brazenness and sense of empowerment that the Pentagon's PR proxies have reaped.

USA TODAY Pentagon reporter Tom Vanden Brook reported on a questionable approach that Leonie Industries used in Afghanistan, costing the U.S. taxpayer hundreds of millions of dollars. Leonie's practices included planting stories into Afghani media outlets, with no indication that a U.S. military contractor had authored them. After reporting closely on the "information operations" in a series of articles, Vanden Brook discovered a peculiar "information operation" had been launched targeting him personally.

Someone, or some entity, had opened various websites and chat accounts that were aimed at discrediting the reporter. Eventually, the minority owner and former president of Leonie, Camille Chidiac, acknowledged through an attorney that he was responsible for opening some of discussion forums.

The episode is a microcosm of the press manipulation that has emerged since 9/11. Through a variety of finessed maneuvers, the U.S. government or its proxies have achieved the Third World gold standard for curtailing press freedoms: controlling access and content. It seems inconceivable this underhanded assault on the press' independence could have been executed without the shocked compliance of the public.

The Pentagon has, through clandestine means, hand selected the journalists allowed onto the war zones. In a series of articles in August 2009, Stars and Stripes newspaper reported just how the Pentagon appeared to be making embed decisions—through a practice the American public had no previously knowledge of. The Pentagon hired the Rendon Group to prepare graded reports on the journalists seeking embed positions, assessing how favorable their coverage of the wars had been. Those graded evaluations would have obviously aided the Pentagon in granting access to those journalists who would report most favorably on the wars. The Pentagon said it did not use the reports in that manner, but cancelled the Rendon contract shortly after the newspaper's illuminating reports.

And importantly, the Pentagon decision to continue doling out contracts to Rendon in 2009 was highly suspect to begin with, given the group's disreputable history. As widely reported, prior to the Iraq War, Rendon promoted million-dollar contracts to Ahmed Chalabi, who, in turn, forwarded fraudulent intelligence reports on Iraqi weapons to the Pentagon. Those flawed reports were used to build the case for war in Iraq and have had a devastating impact on U.S. credibility.

There has been incisive and impartial war coverage, but often it is not authored by the corporate heavyweights. After the AP in

September 2009 distributed to its news clients a photo of a dying Marine, Secretary of Defense Robert Gates personally contacted the agency to vigorously oppose its publication, claiming it would mark an "unconscionable departure from the restraint most journalists and publications have shown covering the military since Sept. 11." Gates was uncharacteristically correct, in that the AP did indeed break from common practice by showing the reality of the war. And Gates' astonishing public rebuke highlights the degree to which the U.S. government is willing to interfere with journalistic prerogatives—just like Third World governments.

The level of the media's war-time omissions are a new American phenomenon. An AP story on the AP photo put it this way: "Critics also maintain some of the [embed] rules [for Iraq and Afghanistan] are aimed at sanitizing the war, minimizing the sacrifice and cruelty which were graphically depicted by images from the Civil War to Vietnam where such restrictions were not in place."

Those attempts to interfere with war coverage add to a series of equally unsettling interventions. The New York Times reported in late 2009 that the Pentagon deployed former members of the military still on the payroll for contracts, but presented as impartial observers, to deliver talking points on the war to U.S. media outlets. In addition, the Pentagon gave the Lincoln Group a multi-million-dollar contract to plant "news stories" that it had prepared in Iraqi media, which was often presented as real journalism. Finally, the Pentagon repeatedly attempted to block Al Jazeera from reporting out of Iraq, after it covered the civilian casualties of the war.

SUGAR-COATED COMPLICITY

"The majority of the media and many notable journalists, more than being submissive and saving their skin, had a good time. They were not victims. Nor were they innocents ... And there is more to reexamine: submission out of fear is one thing, and quite another is the genuflection, sugar-coated and gleeful, of complicity. Of the latter there was too much."

A retrospective on the Argentine media during the Falklands War (translated), by Rodolfo Braceli

"... it was a glorious, wonderful picture that had a lot of people watching and a lot of advertisers excited about cable news. But it wasn't journalism, because I'm not so sure that we in America are hesitant to do this again, to fight another war, because it looked like a glorious and courageous and so successful terrific endeavor..."

Ashley Banfield, April 2003, on coverage of the Iraq War by embedded reporters

Shortly after 9/11, post-boomer Americans saw something they had never seen before: American flags undulating dramatically in the background of news spots, often coupled with a subtle, flapping sound-effect—tacitly tying the wars with patriotism. Just when the media's role became most critical, the U.S. media surrendered its independence.

The media of the Third World has long been the weaker cousin of America's Fourth Estate. Journalists (that often do not come from the moneyed class) are sidelined by high-ranking officials (that have usually accrued generations of privilege) in the Third World. And in terms of U.S. law, the U.S. media has long enjoyed freedoms and rights that even its European counterparts, in reckoning with strict defamation and other speech laws, do not. That distinction eroded dramatically after September 11th and the launch of the wars.

Media outlets entered a competition on who could wave the flag—and therefore support the wars—most emphatically. Under such NCE conditions, a dissenting voice could not be tolerated. On February 24, 2003, less than a month before the invasion of Iraq, MSNBC dumped Phil Donahue. A leaked in-house memo said: "Donahue represents a difficult public face for NBC in a time of war.... He seems to delight in presenting guests who are antiwar, anti-Bush and skeptical of the administration's motives." The memo also said that NBC could be hurt by a perception that it was "a home for the liberal antiwar agenda at the same time that our competitors are waving the flag at every opportunity."

Despite the American media's compliance, the Pentagon has taken pains to make sure media coverage of the wars is even more favorable than it would otherwise be. And in doing so, it echoes the stratagems of Argentina's military junta during the Falklands War of 1982. Like the junta, the Pentagon has maintained a determinative control on safe access to the war zone—through its embed policies—and has attempted to shape that other, all-important aspect of journalistic jurisdiction—content.

The Argentine media was able to maintain some journalistic discretion, despite the quite visible hand of the junta. All the same, the junta exercised tight control over the war zone in the most flagrant of ways: it physically selected the Argentine journalists that were allowed onto the Falklands and checked all news content. It destroyed pictures and documentation that was not to its liking.

It is true that the dangerous conditions in Iraq prevented many journalists from covering the war's fallout for civilians. In effect, the U.S. military's shortcomings in providing security for Iraq protected it from negative press coverage of civilian casualties—at least in the U.S. media. But the U.S. military also played a direct role in controlling press coverage. As a May 7, 2011 article in The New York Times put it: "The military also set strict rules for embedded journalists that kept many graphic images from the public eye."

That article covered an iconic photo that renowned war-photographer Chris Hondros took in January 2005, which broke the trend in U.S. journalism. Hondros photographed a blood splattered 5 year-old girl in terrible despair, after U.S. soldiers opened fire on her car at a dark checkpoint, killing her parents. The military asked Hondros to leave his embedded position after the publication of the photo in the New York Times. (Hondros was later killed covering the war in Libya.)

By controlling access to the war zone and interfering with journalistic content decisions, the Pentagon has resembled one of the most oppressive, and lumbering, military regimes in Latin American history. The Pentagon's interventions are especially excessive when considering how obliging the U.S. media has been.

When Argentina invaded the Falklands on April 2, 1982, many Argentine newspapers sounded off Mission-Accomplished propaganda, claiming that an Argentine government had been established on the island before the war had even begun, while others factually noted that military operations had started. The Argentine media by and large failed to educate the public on the potential costs of a war with Britain.

Indeed, it is difficult to document the U.S. media's failures to report independently, since it has largely committed failures of omission. A failure to cover conditions on the ground has been the overwhelming problem. But a look back at the media's coverage of a pivotal moment in the NCE wars is illustrative.

President Bush has been widely criticized for strutting in front of a Mission Accomplished banner in May 2003. But the role of the U.S. media on that day has largely escaped noticed. And it also projected false triumphalism. Indeed, Bush eventually came under forceful criticism for his myopia, hubris and premature declarations of victory under the now-iconic banner. But the U.S. media failed to counter the self-congratulatory pageantry and spin of that day. Importantly, it has failed to retrospectively acknowledge its missteps.

Some of the coverage, especially televised reporting, sounded more like the accounts of state-run news agencies than anything resembling impartial news reporting. On May 1, 2003, CNN informed its viewers that Bush made a "picture-perfect landing"; was greeted by the roar of the seamen's approval; had underwater survival training to prepare for his flight; and (for those who were wondering) had enjoyed taking the controls of the aircraft and was an "F-102 fighter pilot in the Texas Air National Guard after graduating from Yale University in 1968." The story then quoted an aide to Dick Cheney, who reported that his boss "watched with a big smile." CNN also provided the insights of Rep. Christopher Shays (R-Connecticut): "This president had a right to rejoice. But it was just a compassionate, wonderful speech."

All that was missing in that coverage was a reverential reference to "Dear Leader." In its reporting on Bush's landing and his later speech, CNN and others did not provide a more sober perspective on Iraq to juxtapose with the administration's victory lap. Nor did it feature a single perspective questioning the pretext or need for the war or its amorphously soaring goals. Rather, its featured responses and analysis all focused on the potential danger of *ending* the war too quickly. Bush's Mission Accomplished speech has come to symbolize arrogance and spin. It should also commemorate the mainstream media's failure to juxtapose war propaganda with contextual analysis.

As president, Obama has opposed the fundamental provisions of a media and whistleblower protection bill, even though he had co-sponsored a version of it while in the Senate. The bill would protect journalists from going to jail if they refuse to reveal confidential sources who divulge national-security information. And so journalists remain vulnerable and exposed.

But the problem with the American press is more abdication than censorship or coercion. Obama seemed to have convinced much of the *commentariati* that he had so revolutionized warfare that his Af-Pak strategy could not be judged or put into a historical context of any kind. The boiler plate promotion of the war revolved around Obama and his generals acknowledging the steep challenges of the war, but arguing there was a "newness" to their approach. Much of the media accepted the often repeated and generic argument.

Of all the post-9/11 lapses, the media's forfeiture of its role as watchdog has perhaps been the most serious. The crisis and shock of 9/11 brought the media to heel, rather than marshalling an investigative or analytical zeal. And once that occurred, the popular media just left certain issues off the table. And it has failed to retake them with any vigor.

The media's loss of vitality and feistiness is not as serious as the more injurious co-opting of news outlets in many Third World countries, but it does blur the American distinction. What's more, the failures have aided and obscured all violations. It has therefore enabled the public's complacency.

The tepid news coverage has also reinforced an escapist penchant for R&R info-tainment. U.S. soft, hard and economic power may have been bled profusely by foreign endeavors, but Americans reserve the privilege of retiring to another realm, and watching in awe as contestants cram handfuls of maggots into their mouth before a buzzer resonates—times up!

CHAPTER 12
MAD TV

"Consumers need to be citizens, too," former Uruguayan President Julio Maria Sanguinetti

All societies need their opiates. It's difficult to begrudge individuals and societies their psycho-cultural dependencies. But a shocked and awed society is liable to hit their socio/cultural narcotics especially hard. As America's troubles have intensified, reality TV has become increasingly popular. Despite the criticisms related to quality controls and content integrity, the genre has continued to gain pace, becoming a cultural juggernaut. As James Poniewozik of Time Magazine put it, "In 1992, reality TV was a novelty. In 2000, it was a fad. In 2010, it's a way of life."

Some critics maintain that many reality TV shows reflect and indeed appear to bolster the ethos of the moment. As Francine

Prose put it in Harper's in 2004, reality TV embodies America's cultural degeneration.

Observant readers may already have noted that the guiding principles to which I have eluded- flinty individualism, the vision of a zero-sum society in which no one can win unless someone else loses, the conviction that signs of altruism and compassion are signs of folly and weakness, the exaltation of solitary striving above the illusory benefits of cooperative mutual aid, the belief that certain circumstances justify secrecy and deception, the invocation of a reviled common enemy to solidify group loyalty are the exact same themes that underlie the rhetoric we have been hearing and continue to hear from the Republican Congress.

But even when the collaboration between the military, the government, and the entertainment industry is not overt, these shows continue to transmit the perpetual, low frequency hum of agitprop. The ethics (if one can call them that) and the ideals that permeate these programs at once reflect the basest, most mindless and ruthless aspects of the current political zeitgeist.

As the shows both reflect and promote the zeitgeist, another strange upshot is materializing. In this sense too, America is increasingly resembling a Third World country.

The flourishing of reality TV in America is a strange confluence of first world modernity and Third World escapism. In some respects, reality TV turns on its head Third World concerns regarding honor—with contestants often required to out-humiliate each other on air. Reality TV often takes a modern American tendency to flout preoccupations about honor to an extreme. It often requires a subjugation of an individual's natural pride reflex.

Given the rise of reality TV, Americans sometimes had to be instructed on how offensive the Abu Ghraib abuse was to Muslims. Surely, some of the abuse was designed to inflict actual physical pain, but younger Americans had difficulty understanding why the psychological humiliation was so devastating to Muslim detainees. Those younger Americans saw subjugation through a reality-show lens, something to be striven towards competitively—and televised. They couldn't fathom the gravity of an individual's honor being violated.

So reality TV is a demonstration of American cultural modernity, to some extent. There is much American about it, starting with the fact many of the shows are American innovations. The genre often showcases a traditional American sense of competition, willingness to swallow pride and the pragmatism and mental toughness that requires.

But it is also a perversion of those modern virtues, in other respects. Reality TV is a celebration of all sorts of pettiness, vanity, materialism and exhibitionism. It fetishes meaningless confrontations (it's about RESPEK!) between contestants. Indeed, that aspect of reality TV plays into Third World obsessions about affronts to dignity and *street cred*. The manufactured, made-for-TV confrontations seemed ripped from Latin America's *telenovelas*—or soap operas. And better yet, it's *real!*

A societal thirst for sensationalism is a common trait in countries with few opportunities. Latin America's *machismo* is an outgrowth of such a phenomenon. Men are expected to provide for their families but often lack the means to fulfill hopes and expectations. And so they build an aggrandized view of themselves, and their male power. That fantasy construct, which is not necessarily based on actual achievements, allows that individual to preserve self-esteem and remain the lord of his manor—however modest. Women also preserve some fantastical notions about the power of their femininity, usually connected to virginity or female sexual honor, to bolster self-esteem and grapple with the family's grim, unadorned realities.

But after the economy really began to decline, reality TV in America was no longer just a cultural oddity. Struggling Americans increasingly began to look to reality shows as a source of potential revenue. If ordinary people were now becoming stars, then why shouldn't we? In the reality TV world, we can all aspire. We can all metamorphose. This was painfully demonstrated by the balloon-boy episode and the cash-strapped but socially ambitious White House party crashers. And in this regard, American reality shows are beginning to take on the dynamics of similar competitive shows in the Third World.

Back in February 2003, an article in the San Francisco Chronicle pointed out the differences between reality TV in America and that genre in Latin America. Reporter Daniel A. Joelson wrote from Santiago, Chile: "While reality shows on U.S. TV typically goad well-heeled contestants to perform absurd feats for cash prizes, the shows' counterparts in Latin America can sometimes reflect hard history and harsh reality." He added that a grueling recession in Argentina is "the backdrop for the show 'Human Resources,' in which two contestants vying for a single job recite their personal hardships to win the votes of viewers." But given the state of the U.S. economy, this kind of Third World pop-culture trend is now America's TV reality.

"Today's reality TV is very aware of the state of the union, and some of the most popular shows deal frankly with financial trouble," noted Thor Jensen in January 2012, for RR.com, with shows such as Undercover Boss, which embeds CEOs with employees and is "perhaps the most class-conscious of today's reality TV shows."

Reality-type TV shows are a major source of aspiration in many developing countries—which was so evocatively demonstrated in the Indian movie Slumdog Millionaire. And now in America, people who have been brought to their knees by the global recession are beginning to look at reality TV not as a pastime or entertainment, but rather as a driving hope for a way out of mounting debt and unemployment. Americans are beginning to think they can't make it in the mainstream economy, and are pinning their hopes on something as fantastical as reality-TV stardom.

And if that perception becomes more pervasive, the United States will begin to look socially as demoralized as the Third World. And that phenomenon would then further perpetuate economic decline. In his essay "The End of Multiculturalism," published in January/February 2008 in The National Interest, Lawrence E. Harrison argues that a "progress prone" culture is a vital foundation of prosperity. And central to a progress prone culture is a belief in:

"... education, the belief that a person can influence his destiny, wealth is the product of individual creativity and advancement should be based on merit."

Americans are increasingly losing confidence in America's meritocracy, and the prospect of pulling themselves up by their own bootstraps. In this backdrop, the hopes associated with reality TV are filling the void. With Americans gripped by a sense of impotence, reality TV seems to offer empowerment, and the delusions it nourishes further undermines Americans' will to overcome steep challenges.

Indeed, the popularity of the shows may not only be an indication of America's Third Worldism, they may also be contributing to the Third Worlding of America. As a rule, the shows don't glamorize hard work or cultivated talent. Indeed, they legitimize the breaking-in to a White House event. And they are diverting people's attention from the ongoing events that matter.

That trend is also dangerous for a rich democracy. It could undermine what Harrison calls "social capital," which he believes is another building block of prosperity and development. Harrison cites Roger Doyle's definition of social capital as:

"a high level of trust and tolerance, an egalitarian spirit, volunteerism, an interest in keeping informed, and participation in public affairs."

Certainly, reality TV is detracting, rather than adding, to America's interest in keeping informed and participating in public affairs. Reality TV promotes vanity and consumerism, at the expense of civic values in general. It is diverting America's focus from the threats to its democracy and wealth. As standards in so many areas of the private sector and government were shrugged off after 9/11, Americans seemed more eager than ever for standards to be shed in the way of entertainment TV.

After all, it was a new era, and there was an adolescent, defiant tone to it. America has always indulged escapist TV, to some extent. But reality TV eclipses any of its more modest pop-culture predecessors, which reigned mostly by day but not prime time.

In this dimension, the Third World and a kind of perverse American modernity converge ingloriously. As a result, America citizens appear as disaffected and resigned as their Third World brethren—only occasionally roused from the ever-stranger genre by their fulminating pet pundit, peddling the outrage du jour. We are entranced by the zeitgeist of the era.

CHAPTER 13
A NEW-COMMON-ERA CENTRIFUGE

The 9/11 attacks seemed to create in America a centrifugal force that brings all kinds of human matter into its corrupting vortex. The centrifuge continues to run at high velocity today.

The centrifuge drew in a prominent and unlikely official during the so-called Plame Affair. Indeed, one of the most striking aspects of that saga was the identity and nature of one of the primary protagonist implicated in the "outing" of CIA operative Valerie Plame. Richard Armitage—who is said to be as physically imposing as he is psychologically intimidating—opposed the heady sprint to war with Iraq and the "cooking" of some particularly dubious intelligence as a pretext for that war. And he was known to be fiercely loyal to his boss, former Secretary of State Colin Powell, another U.S. official who was similarly opposed to the most flagrant intelligence "cook outs." And yet despite the well-known reservations of both men in that regard, Armitage played a pivotal role in a plot that revolved around bolstering the credibility of char-broiled intelligence.

Why did Armitage play such a seemingly antithetical role? Unfortunately, both and Powell got caught in the great NCE centrifuge—just like so many officials continue to do today. The foul irony of having one of the strongest critics of cooked-up intelligence personally involved in one of the most craven and unseemly plots to legitimize that intelligence is striking. And it helps to illustrate the dizzying capacity of the centrifuge of the mind.

The particulars of the Plame affair are well-known history now. Joseph Wilson, Plame's husband, was sent on a mission to investigate the credibility of reports that Niger was sending to Iraq fissile material that Baghdad could use to advance a nuclear program. Wilson reported back that the report was not credible. When President W. Bush himself propped up the yellow-cake fantasies in speeches, Wilson called out the White House in an op-ed in The New York Times. The White House and State Department then launched a smear campaign in response, targeting Plame, and compromising Armitage. The facts, of course, fully vindicated Wilson.

Interestingly, the W. White House, which was both driver and victim of the centrifuge, was more than willing to shoot down one of its own in its frenzied race to war in Iraq. Not only was Plame a dedicated, sacrificing operative who labored anonymously at the

CIA, she also appears to have played a role in obtaining the White House's crown jewel of WMD intelligence on Iraq—the aluminum tubes that the CIA said were suitable for use in an Iraqi nuclear program. (The Department of Energy, which was the premier authority on such matters, concluded that the tubes did not appear to fit specifications for use in such a program.)

The CIA's assessment was incorrect. But regardless of the error, it gave the W. White House an invaluable political boost in selling the Iraq war to the American public. The aluminum tubes were so crucial to the White House's case for the Iraq War that they would seem to make Plame untouchable. But the W. White House suffered no such sentimentality. The tubes that Plame and others discovered were leveraged to the hilt, but she as an individual was deemed fit for sacrifice. She was fair game. And Armitage was a critical player in the smear.

The centrifuge has caught many others, including some CIA intelligence analysts that faltered under pressure. President Obama may well be one of its most high powered, sophisticated victims. The president assumed office in 2009 with a stated determination to make at least some symbolic changes, such as closing down Guantanamo and trying terror suspects in civilian trials (sometimes). Not only has he not achieved any of those symbolic goals, he has also opened a new aerial front in America's foreign wars, pioneered phenomenal snooping capabilities through the NSA and conspired with private U.S. corporations and foreign governments to yoke digital information freedom—in the case of WikiLeaks.

In matters of constitutional law, Obama may be one of America's most informed and well rounded presidents—and his administration has also been aggressive in limiting the scope of constitutional rights in terms of free speech, freedom of the media, privacy and due process. He has also made a new record in retaliating against whistleblowers—unmatched even by President Nixon. In doing so, he also publicly condoned the torment of a U.S. citizen who was not even suspected of any ties to terrorist groups, with the forced nudity and exposure and prolonged solitary confinement of Army Pfc Bradley Manning.

Obama is no naïf. He is not some trust-fund president who fell in over his head. He appears to have harbored some worthwhile objectives for America. But the dizzying force of the NCE centrifuge is not to be underestimated.

The power of the centrifuge is cultural, institutional, political. Many other countries have their own centrifuge running. What will it take for America to shut its own down?

CHAPTER 14
LIVE PRESIDENTS

Osama bin Laden once sneeringly referred to Obama as a subordinate "house boy." Surely, the nature of the U.S. executive failed to impress bin Laden much. The president must not only share powers, he must also defend even the foolhardy laws that were passed by previous Congresses and approved his predecessors. In America, it is folly to fetishize the power of the president.

What's more, in the NCE we have seen cultural currents that are born independent of officialdom, such as the Tea Party, gain outsized influence. There is sometimes little that a U.S. president can do to temper the strength of those currents and movements. Indeed, the abuses of the NCE do not all revolve around presidential overreach. Under Obama, Congress blocked efforts by the president to have high-profile terror suspects tried in U.S. civilian courts and to close down Guantanamo. The three cultural furies of the NCE (rage, fear, vengeance) were no match for the power of the president in those cases.

But the presidents have also used blunt policies and abused their powers. The NSA's secret phone snooping program constituted a chilling overreach. There are various culprits of America's afflictions.

There is little question that the American president is ultimately responsible for all the policies he crafts, all the bills he proposes, the statements he makes, and the nature and breadth of the battles he pitches in the courts. And there is no question that both presidents have fought successfully to dramatically expand their powers. During wartime, when the courts are especially obliging to the commander in chief and the power of the U.S. executive is at its peak, a president carries a distinct responsibility for the authority he requests and exercises.

There is never going to be a definitive explanation of why the presidents of the NCE acted as they did. But if both W. Bush and Obama did their part to reinforce America's shock and awe and retrench the nation in its Third Worlding path, then it remains important to place these protagonists in some global and historical context.

THE STORY OF O:

FIRST WORLD PANACHE, THIRD WORLD EXECUTION

The decorous President Obama promised to wage war more gently and politely. He speaks and looks like the consummate First

Worlder: measured, articulate, calibrated. The nuanced Obama has shelved Bush's comic-strip depictions of foreign leaders—and the world.

But all that is the practical equivalent of a good suit. Obama's style is First World but the policies and execution are Third World. He has aggrandized and distorted foreign threats. He has eroded U.S. standards and distinction in legal, policy and moral arenas. Most importantly, he has subordinated the welfare of the country as a whole, and the interests of its citizenry, for the interests of a well-connected and funded elite—a prominent phenomenon in the crony controlled Third World. As a result, Obama contributes and sometimes escalates the policies that are draining American power and character.

Obama has put a First World sheen on Third World policies through a variety of PR tools. But an organizing principle of the spin revolves around a simple, central idea: the United States under Obama does things differently. It wars differently. It suspends habeas corpus selectively and with restraint. It advances on liberties more gingerly. And it puts military men and women at risk with a respectful selectivity.

In order to advance this precision-guided mythology, the Obama administration has, time and time again, insisted it resorts to the unseemly practices of war and security policy with bull's-eye accuracy. This, officials have consistently suggested, is the Obamaesque distinction. Bush dabbled in this PR strategy as well, but the Obama administrated took it to a higher narrative level.

Precision is what still seems to separate the United States from the Third World, as U.S. actions become increasingly similar to those often employed by underdeveloped countries. It justifies a surviving claim to global distinction, despite the errors, violations and setbacks of the NCE. It provides a buffer. But the precision defense rests on an unstable pretense.

President Obama declared that America's extensive drone campaign in Pakistan was a "targeted, focused effort" that "has not caused a huge number of civilian casualties." Obama's cavalier declaration was extraordinary not only because the use of drones is supposed to be secret, but also because it is unsubstantiated. U.S. drones are not precise instruments of war. The idea that the bad guys can be zeroed in on robotically from the air was always exorbitantly improbable in theory and has proved to be untenable in practice.

U.S. practice on detaining human beings also conflicts with the precision myth. The United States is not overly precise or judicious in its approach to detentions, as evidenced by the lower courts' repudiation of the government's reasons for locking up terrorism suspects. As America lowers its due process-standards, it does not look all that different from many institutionally immature, Third World countries.

But it is not just mountain dwelling, turbaned foreigners or American activists who have been harmed by the U.S. government's lack of precision in executing its policies. Importantly, U.S. service men and women have also been victimized. In reckoning with the fickle directives of its civilian overseers, the U.S. military has faltered in protecting the people risking not only life and limb but, outrageously enough, the integrity of their breathing capacity. Some physicians have suggested that the use of burn pits in Iraq and Afghanistan have caused permanent and debilitating respiratory problems for members of the armed forces. And serial suicides demonstrate the burdens and negligence afflicting the corps.

So the idea that the U.S. government puts its military men and women in harm's way only when it selectively deems it imperative to do so is a myth—a sad, insulting one. Individuals have been victimized by silent killers in the air and in the wiring, as the military strives to grapple with the inexorable challenges of a "surge-with-draw" war. As a result, the American distinction has been further minimized, as the nation's professional corps is tragically treated more like the cannon fodder of so many Third World countries.

Obama's superior political skills and finesse have given greater legitimacy to America's failed, enervating policies—lengthening their wretched life spans. And that fits with an identifiable Democratic strategy. Obama represents the return of liberal interventionists who support the wars in the Islamic world, and the bailouts of the banks, but want a more grounded, credible salesman to conduct them. Obama offers a new face, style and political savoir fare to sell the same, self-perpetuating, ruinous policies—and new ones.

Obama rebranded the Afghan campaign—relaunching old-new strategies. The media and pundits parroted the so-called innovations on combat in mindless fashion, without identifying where the real novelty in policy could be found. The opinion elite seemed to subscribe to some archaic gentlemen's agreement, creating a political space for Obama to have his crack at the war, rather than analyzing if his war plans appeared feasible. The interval that the media unwarrantedly granted Obama on Afghanistan needlessly increased the moral, strategic and financial cost of the war and allowed America's honor/warrior culture to extend its influence.

More recently, Obama has given combat a dangerous, no-cost image through his heavy reliance on drone bombings and his warfare-by-mercenary approach. Obama has relied on contractors to the same degree as some Third World countries do in waging their wars. He has deployed the same contractors that have tapped Pinochet- and apartheid-era soldiers—and integrated them into U.S.-led wars under the banner of U.S. contractor companies.

Judging from his statements, Obama understands how civilian deaths challenge the stated mission in Afghanistan. And there is also little doubt that the generals share those concerns. But the realities of Afghanistan have long been crafting U.S. policy, rather than the other way around. U.S. officials watch helplessly as U.S. soldiers come under attack from the enemy, only to see it escape into the primordial fortress of mountains and ravines that abound. And if officials perceive long odds anyway on the broader goals of the mission, they are probably calculating correctly. Given a tug of priorities between the theoretical aims of Washington and the dynamics of the war zone, it is always safer bet to follow the immediate blood flow. And that is presumably the explanation for the current U.S. strategy under Obama—which is the superpower's approach to self defense, rather than any cutting-edge strategy of a global power broker.

Undoubtedly, Obama is a far better interlocutor for military action. Certainly, the Agency seems to think so, especially in regards to America's NATO allies. The CIA stated as much in a memorandum (titled "Afghanistan: Sustaining West European Support for the NATO-led Mission – Why Counting on Apathy Might Not Be Enough") that was made public via WikiLeaks. The memorandum, published in March 2010, suggested that Afghan women be paraded about Europe in order to drum up support for the war—in the name of women's rights. And it held out the hope that the persuasive Obama would wring out more European troops for the Afghan war effort—which, of course, never occurred.

Some Obama defenders have insisted that his mistakes have been driven by pressure from the military brass. But that seems unlikely. Indeed, in the case of the military operation in Libya, it was Obama driving policy, apparently over the misgivings of the military community. In an interview, Bacevich (distinguished author, Boston University professor and former U.S. Army colonel) noted that the officer corps appears to believe "that interminable war is really an unsustainable proposition" and that officers prefer to "lower the interest in military power as the preferred instrument of American statecraft." Given that conviction in the corps, it appears more likely that the U.S. military is a victim of Obama's militarized foreign policy— not vice versa.

AN INVERSE ATA TURK

Obama does not fit into a Third World archetype. He is not the gregarious populist, in the mold of, say, Argentine President Carlos Raul Menem. He speaks well, but is not at all the garrulous Fidel Castro. He is not really a cult figure to anyone anymore, except some particularly listless moderates. He is not outwardly brutal enough to be Putinesque. Nor does he strut like a generalis-simo. He projects a style and image more similar to the techno-crats that rise to power in the Third World, after a crisis, perhaps a little like Prime Minister Manmohan Singh in India.

But something else comes to mind with Obama. He is like an inverse Ata Turk, Turkey's post-WWI leader, who paved the way for secular democracy to gain traction in Turkey. Why? Because Ata Turk had a definitively Third World-style of governing but he was a First Worlder in terms of vision and execution. Obama, on the other hand, is graced with a First World, precise policy style that Europe swoons for, but Third World vision and execution.

Ata Turk put Turkey on the road to secular democracy with a heavy hand. He erected a cult of personality around himself, replete with the hagiographic imagery that is so integral to the blunt Third World PR machine. But in building himself up, he countered the power of the clerics. He forcibly tempered the cultural importance of religion but he wasn't gratuitously authoritarian. It may seem that Turkey has reversed on some of the progress it made since Ata Turk's rule, but it seems more likely that the country has settled on a sustainable cultural equilibrium. The current government has an *Islamish* style and flavor, but the country's secular institutions remain largely intact.

Obama is post-partisan chic in demeanor. He knows how to pepper his speech with the occasional, Third World-style bravado that has become a political requirement since 9/11. But only just so. He is more comfortable when performing rhetorical acrobatics, trying to contort a more humanistic tone surrounding the strikes he presides over. Clearly a gifted orator, he prefers parsing the niceties of just war theory to boasting about drone attacks on Afghans—but he does countenance the latter.

In execution, he betrays the spirit of his own rhetoric. He has not waged the war more respectfully or humanely then his predecessor. All to the contrary, he has escalated the bluntest, most dehumanizing type of type warfare known to man via the drone attack. It is Third World brutality, with technological flourish. It zeroes in on the particular ethnic group making most of the problems for the U.S. mission in Afghanistan: the Pashtuns in Pakistan. Blunt, brutal, victimizing civilian populations, with a particular ethnic group in the crosshairs: the war looks like so many prosecuted in the Third World. What has Obama, and his predecessor, gotten America into?

Given the number of crises buffeting the country, Obama's artful artifice is arising amid a vortex of anxiety and confusion and either insipid or hysterical media scrutiny. The far-right has long entertained political delusions—such as the Obama birth certificate absurdity. Most on the left seem too mystified or depressed to hold him accountable. The country may therefore never see the reason for, and parallels of, its multi-faceted devolution. Obama has been long on hope, short on audacity. His political flair bought the wars time. And that time has cost considerable lives (on both sides) and money.

The president says he hears Lincoln when he writes his speeches. He delivered his oath on the Lincoln bible. He gives little pretense to modesty regarding his place in history. As indeed he should. His will be a consequential presidency.

And given those consequences, will Obama be remembered as a dirt-under-the-nails game changer—in the mold of Ata Turk—or as a sleek, glistening and ineffectual president? Perhaps America knows the answer, but amid the dizzying cultural maelstrom of the NCE, what leadership choices do the American people really have?

OBAMA'S PEEPS

In the Third World, political patronage is a way of life to a much greater extent than in the United States. But after 9/11, for a variety of reasons, crony politics was revitalized in America, to rival the traditions of the Third World. In many underdeveloped countries, those involved with intelligence are the croniest of the cronies, because they are privy to the most unsettling of a government's practices. And so it has been in the United States, particularly when Obama tapped Leon Panetta to be head of the CIA and later to head the Defense Department. The intelligence community's sharp intake of breath was almost audible when the president made the choice.

When Obama chose Panetta—a man with no direct intelligence experience whatsoever—to head the Agency, observers seemed first puzzled, and then became highly critical. Despite Obama's claims that he was going to staff top positions with strong leaders able to push back against his assumptions, the president instead awarded the top post at the CIA to someone who is not an authority on the organization but that the president apparently feels comfortable with. That was his qualification.

Obama's choice had a deep consequence for the United States and its citizens. According to the aforementioned study on drone policy conducted by the Bureau of Investigative Journalism, it was during Panetta's tenure that the drone attacks on rescuers and mourners were executed. When Panetta was replaced by David Petraeus that particular practice was discontinued, according to the study. Panetta, of course, was elevated to head of the Pentagon after his consequential stint at the CIA.

Obama intelligence peeps have been noteworthy in other regards, as well. They create a neat time continuum throughout the NCE. For example, consider James Clapper, who is the head of the entire intelligence community and oversaw the NSA's highly controversial phone snooping program—which Edward Snowden brought to light in June 2013. Upon testifying to Congress about the program, Clapper denied the government was collecting information on millions of Americans but subsequently conceded that the statements he had made to U.S. legislators were "clearly erroneous."

Back on October 28, 2003, Clapper, who was then-head of a top American spy agency within the Pentagon, made some assertions that became more and more audacious as he continued talking. "I think personally that the senior [Iraqi] leadership saw what was coming and I think they went to some extraordinary lengths to dispose of the evidence," said Clapper regarding Iraqi WMD.

Clapper said there was an "uptick" in truck traffic from Iraq into Syria before combat began and even as the war was ongoing. Clapper acknowledged that there were limits to what overhead surveillance (which Clapper's agency specialized in) can detect inside trucks. All the same, he offered this bold claim: "But certainly, inferentially, the obvious conclusion one draws is that the certain uptick in traffic ... may have been people leaving the scene, fleeing Iraq, and unquestionably, I am sure, [weapons] material." He then added, unapologetically, "Based on the evidence we had at the time, I thought the conclusions we reached about the presence of at least a latent WMD program was accurate and balanced."

Clapper's claims relegated, at least temporarily, the WMD debate to an invisible, unknowable realm of classified material, like a desert mirage. The WMDs disappeared into Syria—POOF! But even top officials in W's administration declined to carry on with Clapper's assertions about roving WMDs. Even within the Bush administration, Clapper was a lone extremist in regards to the interpretation of classified information.

A few months after Clapper's statements, in January 2004, then-National Security Adviser Condoleezza Rice—who had claimed notoriously in 2002 that the smoking gun of Iraq's WMD program could be a "mushroom cloud"—downplayed the possibility of wandering WMDs. Rice said that while an Iraqi transfer of weapons to Syria would be serious, she noted: "… I want to be very clear: we don't, at this point, have any indications that I would consider credible and firm that that has taken place …"

Some months after Rice's statements, in June 2004, Defense Secretary Donald Rumsfeld was asked about the possibility of wayward Iraqi WMDs. He said, "Until that can be validated and proven, you'll find people in the administration not talking about it."

But of course, Clapper had talked about it. And in doing so, he proved that not only did he get Iraq's WMD program wrong before the invasion, he then went on to compound his errors by philosophizing publicly, and asserting "unquestionably," after the war had began that Iraq had moved its WMDs to Syria.

Clapper's claims appear to be not only unsubstantiated, but also untenable. Jon Wolfsthal, a non-proliferation expert with the Carnegie Endowment for International Peace, said that a convoy moving WMD would be distinguishable from fleeing Iraqis. Volatile chemical or biological weapons would have to be moved in large, slow-moving tanker trucks with heavy security. "It is all but impossible that significant shipments [of weapons] between Iraq and Syria could take place without us knowing about it," he said. If the U.S. forces had detected such a transfer, he added, "they'd have bombed it."

Flash forward now to June 2010: Obama names this very Clapper to be the head of America's 16 spy agencies. The Clapper case demonstrates how unexamined the 9/11 errors continue to be. America's remains mired in the post-9/11 NCE and the same personalities remain in posts of extraordinary authority. Time seems to be moving in a circle.

The Clapper case also demonstrates the American media's abdication of responsibility on manners of extraordinary importance. Either by design or apathy, the mainstream media and press entirely neglected to report on—even in passing, even after the jump, even in a sidebar—Clapper's remarkably relevant opinions on Iraq's transfer of WMDs to Syria when Obama named him Director of National Intelligence. A few short years later, this official rose to the spotlight after Snowden blew the whistle on dramatic encroachments on Americans' privacy.

GENERALISSIMO W. IN A STETSON

Unlike Obama, President Bush is pure archetype. He seems lifted from the Third World playbook. He was *Putinesque* in his boastful, macho bluster, with an added folksy flair. He brandished all the patriotic props, while he eroded America's distinctive character. He is Third World in both style and execution.

His pedigree is also classic Third World. Rising to power on his father's bootstraps, he established a political dynasty that is uncommon in American presidential politics and rivals those of the Third World. And like the powerful political elite of the Third World, he harbored an aggrandized perspective of the importance of his family and himself.

And that delusion may have fueled the path to war in Iraq. The president seemed to have been more focused on redeeming and validating the Bush legacy in regards to Iraq than with any ill-begotten notions regarding foreign policy.

Indeed, a preoccupation with family honor—a sentiment that sweeps continents in the Third World—may have been an important motivation in Bush's decision to launch the most disastrous war in American history. Of course, it was aided and abetted by those that had other motives. But Bush was, after all, the decider. And he has given us conflicts that keep on giving.

Bush had no ideological or normative penchant for the kind of nation-building enterprise that he ultimately tried to launch in Iraq. As has been well documented, W. was hostile to such notions, and he said so repeatedly before 9/11. When running for president against Al Gore in 2000, for example, W. said: "… I'm worried about an opponent who uses nation building and the military in the same sentence. See, our view of the military is for our military to be properly prepared to fight and win war and, therefore, prevent war from happening in the first place."

And W. clearly felt that Bush family honor had been damaged by his father's decision not to continue on the road to Baghdad and dethrone Saddam during the first Gulf War. Iraq had been central in W.'s mind well before 9/11. According to author Mickey Herskowitz, a ghostwriter for the former president, W. Bush "was thinking about invading Iraq in 1999 … It was on his mind. He said to me: 'One of the keys to being seen as a great leader is to be seen as a commander-in-chief.' And he said, 'My father had all this political capital built up when he drove the Iraqis out of Kuwait and he wasted it.' He said, 'If I have a chance to invade, if I had that much capital, I'm not going to waste it.' "

So in the end, the Iraq War may have been driven more by W's psychological inclinations than ideological dogmatism. W's fealty to his father, which he often expressed in aggressive, profanity-laced terms, has been widely reported and analyzed. There are many examples of W. lashing out at journalists for criticizing his father or failing to praise him, in classic Third World style.

In W.'s Third World perspective, loyalty to his family and himself was always of paramount importance. And in that regard, he demonstrated a conviction that the media was a subordinate entity that should dutifully pay homage to the Bushes. W. crassly expressed such sentiment directly in April 1986, when he approached Al Hunt, who was accompanied by his wife (Judy Woodruff) and their 4-year-old son, and declared: "You fucking son of a bitch. I saw what you wrote. We're not going to forget this." Hunt's offense, apparently, was his failure to select HW Bush as the lead for the 1988 Republican ticket in a short article.

That kind of vulgarity towards journalists is rare in America. But in the Third World, such treatment is not so unusual. Even in the more civilized corners of the Third Worldish world, journalists are merely tolerated, and viewed as a nuisance if they push against official talking points. Consider this colorful exchange between then-President Putin and a journalist who dared question him about Chechnya: "If you want to become an Islamic radical and have yourself circumcised, I invite you to come to Moscow," Putin said, adding, "I would recommend that he who does the surgery does it so you'll have nothing growing back, afterward."

In fact, W. has other *Putinesque* qualities. Both leaders demonstrated noteworthy bravado with *other people's* lives, in fine generalissimo style. After the 9/11 attacks, W. thundered: "We'll get them running and we'll bring them to justice." Putin has a flair for similar talk, when others are doing the fighting: "We shall fight against them, throw them in prisons and destroy them," Mr. Putin said in 1994. Of course, the accuracy of W's and Putin's statements depend on the meaning of the word "we."

W.'s presidency revolved around agitating fear and panic. In the most conspicuous Third World-style, with unabashed redundancy, he conjured the security threat. And in this regard, Bush fits more in the mold of a Third World strongman. Some observers have argued that Bush operated like a WWII-era European fascist, but Bush never erected a coherent nationalist machinery and zeitgeist in all-encompassing, fascist style. Bush's strategy was more circumscribed, and he constantly agitated fear of the foreign threat, in the style of, say, Pakistan's leaders, or even Chavez's Venezuela.

While fascists operate through fear, they tend to be more on the offense, in terms of erecting a towering, nationalist infrastructure and political apparatus, while Bush took a simpler, defensive approach.

That posture can go a long way. By conjuring a sense of insecurity, a government can wield much greater control of a population and uphold itself as the protector of its people. Another bonus of the boogeyman strategy is a government's increased ability to divert greater funds towards the military—and the private sector that feeds from it.

W. presided through intimidation and fear, with an eye towards stifling political debate. U.S. foreign policy couldn't be objectively scrutinized. America was at war. The motivations America's rivals may have for fighting against a military occupation could not be entertained. We're at war. Security legislation could not be objectively evaluated. No time—we're at war. Contracts for servicing the wars could not be bid out. Didn't you hear? We're at war. The war itself cannot be criticized either. Didn't I say? We're at war.

Bush heaped ideological rationales onto the Iraq enterprise, always maintaining democratic objectives so broad and vague that the wars could continue in perpetuity. The means for achieving those broad goals were equally ill-defined. After all, there is no ideology replacement setting on an AK-47.

PART II:
GLOBAL
AFTERSHOCKS

AROUND THE WORLD, CASTING A LESSER SHADOW

PREFACE

The United States remains the preeminent global power of the NCE, even though its economic wherewithal has declined. Despite the setbacks outlined in the preceding pages, the U.S. global lead has been so commanding that America still retains its alpha positioning. Indeed, other large powers have declined in tandem with the United States.

But American soft power has deteriorated more decisively. Largely what can be seen from Europe to the Middle East is a move by governments and the people to establish independence from Washington. America's broad based devolution has not escaped the notice of the world. And the images of a rash and reactive America contend with the idea of a benign hegemon. Across the Muslim arc of countries around the globe, the United States has lost respect through its transgressions. A shocked and awed America has undercut the power of its suasion and its ability to intimidate militarily.

America still has such uncontested geopolitical and economic advantages that the net effect of such a drop in influence is up to debate and interpretation. For starters, the foreign interests of industrialized nations, and even some emerging economies, revolve around energy resources—and therefore oil supplies remain paramount. But even if America's oil-producing adversaries opted against selling to the United States directly, global supplies would not decrease so long as output is sold anywhere else in the world. The most anti-Americans rulers, with the most anti-American publics, must sell their oil to stay in despotism business. And so an America loss of prestige is not expected to impact its access to oil supplies. Unless sea lanes are blocked—a wildly unlikely scenario, given America's naval prowess—oil can be by and large discounted as an interest that needs defending.

All the same, the United States does have more amorphous interests around the world. American citizens can be affected by events occurring abroad. And so the heightened efforts of foreign governments and people to distance themselves from the United States could bear consequences that are difficult to predict. Some of that distancing may help the United States unwind its burdensome self-appointed duties around the world. It could also limit the range of U.S. action.

If America's domestic problems revolve around the American mind, its global challenges also belong to the psyche. America is facing a crisis of global perception. In people's minds, the United States is demonstrating errors of judgment—to the world's great detriment. The American example still burns bright in the global imagination, but the deeds of the recent past contradict it.

The United States can gradually recover its influence. But its stature could also decline more decisively. The current scenario may look bad, but it can still get worse. For now, Americans will have to keep a close eye on the undulating, ever-shifting global landscape of the NCE and execute restrained and intelligent responses.

CHAPTER 15

SHOCKED AND AWAKENED

The Greater Middle East is Roused

The Lion of the Egyptian Revolution

The Revolution in the Greater Middle East is an unpredictable synthesis of incongruous social forces. It has a power all its own. America does not own it. Nor do the Islamists. Some groups, such as the Muslim Brotherhood in Egypt, might command a plurality of support from the public. Recent events suggest, though, that its lack of majority support will demand its pliability for the foreseeable future. Although the Revolution's prospects look dim, its progress could only be expected to come in waves. The spirit of the Revolution is alight even in those countries where the body count of protesters swells in the multiple thousands and where Washington does not support it, such as in U.S.-allied Bahrain.

Abstract theories about the democratizing potential of information freedom exploded into reality in late 2010, as a rebellion that began in Tunisia incited a historic revolution that swept North Africa, spread to the Middle East and is felt in Asia. But there is little question that the revelations of Wikileaks were incendiary because the kindling had already been laid in the NCE. The 9/11 attacks and the actions of a shocked and awed America convulsed the Greater Middle East. And that convulsion culminated in the ongoing, untidy Revolution.

WikiLeaks' disclosures regarding the political corruption in Tunisia and Egypt in 2010 took place within a highly charged context. The 9/11 attacks and the U.S. policy aftermath supercharged the debate in the region. They opened questions about Islam and the authority to interpret it, the morality of the use of force and terrorism in particular and the universality of democracy. The attacks, the wars and other dramatic events challenged standing assumptions and propelled a region-wide conversation.

The campy, Hallmark-style advocacy of democracy of the W. Bush administration appears to have caught the region's attention. From an American vantage point, the pro-democratic rhetoric seems manufactured and expedient—as indeed it was. After all, W. kicked up the utopic, democratic jargon after the complete collapse of the WMD pretext for war in Iraq. And his administration demonstrated the superficiality of its commitment to democracy after the Palestinian elections of 2006.

Nevertheless, the pro-democratic mantras seem to have impressed themselves on the region. If the superpower says democracy enough times, and self-righteously enough, some people around the world might stop and give its prospects some thought. For some individuals, the superpower's talk of democracy highlighted the shortcomings of their government—even when they knew Washington's talking points on Iraq were not the sincerest of gospel. Others appear to have truly believed America was serious about deploying its clout and military power for the sake of democracy abroad, and may have mobilized with that conviction.

In addition, the NCE aggravated an already difficult situation in much of the Greater Middle East, said Ali Allawi, former Iraqi Defense Minister and author, in an interview. "The avenues of escape that used to exist before—the Gulf countries or migration to Europe or, to a lesser extent, the US—have been closed now."

With that closure, the emerging ideas of the region were confined to a political pressure cooker.

What's more, the little noticed American NGOs working quietly on behalf of democracy promotion abroad had more impact in Muslim countries than much of the elite around the world (even in America) appreciated and understood. The pro-democracy NGOs in Egypt, for example, provided foreign activists with practical instruction on political organization and networking, particularly via the Internet. Activists later put those skills to effect, harnessing social networking sites like Facebook—that in the West had been launched with the most frivolous of purposes—to serious political effect.

The impact of the State Department cables that WikiLeaks made public also took the West by surprise. At first blush, the cables seemed much less polemical than earlier revelations, such as footage of civilian casualties in Iraq. Indeed, the West received the cables with some prurient, voyeuristic pleasure, but mostly utter indifference. The situation was far different in the Muslim world.

The cables had an explosive effect on the societies that had been subjected to extreme restrictions on what they could hear, see and read. In effect, they ignited a revolution in Tunisia—that became The Revolution. Western news organizations said they directly experienced the clamoring for information provoked by the WikiLeaks revelations.

As a February 2, 2011 article in the Guardian put it:

"Within hours of the first cables being posted the Guardian started receiving a steady stream of pleading requests from editors and journalists around the world wanting to know what the cables revealed about their own countries and rulers. It was easier to call the revelations unstartling, dull even, if one lived in western Europe, rather than in Belarus, Tunisia, or in any other oppressive regime."

Only in retrospect does it become clear why the seemingly obvious information caught the imagination and indignation of Tunisia's young, reform-minded population. The cables' stark forecast of a limited life-span for the Ben Ali regime became a rallying point—and self-fulfilling prophecy. And that served as a confirmation, in black and white, of a persistent but unrecognized conviction that most all Tunisians' already felt: that the regime had an expiration date. The people decided that the date had come. Where there had once been apprehension about the prospects of a revolution, there was now an affirming belief in the chances for victory.

Equally as important, the superpower was validating the legitimate grievances of the Tunisian population in the cables. And though they were intended for an insider's look only, they were now in the global, public domain. And so the U.S. government could not deny the legitimacy of the rebellion—its State Department cables supported it implicitly. And Washington could not contravene a popular uprising.

And finally, all the modernity of the WikiLeaks phenomenon merged with a time immemorial honor reflex, by revealing Tunisia's corruption and other dirty laundry for all the world to see. The revelations almost seemed to pose a needling challenge to the young generation: What are you going to do about it? Tunisians rose up not only reform to Tunisia—but also redeem it. The youth took the challenge, harnessing concerns about honor to positive effect.

But also, the nature of the Internet itself jarred the population, noted Allawi, because of the "kind of disconnect between the oppressive and authoritarian circumstances and the freedoms of the new information age. So you have access to the Internet, you have access to all these social networks, you have also much more information coming in, while the state continues to behave in an oppressive and controlling fashion" That disconnect heightens a "general sort of climate of malaise," said Allawi.

With all the kindling already available, those factors became politically combustible. And the glare was bright enough for Egypt, and then so many other countries, to behold. The uprising that began in a little noticed backwater spread to an epicenter of the Greater Middle East, and continues to rage there to unknowable effect. Throughout the region, the public is awakening to the false pretexts for coercive rule.

In an April 10, 2011 Op-Ed for the New York Times, Syrian dissident Yassin al-Haj Saleh summed up the awareness, in terms that should also resonate for Americans, for all the reasons discussed in Part I:

The state of emergency, under which Syria has lived for 48 years, has extended the ruling elite's authority into all spheres of Syrians' public and private lives, and there is nothing to stop the regime from using this power to abuse the Syrian population. ...

The official pretext for the emergency laws is the country's state of war with Israel. However, restricting Syrians' freedoms did no good in the 1967 war, which ended with the occupation of the Golan Heights, nor did it help in any other confrontations with the Jewish state, nor in any true emergencies. Because in the government's eyes everything has been an emergency for the last half-century, nothing is an emergency.

A sense of emergency and an under-siege mindset has reinforced the repression of the people of the Greater Middle East. But the people increasingly believe that the emergency has been trumped up. And once the illusion of emergency recedes, the government's yoke becomes intolerable, in the eyes of the people. How everything will play out for the multitude of Muslim humanity is unknown. But Allawi sees a "Second Wave" of unrest to continue playing out for some time to come, with the "ancien regimes" putting up a much greater fight than did the Ben Ali regime in Tunisia and the Mubarak government in Egypt. Pit against the viability of the social movements are what Allawi calls the "three fears" of the Middle East, which were used in the past to justify the oppressive status quo:

Firstly, it's fear that if you have uncontrolled change, or abrupt change, you are inviting foreign powers back into the area in a direct way ... The other fear is that sectarian divisions, which were, to some extent, smothered by oppressive structures, would come up to the fore. And this is what happened in Bahrain and appears to be happening now in Syria. And lastly, although it's muted, is a fear of the breakup of the state. And one state in the Middle East that has already broken up is the Sudan. And there are other candidates for breakup. So these fears, which were used in the past to justify very oppressive or very authoritarian rule, do have some basis, apparently. So you have to also work around these issues.

Those three fears not only led the U.S. to overtly support the dictatorial regimes in the past, it continues to stay its hand going forward. But there is also no compartmentalizing the legitimate anger of the people of the region. And that legitimate anger is directed not only at the regimes and military rule, but at Washington as well—a phenomenon that U.S. officials are abundantly aware of. Striking a policy balance that takes into account the "three fears" and public rage remains America's challenge. In that regard, Washington has done little more than publicly equivocate.

The protagonists of The Revolution do not suffer any such ambivalence. They seek to sideline Washington. In the squares and streets of the Greater Middle East, an organizing aspiration is uniting the varied political factions challenging the despots: driving political reform movements independent of U.S. interference.

And the reformers have been able to marginalize Washington with relative ease. The United States lacks the clout and popularity in the region to meaningfully guide and define the movement. Still, Washington seems to be unable to resist a compulsion to put its stamp on the uprisings, even though Washington is surely cognizant that its involvement imperils the vitality and integrity of the uprisings. As Bacevich (distinguished author, Boston University professor and former U.S. Army colonel) put it in an interview:

"The Arab uprising more broadly presented evidence of this enormous wave of change in the region, prior to the U.S. intervention in Libya, occurring without the United States playing any kind of particular role. To overstate the case, you could say that the Arab uprising had seemingly made the United States more or less irrelevant to the region's future. And intervening in Libya against Qadaffi probably, in some people's minds, seemed to be a way, to restore some semblance of relevance. I know some people in the administration have used this phrase: being on the right side of history, which leads you to think that some people imagined that intervening in Libya against a bonafide bad guy like Qadaffi would enable the United States to reposition itself on the right side of

history. I don't think that's really going to be the outcome, but that could have factored into the thinking in the administration."

Recognizing the collapse of regard for Washington, the regimes have also become emboldened in pushing against U.S. influence. During a July 2011 visit to Washington, Maj. Gen. Mohammed al-Assar, a member of the Supreme Council of the Armed Forces, criticized the United States for funding pro-democracy NGOs that are clashing with Egyptian officials. Al-Assar said that Egyptians were opposed to such "foreign interference," and claimed that at stake was "a matter of sovereignty." Amid controversy about U.S. funding of NGOs in Egypt, the USAID Director Jim Bever left his post in Egypt.

The Egyptian's wariness of U.S. interventions was also illustrated in the July 31, 2011 issue of a state-run magazine. The magazine's cover featured U.S. Ambassador Anne Patterson holding a burning wad of dollars to the wick of a bomb wrapped in an American flag. The cover read: "The ambassador from Hell who lit a fire in Tahrir."

Despite Obama's refined oratory in the region and the campaign in Libya, opposition groups remain antipathetic to Washington. That is the general the sentiment on the street. American popularity has plummeted under Obama in Muslim countries. According to a 2010 survey by the Pew Research Center, U.S. popularity in

Egypt dropped to a five-year record low, with U.S. favorability registering at just 17%. In Pakistan, American favorability stood also at just 17 % and in Jordan it was only modestly higher, at 21%. Only the Lebanese gave the United States majority approval, at 52%.

ANTI-AMERICASTANS

There are a host of causes for the anti-Americanism that mingles with the revolutionary zeal of the Muslim world. But the public is harboring wariness, and even rage, towards the United States for founded reasons. In Egypt, America had for decades bolstered not only the political power of leaders like Hosni Mubarak, it also despicably enhanced their repressive capabilities by providing U.S. security aid that went towards purchasing the hardware that was used against protesters.

What's more, indignation over the terms of the Egyptian-Israeli relationship circled Tahrir Square. Taking a look back at the years after Egypt penned its peace accord with Israel, and then suffered the assassination of its leader that inked the accord, it seems that the Egyptian people were at least resigned to tolerating the peace agreement—and the Mubarak dictatorship that followed it. Much of the West understood that the peace agreement could come at a cost to the democratic evolution of Egypt, since it would take a heavy hand to enforce it. But that was a compromise of competing ideals the international community was willing to make.

Egypt and Israel therefore had several years to prove to the value and integrity of the peace agreement to their own countries, the region, and the Islamic faithful around the world. The value of the pact to the Mubarak government was glaringly apparent—it received millions of dollars for its adherence to the agreement and hoarded the money in the most rapacious manner imaginable. But no one made serious efforts to demonstrate the dividends of the U.S. aid and the peace agreement to the Egyptian people.

It was also in Israel's interest to illustrate those dividends. But Israel seemed to operate with the assumption that the sustainability of the peace accord (by way of Mubarak's rule and U.S. security aid) was automatic and a foregone conclusion. And that seems to be the reason Israel failed to invest its political and creative energies towards proving the value of that accord to the Egyptian people. What's more, its policies towards the Palestinians and other neighbors seemed based on the idea that since the accord was in effect bought and paid for by Washington, Egypt's deferential and obliging relationship was in the bag—so to speak. In retrospect, that was not a wise policy. Looking back, there was never any good reason to bank on the indefinite survival of a bought-and-paid for regime carrying out the bidding of its bankroller. Client regimes have a history of failure.

The Mubarak regime also appeared oblivious to potential threats to its longevity. The regime operated under the assumption that as long as it remained deferential to the peace accord and

Washington's and Israeli interests, that the U.S. checks would continue rolling in—regardless of how it brutalized and repressed its people. Those checks seemed to assure Mubarak's political survival, until suddenly they didn't.

Future players may be more apt to spread the wealth. Allawi maintains that the idea of a U.S.-aligned youth movement dominating the Revolution in the Greater Middle East is something of a Western delusion. Although that group does play a role, it is not the central force. Allawi describes the Muslim Brotherhood as the most organized player.

So the Western daydream for the region will not come true. But the people of the region may still come out with something. The idea of more distributive governments may not quicken the Western pulse, but it offers the people access to desperately needed services and an improvement from the kleptocracies of the moment.

There is little question that Washington will have less sway over those governments and that they will not be so easily co-opted by cash. That fits in with a global, not just Islamic, trend. Even the wealthy countries of the world will make common cause with Washington only if it suits them—as NATO has done in Libya. When it doesn't, those countries are shrugging off U.S. entreaties—as evidenced by Britain's exiting of Afghanistan. This trend is apparent with another major power broker of the Muslim world.

THE BRIDGE OF CIVILIZATIONS DRIFTS EASTWARDS

Turkey has long been the cultural nexus between East and West. Ankara has offered its hand in the Middle East crisis, it tried to broker the voluntary exit of Moammar Qadaffi from Libya and it has developed solid diplomatic relations with the nemesis of the West (Tehran) while maintaining good relations with the West itself.

But Turkey's orientation is turning decidedly eastwards, and the opportunity for leveraging Ankara's mediation skills and savoir faire may be closing. The Turkish people are losing their penchant for the all things Western—including institutions. That trend will probably gain momentum going forward. And while Ankara is surely loath to forfeit its unique role as cultural translator and power broker, it would ignore the will of its own people only at its peril—as the ongoing and proximate Revolution so poignantly demonstrates.

The Turkish street has become unsympathetic towards the United States. In recent years, the image of the United States has been largely negative in Turkey. According to a Pew Research Center Survey, "Turkey was the country in which the U.S. received its lowest favorability rating in every Pew Global Attitudes survey conducted between 2006 and 2009. [In 2010], just 17% of Turks have a positive opinion of the U.S., tying Turkey with Pakistan and Egypt for the lowest U.S. favorability rating among the 22 nations surveyed."

So America in general may not be able to count on Turkey to bridge gaps and intervene on its behalf in the Muslim arc countries—the way it has in the past. Meanwhile, Turkey is expanding its economic links, and power, in the Greater Middle East. That expansion, and shift in orientation, upholds not only economic interests, it is also more congruent with the public mood.

The people of the Greater Middle East want to shape a new destiny. They want to be their own agents of change. If the NCE for America has been a time of shock, awe and delusion, for the Muslim world it is a time of awakening: a rude and violent and still uncertain awakening, but an awakening nonetheless. If America respects the independence of region's movements it could eventually recover its soft power. But there is no question that regard for America has fallen several notches and that the ideological terrain has become treacherous.

CHAPTER 16
AL QAEDA GENERATION XXX: RATED FOR BLOODTHIRSTINESS
And the Base is Scattered

Bin Laden's management style was so 2001. In the NCE, international jihad is much more dispersed, localized and, in a way, democratic. There is no single controlling authority or unifying agent for the groups that wage Islamic, or Islamish, jihad around the world. By the time of bin Laden's death, he was an inspiration figure just barely. The wars of the NCE have rallied violent anti-Americanism that has organized into dispersed jihadi groups.

The April 2013 bombings on a Boston marathon represent the new face of jihad. The perpetrators appeared to have acted alone, indoctrinated, in part, via the vast realm of cyber jihad. While certain clerics may have commanded ideological clout, there was no outside controlling authority.

There are now so many autonomous jihadi groups scattered around the world that America faces steep challenges in infiltrating them. Americans hardly had time to celebrate bin Laden's death when radical Islamists stormed U.S. outposts in Egypt and Libya—killing a number of Americans, including the U.S. ambassador to Libya. Just after America proved its phenomenal reach and surgical lethality with the bin raid, the al Qaeda spin-off groups demonstrated a reach and brazenness all their own.

And as the groups become more decentralized, they have also become more brutal. In an interview, author and terrorist expert Lawrence Wright characterized the current, post-bin Laden leadership:

The leaders of al Qaeda after bin Laden are more radical, or at least more bloodthirsty, than bin Laden. This is especially true of Ayman al-Zawahiri, who has been the intellectual and moral force behind al Qaeda proper since its beginning…Without bin Laden at the head, al Qaeda faces an existential moment. However, Zawahiri has the experience of rebuilding a terrorist organization – his own Al Jihad movement…The movement is in disarray, but it is certainly not leaderless."

Bin Laden's death, while welcomed in terms of justice, could have unpredictable consequences in practical terms. With bin Laden gone al Qaeda may command less clout, but his successor could prove more brutal and cunning.

Surely, bin Laden wasn't exactly a figure of mercy or moral rectitude. It is difficult to conceive of a more brutal terrorist group then the one that bin Laden led, with its homicidal inclinations climaxing on 9/11. And yet, bin Laden's terrorist group may be defined by greater restraint then the next generation al Qaeda and its spin offs. Indeed, when he witnessed the beheadings and no-holds-barred violence of al Qaeda in Iraq as led by Abu Musab al-Zarqawi, bin Laden protested, presumably due to concerns over al Qaeda's PR. And because bin Laden is known to have exhibited charisma and mystique, he was less reliant on appealing via brute force and terrorist "victories" in order to win recruits and influence.

But al Qaeda's apparent successors don't lay any claim to even those flimsy human sensibilities. And the relative radicalization of al Qaeda is not unique. The trend also appears to be manifested in the new Taliban generation. The head of Afghanistan's Taliban, Mullah Omar, is more restrained then the new-generation leaders of Taliban offshoots, such as the heads of Pakistan Taliban. The brutality and radical nature of the new groups was succinctly demonstrated in the summary execution in 2010 of Brig. Sultan Amir, more commonly known by his nom de guerre, Colonel Imam.

Iman, formerly Pakistan's consul general to the Afghan town of Herat and a member of Pakistan's intelligence service, had played a pivotal role in nurturing and supporting the Taliban in Afghanistan, with an eye towards bolstering Pakistan's control and sway over its neighbor. But his bona fides in supporting the old-guard Taliban meant little to the Pakistan Taliban that captured him in North Waziristan in 2010. The Mehsud clan that controls the area ignored the alleged interventions of Mullah Omar and others to spare Imam, and executed him after the Pakistani government refused to release some prisoners as the clan had demanded. The Pakistani Taliban and other new generation jihadi fighters in Pakistan and Afghanistan do not seem to heed the orders of the old-guard, or subscribe to any of its limited code of conduct.

Imam's killing pithily demonstrates the dangers of "riding the tiger," as Pakistan's strategy of supporting the Taliban and terrorism in India is sometimes described. It also demonstrates that Washington's strategy of decapitating jihadi groups can deliver inconclusive results. While such a strategy does create a leadership vacuum, that benefit is often temporary—and sometimes opens the way for more violent leadership. Indeed, jihadi groups seem to have a long established custom of establishing a capable successor, even while a leader remains alive.

Washington was correct in launching the 2011 bin Laden operation in Pakistan, primarily for reasons of justice and accountability. Indeed, the operation was successful in meting out justice—a barbaric justice, perhaps, but justice nonetheless.

All the same, Washington's broader military action has spawned a virulent and decentralized form of jihad across the globe. And now U.S. officials have a limited range of action for responding effectively. America should certainly take all legitimate covert and overt action against those groups that are plotting to harm the United States. But the elimination of one group or leader can also birth a more violent one, particularly given a certain cultural backdrop that the United States has no control over.

CHAPTER 17
ALL THE KING'S WIVES
Polygamy Central Thrives

The gold-plated Saudi royals don't make uncouth declarations against the United States, the West or Israel. But the beguiling Saudi elite is the largest and most underhanded supporter of terrorism. Saudi Arabia is the lead underwriter of Jihad Inc., providing the ideological pretexts and financial wherewithal for waging jihad. All the while, it is sure to uphold all social graces with Saudi flourish, always brandishing the tantalizing potential for Western companies to penetrate the country's barricaded industries—and often slamming shut that prospect at the last minute.

The crippling of America's clout has made Washington more reliant than ever on the kingdom—given Washington's submissive hope that the Saudis will crush Islamic militants. And, indeed, the

Saudis do police their own borders well. The problem, though, is Saudi activism abroad.

The Saudi's predilection for jihad has wreaked havoc in many parts of the world. And while social upheaval is gripping much of the region, the Saudis have mobilized to underpin and implant their ideologies, and interests. In an interview, former Iraqi Defense Minister and author Ali Allawi said:

"I think the Saudis are trying to organize a counter-revolution. They are relying on disparate groups to do that. They are ideologically Wahabis, and so on. They are using the former plutocrats where they can find them to bring them into some kind of organized form. So they are doing that a great deal in Egypt now. They are also trying to control the pace of change by, in some ways, sort of hijacking the other Gulf states."

Indeed, the Saudis have long been transgressing against the richness and strangeness of cultures around the world. Because not only is Saudi Arabia creating and funding jihadis and incubating future generations of angry men that could lash out in unpredictable ways, it is also the great, cultural and religious juggernaut of the Muslim world, eradicating the ancestral idiosyncrasies of foreign countries by funding its kind of madrasasas. It is a cultural Starbuck's, trumping national histories and supplanting varied and intricate customs with a monolithic, generic and uncompromising brand of Islam.

Watercolor of Afghan woman and child by Charles W. Barlett from 1920, depicting dress before the Saudis trumped native customs.

Regrettably, the Saudis have been mobilized by the global tumult of 9/11 and the political upheaval that struck the Greater Middle East in 2010. They have found increased motivation to co-opt foreign politicians and intrude on customs and sovereignty. Washington is as impotent as ever in countering those Saudi actions, given its fall in prestige. It is more dependent than ever on the kingdom's counter-terror cooperation. But the influence of the Saudis is diametrically opposed to America's interests and security and to its cherished values and principles.

But perhaps the most damning Saudi phenomena are the country's own social demographics and their nurturing of fundamentalist Islam. Saudi Arabia is not only funding and indoctrinating the jihadis of the globe, it is also creating the conditions for large-scale societal dysfunction that could incubate generations of angry, deprived men.

Polygamy is one the most injurious social practices continuing in the modern world. Of all the resources for one person to hoard, the taking of multiple wives (which in a social sense is a resource) is the most threatening. If a traditional society lacks a woman for roughly each man that wants to take a wife, a dangerous discontent undoubtedly will arise. When that discontent merges with a militant form of Islam, the potential for a violent lashing out heightens.

In many Muslim countries, polygamy is now rarely practiced and is often frowned upon. In Turkey, polygamy is against the law. When the Muslim's Prophet Mohammed advocated for polygamy, he did so with some important caveats and under distinct social conditions, whereby many women had been left widowed by war. All the same, the practice is still broadly practiced in Saudi Arabia. Data is hard to find, but statistics from King Saud University show that men taking second wives are the cause of 55 percent of divorces in the Kingdom.

There are no apparent precedents for enlightened polygamy. That practice has consistently involved the subjugation of girls, women and young men looking for a bride, even when it is practiced within extraordinarily wealthy countries, like the United States, by break-away Mormon and other sects. Those polygamous communities in America create rigidly hierarchal theocracies that are thoroughly undemocratic, as illustrated so grippingly in Jon Krakauer's *"Under the Banner of Heaven."*

Paul H. Rubin, the Samuel Candler Dobbs Professor of Economics and Law at Emory University, offers a compelling explanation of why polygamy conflicts fundamentally with democracy in a study for the CATO Institute:

"There are two reasons why it is difficult and may be impossible for polygamous societies to become open and democratic. First, the opportunity to acquire many wives creates a powerful incentive for seeking power. Second and more importantly, polygamous societies create tremendous internal tensions. In particular, in societies where some males have more than one wife, other males have none and may not have prospects of marrying. Those males —

typically young — are a destabilizing force in society, and it may be necessary for society to be repressive in order to control them. Of course, as we were reminded by the recent raid on the Texas ranch owned by a religious sect that had broken away from the Mormon Church, there is still some incidence of polygamy in the West. Interestingly, such sects often appear to be run dictatorially. They also oftentimes expel young males (called "lost boys") to reduce competition for wives. It is easy to see that such homeless boys could be a highly destabilizing force. Only a powerful authority would have the ability to force such an expulsion.

For current-day societies with poor access to modern medicine, the subjugation of women may appear a requirement for a society's survival. Without that subjugation, an unknown number of women could decide against leading a married life that involves repeated, phenomenally painful and life-threatening child birth. For such a society to survive and expand, it denies women their ability to opt out of marriage by precluding their ability to generate or inherit wealth and enjoy other rights. In those societies, women can hardly imagine the concept of having options, since their lives have been strictly conscribed since childhood. Not too long ago, Western societies broadly repressed women in concrete and conceptual respects, before the advent of modern medicine and other benefits of industrialization.

The self-entitled Saudi regime has enough wealth to prevent such poverty and medical scarcity, but chooses instead to keep for itself the bounty of the country's oil industry, which generates much cash but few jobs. Certainly, Afghanistan is so poor in terms of actual wealth and raw resources that it is unsurprising that its tribes maintain the logic of female repression. Potentially, if Afghanistan were to evolve economically, if marriage and child birth became a more attractive prospect, that repression would become less expedient. And for Afghanistan to progress, it need only regress, paradoxically enough, to its once broad observance of the more tolerant form of Sufi Islam, which Saudi money and influence has effectively suffocated.

The U.S. model, as an alternative to the retrograde Saudi juggernaut, is losing appeal as the people of the world sour on the United States. At a crucial time, during a vital contest in ideologies around the world, the Saudi ideology is being bolstered. A shocked and awed America is handicapped in its ability to respond effectively. Looking around the world, it becomes apparent there is no alternative that offers America's global luster.

CHAPTER 18
AXIS OF DEFIANCE
North Korea and Iran Thumb Their Noses

Since 9/11, the United States has been playing a high stakes game of geopolitical chicken with Iran and North Korea. Immediately after taking office, W. Bush tossed aside the rapprochement that his predecessor had established with North Korea under the Agreed Framework deal. Then, the W. administration accelerated the brinkmanship, provocatively claiming Tehran and Pyongyang and Iraq formed an Axis of Evil.

Once a confrontational U.S. foreign policy is unleashed, it is difficult to reverse, even by a president who once claimed he would do so. Obama continues to escalate the sanctions pressure on Iran, even though President Ahmadinejad supports the kind of nuclear deal—entailing outsourcing the enrichment of uranium—that Obama had advocated for on the campaign trail, according to documents published by WikiLeaks. What's more, the 2007 National Intelligence Estimate said that the intelligence community has found no evidence that Iran is developing, or trying to develop, nuclear weapons.

Seymour Hersh concluded in June 2011, based on extensive interviews with members of intelligence communities around the world, that "the U.S. could be in danger of repeating a mistake similar to the one made with Saddam Hussein's Iraq eight years ago—allowing anxieties about the policies of a tyrannical regime to distort our estimates of the state's military capacities and intentions." In an interview with Antiwar's Scott Horton, Hersh said that coming to such a conclusion was, in the eyes of many, akin to being "an advocate for incest." Indeed, challenging the trumped up claims of Iran's nuclear threats remains a thankless task in a shocked and awed America.

Washington has been unwilling or unable to reestablish a constructive relationship with Tehran. And while the relationship remains on deep ice, the nonproliferation threats that the pre-9/11 rapprochement was geared towards addressing rage on. And what remains clear is that, partly as a result of America's confrontational posturing, the Axis of Evil regimes have become more bellicose since 9/11. In Iran's case, that hostility appears to be rhetorical. In North Korea's case, actions have accompanied the fighting words.

Some of the tyrants of the Greater Middle East are now facing a limited political (and maybe physical) lifespan, given uprisings that have swept the region. But the rogue's gallery remains largely unscathed—and even emboldened since 9/11. The predictions about the impact of the Iraq War are now so clearly inaccurate that it may seem uncharitable to unearth them. But since Washington seems frozen in a NCE mindset on matters of foreign policy, it remains important to recount the more fantastical forecasts. In his 1999 book, David Wurmser (who has been special assistant to U.S. Ambassador to the United Nations John Bolton), said "Launching a policy and resolutely carrying it through until it razes Saddam's Ba'thism to the ground will send terrifying shock waves into Tehran." Clearly, Tehran is not terribly terrified.

Indeed, its sphere of influence has expanded, as the Shia government in Baghdad aligns itself with its theological brethren in Tehran. The Shia populations across the Middle East have also become emboldened—lashing out after enduring, in many cases, intolerable abuses at the hands of despots who shower their own tribes with preferential treatment. A sustained, region-wide Shia uprising could continue to strengthen the hand of Iran.

Tehran has issued Washington graphic, belligerent warnings since 9/11/01. On July 2004, Iran's supreme leader Ayatollah Ali Khamenei thundered at Washington: "If the enemy attacks our scientific, natural or human technological interests, the Iranian people will cut off its hand without hesitation and place in danger the interests of the aggressor everywhere in the world."

And the theocracy has not hesitated to bring out the iron fist to crush democratic progress. In the February 2004 parliamentary elections, the mullahs on the hardline Guardian Council disqualified about 2,500 pro-reform candidates from running for office. Those disqualified included 80 sitting lawmakers. About 124 lawmakers in the 290-seat Majlis, or parliament, resigned before the election in protest of the disqualifications. Democratic reform in Iran has suffered reversals, rather than progressed, in the NCE.

The Iranian President Ahmadinejad has alarmed the international community by suggesting, for example, that Israel should be wiped out. With the Wikileak Awakening sweeping the region, Iran cracked down with mortal force against protestors and has imprisoned distinguished members of the opposition.

Most importantly, Tehran continues to make clear that it will dictate to the international community the terms under which negotiations over its nuclear program can be discussed. After the release of a U.N. report claiming that Iran's activities appear to have both civilian and military applications, Ahmadinejad came out swinging, declaring "This nation won't retreat one iota from the path it is going"—certainly not the declarations of a cowed power.

But Iran has been a tentative and calibrated power next to North Korea's defiance and bravado. Pyongyang has engaged in a crescendo of defiance since 9/11. While Tehran is needling the West with its posturing, Pyongyang has been slapping it in the face.

In October 2002, with America on the path to war in Iraq, Assistant Secretary of State James Kelly said that North Korean officials had told him that their country had been secretly pursuing the development of nuclear weapons, in violation of the 1994 Agreed Framework deal. Washington responded in November 2002 by cancelling fuel-oil shipments to North Korea and halted construction of light-water reactors, benefits that North Korea was formerly entitled to under the agreement.

North Korea responded one month later by reactivating its shuttered Yongbyon nuclear reactor and throwing out international inspectors and then, the following January, withdrew from the Nuclear Non-Proliferation Treaty altogether. In July 2003, the regime claimed it had made enough plutonium to make nuclear bombs and later that year, it said it reprocessed 8,000 nuclear fuel rods, enough material for up to six nuclear bombs.

North Korea made clear its motivations for such defiant actions. In June 2004, the regime's state-run Minju Joson newspaper said:

"The U.S. is finding itself in a tighter corner as the days go by due to its foreign policy failure [in Iraq]. It is now under fire at home and abroad ... The U.S. charged the DPRK [Democratic People's Republic of Korea] with 'nuclear and missile proliferation' by absurdly linking its increase of nuclear deterrent force to terrorism in a bid to deliberately hype the urgency of the situation and induce the international community to support Washington's pressure upon the DPRK ... The U.S. is using the same method in Iraq."

Sensing U.S. weakness, North Korea ratcheted up its nuclear ambitions. Perhaps Iraq also illustrated to North Korea and the world the perils of disarming. U.N. weapons inspectors had certified that Iraq had disarmed 90-95% of its WMD capability in 1998, before the inspectors were withdrawn from Iraq by the U.N., in anticipation of the U.S. and British Desert Fox bombing of the country. After disarming, Iraq was invaded in March 2003. As if heeding those lessons, the North Korean foreign ministry said, after six-nation talks collapsed in August 2003:

"How can the DPRK trust the U.S. and drop its gun? Even a child would not be taken in by such a trick. What we want is for both sides to drop guns at the same time and coexist peacefully."

Remembering that Washington had pursued Iraq's disarmament and then, in short succession, regime change, North Korea was clearly wary of forfeiting its nuclear deterrent. If anything, Washington's Iraq campaign stiffened Pyongyang's determination to acquire a nuclear capability.

It is true that North Korea has long been a rebellious and often belligerent regime. But back in 2000, North Korea had launched a global charm offensive. That year, South and North Korean leaders held a historic summit and took a series of measures to open up relations. In May 2001, an EU delegation headed by Swedish

Prime Minister Goran Persson visited North Korea to support the rapprochement. It was the highest-level Western diplomatic mission ever to travel to North Korea. About three months later, North Korea's leader Kim Jong-il visited Moscow for the first time.

Something clearly happened to change Pyongyang's disposition— or its calculations. Bush's statement in January 2002 identifying North Korea as part of an Axis of Evil did nothing to cow the hermetic and starving communist state. After engaging in coy brinkmanship for years, North Korea in 2006 dropped a bomb, literally. In July of that year it test-fired a long range missile, which performed badly. The bravado was there but the know-how had not yet caught up. Later, in October 2006, Pyongyang test fired a nuclear weapon for the first time.

And so on October 2006, North Korea's smoking gun became a giant mushroom cloud—to borrow a turn of phrase. As Washington was flexing military muscle, the United States and the rest of the international community lost ground in the nuclear non-proliferation effort. It was later verified that Pyongyang had test fired a plutonium bomb that October, producing nukes from its plutonium assets that had previously been frozen under the Agreed Framework deal of 1994.

In May 2009, North Korea said it successfully carried out an underground nuclear test, eliciting howls of protests from Washington, Beijing, Moscow and others. And then it added it did not see itself bound by the 1953 truce that ended the war between the two Koreas. And in March 2010, North Korea brought already tense relations to a fever pitch, by sinking the South Korean warship Cheonan. And in case there was any doubt about North Korea's audacity in the NCE, Pyongyang showcased a vast, secretly built facility for enriching uranium at its Yongbyon complex to an esteemed visiting American scientist.

But North Korea's most significant show of defiance was the long-range rocket test it conducted in December 2012—because it dashed hopes for a more conciliatory regime under the country's new ruler, the youthful Kim Jong-un. And based on satellite imagery, some observers believe North Korea is preparing for its third nuclear test at the Punggye-ri nuclear test facility.

The United States before 9/11 was able to project influence and the suggestion of military might without firing a shot. That aura of prowess has been dispelled. After Washington expended so much firepower and so many troops in the wars, America's power by suggestion is severely curtailed. A shocked and awed America has provoked the increasing defiance of its adversaries—and the alienation of its closest allies.

CHAPTER 19
WEST VS. WEST
A Clash of Civilizations

The streets in America ran red after 9/11—with French wine. A shocked and awed America was indignant over France's decision to sit out the Iraq war, while France remained contemptuous of Washington's reckless war schemes. Animosity engulfed American and French publics, and conflagrated old Europe.

In June 2011, outgoing Defense Minister Robert Gates reflected the trans-Atlantic rift, when he told a European think tank that the NATO alliance faced "dim, if not dismal" prospects. "Future U.S. political leaders—those for whom the Cold War was not the formative experience that it was for me—may not consider the return on America's investment in NATO worth the cost," he said. Indeed, the alliance has been under unprecedented duress in the NCE, with Washington increasingly frustrated with

European reluctance to back U.S. military engagements, and much of Europe bitterly resentful of the burdens America has hoisted onto NATO.

The loss of bonhomie could amount to nothing. Or it could have profound consequences. It is a known unknown—to borrow a familiar term. The main problem is that America seems hell bent on getting itself into trouble in strategic and economic terms. And so the loss of friends becomes more foreboding. If the United States seemed poised to make better decisions (foreign and domestic), then the trans-Atlantic cultural divide could be more easily shrugged off. It might amount to nothing more than a European snub of color-clad Americans on vacation.

But Europe's enduring antipathy for the United States could be more consequential, during the NCE. And despite the high hopes, there is nothing America's suave and agile Obama has been able to do about it. Europeans may swoon over Obama himself, especially as he scaled vertiginous heights of pedantry during his Nobel acceptance speech, where he cited glistening doctrine in his circuitous musings about fair war theory. Obama distracted the Europeans from the reality of an escalated, politically triangulated war, for a moment. But even as the Europeans applaud Obama, they don't approve of his foreign policies and certainly don't want their countries embroiled in them.

America's missteps are not only noted in Europe with detached, idealistic contempt. They reverberate in Europe. They are felt on the streets. For starters, Europe co-exists with Islam. It is not only geographically close by. In much of Europe, the immigrant population is mostly Islamic. And in some countries, it represents double-digit percentages of the total population.

For all of Americans' problems with Islam around the world, the Muslims residing in the United States are more quiescent than those living in Europe. The demographic has greater opportunity for social/economic mobility in the United States than it does across the Atlantic—even though America's ladder has become more difficult to scale since 9/11. Polls indicate that the Muslim population in the United States is happier than in many other parts of the world. Americans tend to maintain a live and let live attitude towards all sorts of individuals living in their midst. Americans are more exposed to, and have a greater tolerance of, religious fundamentalism that often maintains a hierarchy between the genders.

Many Europeans are staunchly intolerant of intolerance. So Europe has a more precarious social and cultural balancing act to pull off, in regards to Muslims. And the relationship between Europe and its Muslim inhabitants has become more strained.

The great achievements of Western Europe require great exertion and perspiration to maintain. Western Europe lacks America's self-generating viability. It does not quickly integrate its immigrant population, the way the United States has been able to do. The broad safety net it offers doesn't quite compensate for its more limited opportunities. Keeping the enormous bureaucracies functioning, preserving support for European integration and dealing effectively with newly established diversity pose steep challenges.

More recently, a growing nationalism, hostility and discontent have made those challenges more daunting for European governments. While Europeans may be increasingly sympathetic to Muslims living in Muslims countries (particularly those who come under attack by non-Muslims), many do not extend those feelings towards the Muslims living in their own countries. And that anti-Islamic sentiment—in the domestic sense—has strengthened the hand of scrappy, nationalistic political parties across Europe.

Europe is not only lashing out at its Islamic populations. It is in conflict with itself. European elites exist above the fray, unmolested by the Islamic street that has become increasingly segregated and disaffected. Among the Europeans that cross paths with the Islamic communities, there is smoldering hostility, even hatred. The rise of that anti-Islamic sentiment, in turn, is strengthening the hand of Islamist fundamentalists on the continent. The more rarified reaches of the European social strata maintain a more detached and broadminded tolerance. As Europe grapples with how to address its social rifts, its police state grows.

The social gulf in European perception is reflected in polls. According to a 2010 German Marshall Fund poll, 21 percent of the European public said fighting terrorism was a top priority, with only the managing of the global economy coming in as a higher priority. But only 5 percent of European leaders identified terrorism as a top priority. The social divide is also reflected in regards to predominantly Muslim Turkey. According to the poll, 51 percent of European leaders favor Turkey's joining the

European Union, while only 22 percent of the European general public supports Turkey's membership.

When America executes or backs military strikes that inflame Islamic people, the European "street" is affected. The Europeans are nonplussed by that. They face considerable challenges in dealing with the Islamic demographic even without America inflaming that population with anti-Western enmity. So the Europeans begin to look across the Atlantic with disdain. And needless to say, they share that antipathy with many Muslims.

When the United States celebrated the killing of Osama bin Laden in Pakistan in May 2011, Europe watched with contempt—and concern. The editor of France's weekly L'Express, Christophe Barbier, said: "To victory one must not add provocation," adding, "To cry one's joy in the streets of our cities is to ape the turbaned barbarians who danced the night of Sept. 11. It is to tell them the ghastly competition continues between them and us." And the French and other European nations have much to fear about that ghastly competition, because it could be fought in their streets.

European perceptions of a macabre and barbarous American celebration in wake of bin Laden's killing also reflect a trans-Atlantic culture gap that has become more pronounced in the NCE. The European elite was struck with a powerful sense of American "otherness" after U.S. citizens celebrated bin Laden's killing. As one German commentator (Jörg Schoenenborn) put it: America is "quite a foreign land to me. What kind of country celebrates an execution in such a way?" But it was not only the German elite that was put-off by the post-mortem jubilee. According to a German public television (ARD) poll, only 28% of Germans believed the death of bin Laden was a reason to be happy, and 64% said happiness at his death was inappropriate. And only 42% believed that the United States had a right to kill the al Qaeda leader. Another 52% thought the United States should have arrested bin Laden and delivered him to the International Criminal Court for trial. Interestingly, some 79% said they expected terrorist attacks to happen in Germany in wake of bin Laden's death.

There is also a deeper and more fundamental trans-Atlantic divide regarding the use of force, even as a means towards desirable goals. The German Marshall Fund's 2011Trans-Atlantic Trends poll found that 75 % of the U.S. public believes that war is some-times necessary to obtain justice, while only 33% percent of the European public agrees with that sentiment—demonstrating a robust skepticism of the use of military force.

As Europe comes to see the United States with renewed skepticism on military matters, it takes a darker view of U.S. global influence in general. And that kind of loathing multiplies. Like many Eastern civilizations, Europeans are wary of American cultural hege-mony—and the consumer-driven materialism it injects in their society. And they are at a loss as to how to insulate their countries from America's cultural impact.

And, of course, there is profound alarm about America's com-mand of the global economy. Prior to 9/11, much of the world was tolerant or at least agnostic about America's military and financial dominance. Needless to say, that is longer the case. The worst financial conflagration to hit the world since the Great Depression was incontrovertibly made in America, compliments of gratuitous greed, corruption and stupidity on Wall Street and Washington. And that financial meltdown is also tied directly to 9/11 aftershocks.

The world's anger is unfortunately not targeted exclusively on fat-cat bankers and their accomplices in Congress, the White House and the Fed. It is directed at America in general, even though most of America is also the victim. And Europe and the Muslim world clearly have in common that economic rage focused at the United States. After all, they have been personally and deeply hurt by the financial troubles.

Europeans, like so many in the East, also fear America's outsized influence on global food trade. The use of antibiotics and hormones on U.S. livestock has driven down the price of U.S. food exports—and imperiled the livelihood of more traditional farmers elsewhere. Europeans see those developments with deep misgivings, since they are not only focused on food quality and safety, they are also protective of old agrarian traditions—just like so many Islamic societies.

The United States and old Europe undoubtedly have much in common culturally. And the West is so culturally distinct from Islamic worlds that many experts have been calling for a clash of civilizations between those two worlds. But despite Western bonds, European *sympathies* have been moving eastward, particularly since 9/11. According to 2010 surveys carried out by pollster and strategist Stanley Greenberg, and sponsored by the American-Jewish organization The Israel Project, there are stark differences in the way United States and Europe view Israel. Although the surveys show that U.S. support has been dropping since 2009, a sizeable 51 percent of Americans said the U.S. needed to support Israel.

Greenberg's surveys detected much chillier attitudes in Europe towards Israel. In Sweden, 49 percent saying their feelings toward Israel were "cold" or "very cold." In France, 24 percent said they felt "warm" or "very warm" feelings toward Israel, while 31 percent felt cold or very cold feelings toward it. In Germany, 19 percent of German respondents said they felt warm or very warm feelings toward Israel, while 50 percent responded they experienced very cold or unfavorable feelings toward Israel.

Put simply, much of Europe (both new and old) sees the United States as supporting Israel's victimization of Muslim populations and as a fumbling, errant, top-heavy superpower, foolishly harming Islamic civilians in the conflicts it wages or backs. So Europeans have grown contemptuous of America and Israel, and sympathetic to the victimized people enduring the gunfire and drone attacks. Europeans are beginning to view themselves as the industrialized world's counterweight to America, championing America's victims.

Undoubtedly, a gaping cultural chasm separates European and Muslim worlds. While Europeans limit the impact and role of institutional religion in government with conviction, many Muslims embrace it with anti-Western defiance. And while Europeans are profoundly skeptical of resolving threats and differences through the use of force, much of the Muslim world is at least ambivalently welcoming the rise of Muslim fighters to beat back American ambitions.

And so America has more in common culturally with Islam than does Europe. Since 9/11, many Americans have turned towards religious activism, seeking to tie together the political, spiritual and even military spheres. Americans widely believe in the use of force to obtain security goals, particularly if it is waged robotically and claims only foreign victims. And many are disinclined to nit-pick on how, or on whom, that force is applied. And it seems that the more the United States and Islam share common cultural inclinations, the more deeply embroiled in hostilities they become.

Meanwhile, Europe and Islam (as incongruous as they may be culturally) increasingly share common interests that bond the civilizations, in wake of 9/11. Both view American military and economic power and encroaching cultural influence with alarm—and they share an uncertainty on how to counter the world's only superpower. Europeans maintain good feelings toward NATO, but not its most ambitious mission—in Afghanistan.

Europeans then, feel warm and fuzzy towards the US president and NATO, but have been unwilling to put up more invest-ment—in blood or money—to further the most defining goals of either one. Obama was not able to slow the European exodus from Afghanistan and Europe is intent on staking out a foreign policy that distinguishes it from America. America's relationship with Europe has become unmoored. And NATO is providing a most ambiguous anchor, since it is unclear just what a common defense entails in an age of non-state, asymmetrical attacks.

What's more the cultural clash between Europe and the United States seems fated to worsen, because as the two drift apart, they are increasingly unable to influence one another. And that marks a worrisome break from the past. European cultural currents have always been felt in the US, and vice versa.

A hermetic America devoid of European influence is not a welcomed prospect. Already, the hard-line right carries too much clout. And if Europe shrugs off U.S. sensibilities it could see its multi-tentacled, European police state grow even larger and its dizzying array of bureaucracies continue to multiply.

The world at large intrudes more heavily on Europe. And Europeans have a tangible understanding of tribal, religious, ethnic and cultural issues that are barely visible in America. Europe can impart that understanding to America. Europe's melting pot does not burn as intensely as America's, and some ancient customs brought from the Third World are more apparent on the continent. And of course, Europe offers America a long perspective—gained from enduring horrific war on its own soil and other upheaval.

In turn, America's matter-of-fact and upbeat perspective on global challenges can counter European apprehensions to act when necessary. And America's healthy skepticism of foreign aid, multiculturalism, an intrusive government security apparatus, and a roving nanny state balances Europe's adherence to such propositions.

At first blush, it may not seem to matter much that Europe sees America as a trigger-happy superpower that is bound to bloody itself. Europe is not especially economically, militarily or politically equipped to either harm or help America. Europe, in turn, may not need American help either, since the security threats it faces are not as severe as the ones the U.S. has created for itself.

But America faces asymmetrical threats. And they are global. America still benefits from maintaining solid relationships with governments that share many of its principles and values. If America and Europe could get the balance right, and mutually and beneficially influence each other, they could reach a sustainable consensus for effective global action.

The US and Europe could form a working agreement along the following parameters: they will not enforce desirable outcomes (democracy, human rights, women's rights) at the point of a gun; they will not allow humanitarian missions backed by military firepower to morph into roving, transformational enterprises; and they will more selectively define what NATO's common defense obliges member countries to do. America and Europe could also agree more decisively on techniques for countering terrorism. But such a basis for cooperation could falter if America and Europe remain, culturally, oceans apart.

The trans-Atlantic chill is liable to intensify, rather than recede, if further intensified by continued economic troubles and ascendant cultural and political movements. Another terrorist attack or a new cycle of Israeli-Palestinian conflict would also further injure regard and relations. The most critical factors are not the governments involved, but the mood of the European and American people themselves.

CHAPTER 20
IN THE NAME OF THE MOTHER

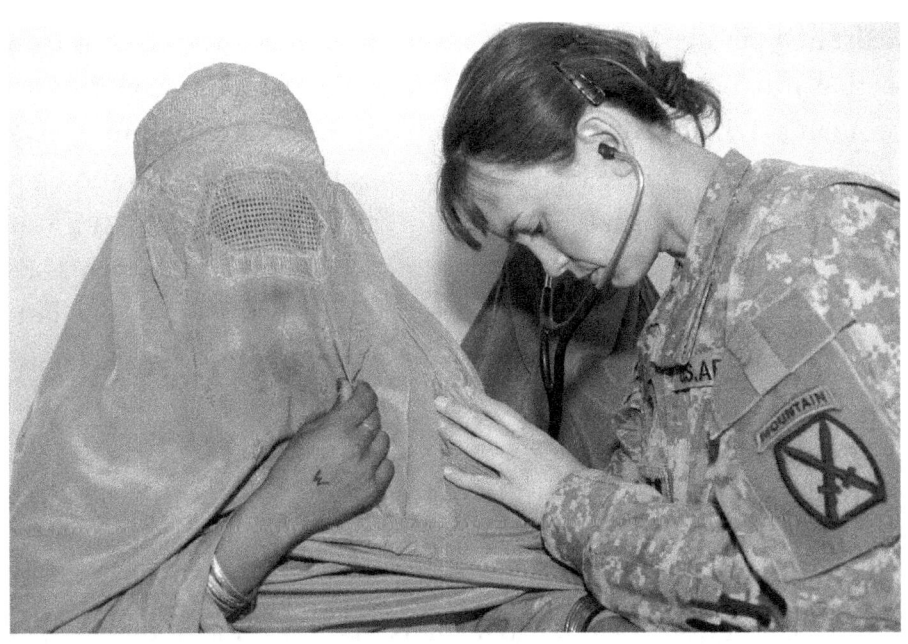

An integral part of Washington's narrative on Afghanistan is that, apart from killing off terrorists, the United States is leveraging its hard and soft power capabilities to advance its soft interests. The women's rights cause injects the U.S. enterprise with moral import. But the hard power America exercises undercuts the soft power it is trying to project.

"We will not abandon you, we will stand with you always," Secretary of State Hillary Clinton told Afghani women in May 2010. But the death toll of U.S. military action competes with that luminous sentiment. And the United States has largely failed to meaningfully improve the lot of Afghani women.

As Ms. Clinton is no doubt aware, the laws of Afghanistan often exist in a parallel universe that rarely intersects with the country's actual inhabitants—particularly female inhabitants. Establishing woman's rights in Afghanistan could only be an arduous undertaking, even under more peaceful circumstances. Women's subjugation in Afghanistan has been reinforced for centuries by cultural factors and, in more recent decades, by the ravages of war. U.S. officials and commanders have resorted to policies that may bolster tactical military objectives, but undercut the efforts being made to improve the environment for women.

Washington has targeted and weakened the Taliban, but has also enriched and empowered other notorious warlords that are brutal, unaccountable and fiercely hostile to women's rights—and children's rights. Indeed, tribal chiefs, such as some of the leaders of the Shinwari tribe, have received significant U.S. funds for fighting the Taliban. The war seems to have transferred power from one group of armed and arbitrary fundamentalists to another group of armed and arbitrary fundamentalists. The warlords have also become richer and more powerful by the resurgence of the heroin trade—which has functioned like a natural stimulus program for warlords.

What's more, there are indications that, amid the wreckage of war, the Afghan security forces are involved in a web of horrific abuse that targets not only women and girls, but also young boys. Washington has further strengthened the already heavy, barefisted hand of warlords and undisciplined police recruits—at the expense of women and children.

Washington showered millions of dollars on North Alliance commanders but, as former Afghani Parliamentarian Malalai Joya, put it in her book "A Woman Among Warlords":

"They were the same extremists whose militias had pillaged Afghanistan during the civil war… The Western media tried at the time to portray these warlords as 'anti-Taliban resistance forces and liberators of Afghanistan,' but in fact Afghan people knew they were no better than the Taliban." Joya quotes an Afghan proverb to describe the phenomenon: "It's the same donkey, with a new saddle."

WOMEN IN THE FOG

So life remains repressive and brutal in Afghanistan for women and children. Although data on conditions for women in

Afghanistan is hard to come by, the information that does exist illustrates a dire existence for the society's most vulnerable individuals.

Afghanistan came dead last in a ranking of the best to worst places to be a mother, in a May 2011 report by Save the Children. According to the study, Afghanistan has the highest lifetime risk of maternal mortality and the lowest female life expectancy in the world. It also places second to last on skilled attendance at birth, under-5 mortality and gender disparity in primary education. Performance on most other indicators also places Afghanistan among the lowest-ranking countries in the world. The typical woman in Afghanistan dies before she turns 45 and has fewer than five year of education. One woman in 11 dies in pregnancy or childbirth in Afghanistan and 1 child out of 5 dies before the age of 5. "At this rate, every mother in Afghanistan is likely to suffer the loss of a child" in Afghanistan, said the study. The study's findings indicate that it is more risky to give birth than to fight in Afghanistan.

In a report released in March 2011, the United Nations Assistance Mission in Afghanistan said: "The conflict continued to have a devastating impact on women and children," with 1,175 women and 555 children killed in 2010. The report said more women and children were killed and injured in 2010 than the year before. Women casualties increased by six percent and child casualties increased by 21 percent from 2009. Over the past four years, 8,832 civilians have been killed in the conflict, with civilian deaths increasing each year, the mission said.

In March 2011, the Afghan Independent Human Rights Commission said that deteriorating security in large parts of the country, a growing culture of criminal impunity, weak law enforcement institutions, poverty and other factors had contributed to increasing violence against women, such as rape and torture. Given these bleak and brutal conditions, women in Afghanistan often resort to the unthinkable: they set themselves on fire.

Many reports provided chilling anecdotes of the practice, but no statistics. A November 2009 human rights assessment prepared by Canada's Foreign Affairs Department documented a skyrocketing suicide rate among Afghan women, according to the Canadian Press and CBC News. The report found that "Self-immolation is being used by increasing numbers of Afghan women to escape their dire circumstances and women constitute the majority of Afghan suicides."

CHILDREN IN THE FOG

It should come as no surprise that the war in Afghanistan has been especially hard on children. The children of Afghanistan have not only had to tolerate depravations, they have also had to tolerate depravity. Warlords that operate above the law are the guiltiest abusers and some have benefited directly from U.S. funding, granting them even greater power to inflict widespread harm and suffering on more children. The members of the Afghan Police force that America is standing up are also notorious perpetrators of the most horrific child sexual abuse. The fact that Washington effectively uses its resources and soft power to do some good on the margins by opening schools and clinics does not obscure this abuse.

Even under ordinary circumstances, children are by far the most powerless members of any society and that is particularly the case in traditional cultures. Children are not protected by virtue of their gentle features and soft voices. Children have no resources, no constituencies. And in traditional societies, where the elder is often venerated, the desires and needs of children are roughly subordinated to the preferences of family, clan or community. Indeed, there is little sense of childhood. Children, even male children, are obliged to further the interests of tribe and family. In a time of conflict, the welfare (and even physical integrity) of children is more dramatically marginalized, as can be seen in Afghanistan.

In a landmark documentary aired in April 2010, Frontline revealed the extent of warlords' abuse of children. Wealthy predators pick up destitute children, and corner them into a life of sexual abuse and servitude. Often, boys known as bacha bazi (which means boy play) dance for the warlords and his guests at parties, and then endure repeated sexual abuse. A warlord's bacha bazi harem is recognized as a status symbol in some circles in Afghanistan. The practice was banned under the Taliban but has resurfaced.

The abuse of children in Afghanistan has been so sickening and shocking that some eye-witnesses of the practice have come back to their home countries with post-traumatic stress disorder. In June 2008, a Canadian soldier told the Toronto Star that he had seen injuries sustained by a boy that was raped by an Afghan soldier at one of the Canadian outposts in Kandahar. The boy's intestines were falling out of his body, a sign of trauma from anal rape, the soldier said.

These accounts have been corroborated by the State Department's remarkably truthful annual human rights report. Its report on Afghanistan, released on April 8, 2011, said that "Child abuse was endemic throughout the country, based on cultural beliefs about child-rearing, and included general neglect, physical abuse, sexual abuse, abandonment, and confined forced labor to pay off family debts. The Ministry of Labor, Social Affairs, Martyrs, and Disabled (MOLSA) stated that police frequently beat children." The report also said "Sexual abuse of children remained pervasive. NGOs noted that most child victims were abused by extended family members. An UNHCR report noted tribal leaders also abused boys. ... According to the AIHRC, most child sexual abusers were not arrested."

Despite U.S. efforts to promote and cajole U.S. values in Afghanistan, paltry U.S. resources went towards helping the children of Afghanistan. "NGOs estimated that there were 37,000 street children in urban areas. Street children had little or no access to government services, although several NGOs provided access to basic needs, such as shelter and food. Living conditions for children in orphanages were poor. Children in orphanages reported mental, physical, and sexual abuse; were sometimes trafficked; and did not always have access to running water, winter heating, indoor plumbing, health services, recreational facilities, or education."

The American public first became aware of the scale and nature of child sexual abuse through the Frontline documentary. But what the American public may not be as familiar with is a State Department cable, published by WikiLeaks as one part of a large body of cables, which suggests not only a shocking callousness on the part of an U.S. official towards the sexual abuse of children, but also a degree of U.S. complicity in the practice through the apparent participation of U.S. contractor DynCorp. in procuring a child for Afghan police recruits to abuse. The cable—which was released on December 2, 2010 and documents a meeting between U.S. assistant ambassador, Joseph Mussomeli, and Afghan Interior Minister Hanif Atmar—also provides a window to pronounced Afghan concerns over the abusive acts of U.S. contractors and a cavalier indifference of U.S. officials towards those acute concerns.

The lack of progress for the children of Afghanistan under U.S. occupation showcases the limits of America's hard and soft power. The United States should not be expected to triumph over ancient cultures and phenomenally difficult circumstances. But when the superpower legitimates its occupation in part on vaunted values, it creates expectations that will not be fulfilled.

RATIONALES IN THE FOG

There are underlying reasons why Washington cannot advance its soft interests in Afghanistan while it is engaged militarily there. Women do not fare well during war or in the post-war period in tribal societies, where a victor's justice prevails and the most productive, and brutal, use of force gains currency. Anywhere where might makes right, women are going to face tough terrain. After all, women's rights depend on an idea that contradicts the power structure of traditional societies, particularly in war time. Women cannot compete in the might, or brutality, department. And that reality is even tougher for children.

The development of women's rights and abilities is not the default order of society. That default centers on strongmen that offer "protection" and subjugation of the rest of the population—and the society evolves (or not) from there. The wars, including U.S. aid, tend to favor the interests of well-armed chieftains who can protect the community from outsiders, or the marauding members of the National Army and Police, who often have no blood ties to the territory they are policing, and abusing.

When the survival of the clan appears in jeopardy, the men with the guns are paid with power, deference and homage. The aspirations and rights of the individual are subjugated for the perceived good of the clan. It goes without saying women's welfare, to say nothing of rights, is threatened, as is the safety of the fair-minded advocates for them.

The ascendance of women in a community depends on the rule of law—and a certain abundance. When the society is so evolved that it can accommodate the aspirations of the individual in diverse ways, the rights of women are respected. Indeed, such a thriving community can accommodate an eclectic array of personal fulfillment, including those that are downright subversive in less privileged societies. If security and resources are scarce, girls and women are swiftly made to bow their heads and make all the practical, emotional and intellectual sacrifices.

Women are often seen as the pivotal threat to the stability of societies in poor and tribal communities. A good deal of energy, custom and religious law is geared towards preventing the temptations posed *by* women or *of* women. In many impoverished and tribal societies, civilization revolves around the human triumph over sexual impulses. Surrendering to those impulses could destroy the social order, undermining what advances the community has achieved. Putting the onus on women to maintain sexual prudence may have been inspired by both pragmatism and bigotry. Women may have seemed easier to control then men, and the responsibility to maintain purity was and continues to be put on women, even in the case of rape, in many societies around the world.

Some of the most zealous agitators for U.S. strikes are so often keen to highlight the cultural and social deficiencies of the region. But they do not typically come full circle on their argument. They fail to acknowledge the harm that the use of force is causing the already struggling communities in Afghanistan. They often fail to even try to prove convincingly, and with data, that the use of force is helping women. What those advocates and social critics do help to reinforce, though, is a sense of otherness—critical to the hardening of the heart for the killing of those different from us, in terms of ethnicity, value system and religion. And in that regard, they are the intellectual architects of further abuse of women and children—not to mention the harm to America's image abroad.

Washington has never settled conclusively on an objective for Afghanistan. The rights of women and children are promoted sporadically, but at other times Washington is focused on killing terrorists. Despite the lack of consistency, the United States heightened the world's expectations, due to its own claims and rhetoric. In doing so, Washington has showcased the limits of its competence in the foreign theatre. The fact that it has all been a mostly impossible task anyway doesn't deflect the damage to U.S. clout.

PART III:
PRESCRIPTIONS,
A CLARIFICATION
AND A QUIBBLE

The preceding pages offer a snapshot of what America looks and acts like today and how it is regarded around the world. Some readers may concur with the snapshots and agree that America has indeed been shocked into a Third Wording cycle. Even so, they may still believe that the circumstances surrounding 9/11 left America with no other alternatives. But U.S. actions may be understandable under the circumstances and still not be inevitable. Just like children, nations can make good choices, or bad ones.

And so the following pages offer some better choices that go beyond ending conflicts and spending less money. These recommendations are as much about the nation's character as a call to particular action. They offer an alternative view on policy and posturing that breaks with the NCE mentality the country is mired in. America's policies should come as a natural outgrowth to this philosophy. Finally, a quibbling thought is offered on why the American devolution parallels a Third World, and not imperial, decline and a parting caveat is provided on multiculturalism.

CHAPTER 21
NOBODY PUTS HEGEMON IN THE CORNER

American power has long been controversial. It has become particularly reproached in wake of 9/11. Washington's attempts to intervene abroad, exerting what once seemed like limitless military and economic superiority, have turned out badly. After expending so much blood and treasure, it's difficult to perceive any substantive gains—while the losses are staggeringly and conspicuous.

By taking on war on two difficult fronts, the United States squandered its aura of boundless military might. And now, America appears to be suffering a natural decline, after military overreach abroad. American power, it seems, is suffering a justified correction. The hyperpower has got its nose bloodied, and that is all to the good—many would argue.

Some observers believe that America's overreach was inevitable and that, as a nation gains predominance, it becomes corrupted by its power. And that may well be. But America's economic sway should be given as long a lifespan as possible.

As America's economic retraction continues to create a vacuum causing untold suffering and privation around the world, what power—or even group of powers—will reignite the global economic engine? In the face of waning U.S. clout, what power, or group of powers, will address the pressing, global issues of the moment, such as non-proliferation and the evident turbulence in the climate? What other power, or group of powers, can address human and civil rights and the onward march of democracy? Could it be Brazil, Russia, India and China, otherwise known as the BRIC nations? That question hardly needs answering. And there are powerful and entrenched reasons why those countries will not rise to the occasion.

In absolute terms, America's global legacy can be vehemently and righteously criticized. In relative terms, the U.S. record is more difficult to lambaste. America looks a lot better in comparison to other countries. And when U.S. foreign policy is measured against America's phenomenal global power, its involvement abroad seems somewhat more judicious, relative to the actions of other great powers throughout history.

Arrogance is the first cousin of stupidity. And in the NCE, Washington has committed foreign and domestic errors of dumbfounding ignorance, arrogance and even stupidity. And the world has been given a ringside seat to the outrageously flawed policies, perpetrated by U.S. policymakers schooled at some elite American institutions.

The neoconservatives that were tapped to justify and orchestrate the Iraq War revealed the depths of such myopic arrogance. Indeed, it was not only the mistakes that were actually committed that demonstrated those depths, but also the general ideas that the neoconservatives planned to eventually execute, such as the privatization of Iraq's oil industry.

Such a lack of understanding of the culture that the neocons were operating in was inexplicable. The Iraqis have yet to decide how they will ultimately distribute oil revenue among themselves. The idea that they would forfeit control of their oil resources—of which they are vehemently protective of—to an occupying, foreign power was always a non-starter.

So mistakes have been made—mistakes of enormous consequences not just for U.S. targets, but also for America itself. Undoubtedly, America's has self-inflicted blows to its credibility and leadership. And so humbled, it may seem the United States should probably lick its wounds and keep its head down.

But there is still a chance that America could retake the mantle of tolerated superpower. If it is to do that, the country must project leadership and clout by example. It should rely more heavily on overt, rather than covert, global action. It should intervene militarily in countries only to safeguard vital national interests, rather than special-interests and corporate advantage. Instead of inserting itself by force to spread democracy, it must take democracy and civil liberties seriously at home during wartime—and provide a compelling model that the world will strive to emulate. The world might accept an American superpower, as long it acts predictably and reasonably.

The United States can and should adjust its relationships with foreign governments according to values and principles. As a tolerable hegemon, America must downgrade its alliances with tyrants to merely procedural relationships—which would include information sharing on terrorist threats and the like but not a broad, enduring alliance. After all, America need not extend to strongmen such a legitimizing honor. The tyrants are just as interested in sharing information as America is. The Islamic militants have them in their sights, too.

The United States should maintain alliances with like-minded and principled countries, but not if those alliances come with a price tag and the ties must never be unconditional. If America should choose to back up humanitarian missions with firepower, it should not do so alone and should act in legitimate concert with other nations and with Congressional approval. Washington must also maintain limited and defined objectives. At any rate, the United States should resist the temptation to come to the rescue on its white F-16s. In times of natural disaster abroad, America should be first on the scene to provide humanitarian—but not transformational—aid, as long as it can afford it.

America must scale back dramatically all of its foreign policy interventions—so that its actions take on consistency and coherence.

That includes moving swiftly to shelve security aid, which feeds the industrial-military complex at home. The armaments bearing the label "Made in America" that were used against the Egyptian people illustrated the evil that U.S. security aid abets. If foreign governments need such help from America, it is usually for the wrong reasons.

And importantly, America must decriminalize drugs to end the global drug "war." This prescription is not related to 9/11, but the challenges of the NCE make such changes more urgent. By doing so, America would cut the profit of the warlords enriching themselves on the heroine trade—some of whom target and kill U.S. troops. Such a move would also undercut the most sanguinary criminal gangs of the world—overnight.

American police officers should not have to risk their lives to prevent adults from sticking needles in their arms or shoving bimbo powder up their nose. If America took these steps, many of the innocent Latin Americans caught in the murderous cross fire of the drug war could reclaim their countries. Law enforcement is not responsible for saving people from themselves.

A policy of restraint would not require the United States to sit in the global corner. Bolstered by solid prestige, America should be a supporter and interlocutor for the values it upholds at home. It should condemn forcefully when appropriate and take the lead in doing so. Backed by an adherence to U.S. law and traditions and a robust economy, the United States would have ample ability to project its alpha influence.

The Founding Fathers and many of their descendents certainly upheld such discerning restraint, and American presidents have long adhered to such principle. The words of John Quincy Adams may well be overexposed today, but he voiced the sentiment so well as secretary of state in 1821 that it deserves repeating:

"Wherever the standard of freedom and independence has been or shall be unfurled, there will be America's heart, her benedictions, and her prayers. But she does not go abroad in search of monsters to destroy. She is the well-wisher to the freedom and independence of all. She is the champion and vindicator only of her own."

That sentiment appears modern and cutting age today—after the excesses and hypocrisy of neocon and Obamaesque interventions. U.S. officials have tried to shed them off and in doing so have caused great harm abroad and at home.

America need not be liked for obsequious benevolence nor feared for reflexive violence—but it must be respected. U.S. military power should be reserved for vital interests. And even then, it must be swift, lawful and proportionate. If Washington is seen acting predictably and credibly, America could eventually regain the soft power it once projected.

The world knows that America has been the best place for immigrants to make a bid for the middle class. If Washington can get its policy balance right, the people of the world may remain at least agnostic about U.S. economic prominence, once again. If America is interested in safeguarding its strategic interests in the long term, it must make its economic vitality the priority.

Americans in the NCE are potentially in favor of such a prioritized approach. According to a comprehensive 2010 German Marshall Fund poll, 74 percent of the American general public and 78 percent of America leaders agree economic power is more important than military power in world affairs. If U.S. leaders explain the economic costs of military exertions abroad, the American people are apt to prioritize U.S. economic power over tactical victories.

America was not predestined to be a First World power. It arrived at such an achievement through the strength of its institutions, the integrity and balance of its form of government, and the pragmatism and hardiness of its people—with some tremendous geopolitical advantages thrown in. God may or may not smile on America. But the United States can sustain its alpha power only if it reclaims those achievements.

America's compelling revolutionary past and its unique institutional freedoms enable it to claim a natural leadership position. It is situated to influence and inspire. It has an array of advantages that command regard—as long as it is discriminating in its missions and actions.

CHAPTER 22
SO KEEP IT LOCAL

The implosion of the life and work of Greg Mortensen in May of 2011 provides a succinct parallel for the folly of U.S. policy, particularly in the NCE. The downfall seemed like a tragic turn for a flawed but well intentioned man. But the apparent factual inaccuracies in the book that chronicled his life, "Three Cups of Tea," now seem to point to a sweeping and recidivist tendency of the United States and other Western nations.

Industrialized countries cannot seem to rid themselves of the notion that some white male has to come to rescue of some poor country that has invariably suffered the brutality and domination of other white males. Such a narrative closes a neat circle for Western society, righting the transgressions of the past—thereby redeeming the West—while at the same time reinforcing white male domination. The white male, whether he be turning his magnanimous attentions towards South Africa or Afghanistan, reinforces the lord and vassal power structure the West can't seem to wean itself off of, since the rescuer brings resources the Third World country is desperate for.

The factual shortcomings of the Mortensen story highlight the perils of this Western fantasy. And when author Jon Krakauer revealed the inconsistencies of "Three Cups of Tea," he put the Pentagon on the defensive, since it had championed Mortensen and his work. Mortensen had in effect helped Washington promote the war on idealistic terms, and he was therefore quite useful. Mortensen supported the occupation of Afghanistan while at the same time appeared to be spearheading—with superhuman competency—the opening and running of schools throughout the country. He seemed to personify and perpetuate the fiction that a white-male transplant could come into a foreign country, bring his superior know-how, and create the mythologized transformation that Washington promised for both Iraq and Afghanistan. It turns out that Mortensen was not able to keep running all the schools he opened, and the book on his life was inaccurate in a host of ways.

The West would do far better by supporting local groups and individuals if they are to do anything at all to help the Third World. In Afghanistan, a women's group that pre-dates the Soviet invasion has successfully erected schools throughout the country—and kept them running. During the Taliban rule, the group continued to run a network of underground schools, using the basements of supporters and drawing on native resources, networks and strategies to keep schools in session.

The reason most Americans have not heard of this group is that it does not conform to the Western fantasy outlined above. The Revolutionary Association of the Women of Afghanistan opposes the U.S.-led occupation. It challenges today's warlords. It also opposed the Soviet occupation and defied the Taliban. Simply put, RAWA depends on members with nerves of steel. And those people do exist in Afghanistan, just as they do around the world.

The fact that Washington, by way of its incorrigibly flawed policies, found itself having to throw its support behind the factually challenged Mortensen, rather than an established, native and competent organization like RAWA, is illustrative of Washington's policy folly. Principled, local assets like RAWA that are sincerely working towards progress in their countries are never going to conform to Western rescue fantasies, and they are most definitely not going to support a foreign occupation of their own country.

Since Washington found itself locked into Mortensen's embrace, and then soiled by the latter's collapse of credibility, it should also question the policies that brought it to that union. It is true that Mortensen and his half-truths and half-endeavors were long forgotten by the next news cycle and the West can find another white poster boy to replace its delegitimized altruist. But such a move will not ultimately help Afghanistan and Washington will sink further into its nation-building quagmire.

Wealthy countries should begin thinking seriously about championing the work of local people, women even (and brown women at that!) who are laboring without fanfare to advance the welfare of their fellow countrymen. In one fell swoop, the West would thereby come upon a strategy for advancing development and human rights with the necessary cultural acumen.

Afghanistan's recovery will be neither swift nor tidy. The wars on its soil have done significant damage, and there is no papering over that tragic fact. But as Afghani former Parliamentarian and author Malalai Joya has so logically maintained, Afghanistan's war-related wounds cannot heal until conflict ends and Afghanistan retakes power and responsibility over itself. Joya herself was educated at an underground RAWA school in Pakistan. She is a living testament to the power and unrelenting bravery of native reformers, amid the terror of war.

Supporting local groups may not prominently spotlight American might, but it could be moderately helpful in reinforcing the arduous efforts of Third World reformers. Eventually, such well placed U.S. support would be recognized—just not in accordance to a four-year election cycle.

CHAPTER 23
SUDDENLY, A DRONE

When Americans think back to 9/11, they often remember the crystal clear sky that day in New York. They imagine people rushing in the early morning to fulfill their responsibilities. They recall a sense of everydayness, pierced by the mangling of plane and building and flames and people. They think of destruction that puts a stain on humanity itself. Just as soon as the attacks became an act, they also became a symbol.

As Americans remember the savagery of those attacks, they might stop for a moment and wonder what it is like for innocent people—also going about the cherished, mundane activities that are the bulk of human existence—to come under attack with no warning whatsoever by a robotically controlled U.S. drone. To some Americans, imagining that unseemly scenario smacks of disloyalty to country. Many who see drone attacks as a necessary evil stridently oppose considering the damage they wreak.

Obama joked in May 2010 about the silence of the drones, in warning the Jonas Brothers to keep their distance from his daughters. "But boys, don't get any ideas. I have two words for you, 'predator drones.' You will never see it coming," he said. Indeed, the drones are quiet. And unfortunately, Obama's pathetic attempt at levity traveled around the world and was heard in the affected and victimized countries.

There are pressing and pragmatic reasons for taking the time to consider in all seriousness what drone attacks do—and what it is like to come under their mechanical and merciless fury. Pakistanis certainly discuss the horror of the drone and for that reason alone, so should Americans. Efforts to block debate about the drones in America do not stop the image-laden controversy from being aired around the world. And so attempts to cordon off such a discussion in America is a futile and vainglorious exercise. Americans have the right, and indeed the need, to see what foreigners see. And then they can decide for themselves whether or not such attacks are advancing American interests.

The drones have mistakenly targeted wedding parties, funerals, children at play. Their impact is horrific, tearing apart the human body. Many Americans naturally want to be spared the details. But the rest of the world is bearing witness.

The Pakistanis whose lives have been shattered by the drones have often been left with nothing left to lose, and a seething rage. Many have turned to violence against American troops for retribution. And so a drone attack can be a life or death matter for those serving in Afghanistan. And if the fury is intense enough, and the victim determined, a drone attack might come to be avenged on American soil.

Those who are not personally affected and propelled into the depths of anger and suffering still take due notice of the attacks. And in a broad sense, those perceptions limit American legitimacy. Foreigners will always be predisposed to wariness by the scale of American power alone, and so Washington needs as many chips as possible. The drones reduce America's chips.

The Greater Middle East is focused on America's deeds, rather than Obama's fluency. America is injuring its image at a time that it is critically engaged in a contest of ideas. These attacks are particularly difficult to justify, since so many of those targeted have not had even the remotest involvement in 9/11.

CHAPTER 24
AMERICA MAKES ITS OWN INVITATION
Operation bin Laden, and Others Like It

The shots that killed bin Laden traveled around the world. The world collectively drew in its breath sharply with those shots. The bin Laden operation showcased a very singular type of global power and lethality.

How powerful does America look when it can swoop into a remote and highly hostile foreign country, in the midst of a foreign army garrison, and leave swiftly with its man? How agile does America prove to be when it can complete such a phenomenal mission with so few people involved? And how surgical, controlled and proportionate did American power appear when it zeroed in on its highest-value human target, and cause such minimal collateral fatalities?

The bin Laden operation dramatically demonstrated to the world that, regardless of where an individual may be hiding, U.S. forces can penetrate it. And it makes its own invitation. Regardless of whether or not some Pakistani officials knew the operation was coming beforehand, they certainly didn't favor it.

And while the mission proved that there is no quarter of the world closed to American penetration, it also demonstrated that America's human, special-operations' capabilities are every bit as advanced as its technological hardware. This was a revelation because the United States has been depending so heavily on robotic killings from the air.

Assuming that Washington had, and continues to have, a substantive reason for linking bin Laden to the 9/11 attacks, then it was not only justified in piercing Pakistani sovereignty in order to seek out the al Qaeda chief, it had a constitutional imperative to do so. Regardless of how the United States might be provoking the jihadis, violent actions against American civilians are illegitimate, immoral and must be punished. Only by taking such action would the U.S. government uphold its compact with its citizens.

The operation was distinct from other manhunt missions supported by intelligence operations. It did not occur in a country under U.S.-led occupation. It did not occur in a Western country. It occurred in one of the most inhospitable human terrains on earth—and with uncertain (perhaps grudging?) consent from authorities of that country. The success of the mission proved what

America has the capability to accomplish under some of the most difficult circumstances imaginable.

Compare that show of U.S. force to the revelations of the occupations in Iraq and Afghanistan. Those occupations have showcased the limitations of America's hard and soft power. They have showed the fiscal damage that wars can cause even to a superpower. They have illustrated, in grim reality, America's willingness to use blunt instruments of war and thereby sacrifice the lives of foreign civilians—civilians that the U.S. government does not even count. The images of the war's victims have travelled the world, except, for the most part, in the United States. In short, even though the wars were sometimes defended on the grounds that they were needed to demonstrate American strength and power, they have nevertheless demonstrated a host of weaknesses.

And so a natural question emerges from the bin Laden operation, and all the wreckage of the NCE: can the United States perform missions like the bin Laden operation, without the need for massive troop deployments and occupation? Many Americans put the bin Laden mission and the occupation into the same mental category. But indeed, they belong to separate spheres. And according to W. Patrick Lang (former head of human intelligence collection and Middle East intelligence at the Defense Intelligence Agency and recipient of the Presidential Rank of Distinguished Executive award), it is possible to do one without the other.

The occupation of Afghanistan, Lang said, has been based on the precepts of COIN, which is really "armed nation building" and is the broad policy that the Obama administration applied in that country. At the same time, the United States has been running Joint Special Operations Command (JSOC), which joins the intelligence community with elite special forces to find the terrorists. Lang believes that nation-building COIN should not be conflated with JSOC terrorist-hunting operations. And Lang said that the individuals who claim that JSOC missions (like the one that killed bin Laden) have to be run in conjunction with COIN are mistaken:

"They're just wrong. People who say that, well they have an axe to grind. These are COIN partisans. In fact, if you have a base, you can recruit people to spy upon the enemy out of the countryside, in what we would call a denied area. You can do that. I've done it so many times. I did it Soviet Union, East Germany, Vietnam and any number of other places. And if you're any good at this, you can recruit people to spy for you," said Lang.

Obama bought time politically to continue the war in Afghanistan with the killing of bin Laden, but to the close observer, the raid delegitimized that prolongation and the Afghan occupation as a whole. The bin Laden raid demonstrates that the U.S. government could have best upheld its obligation to the citizenry by deploying its key assets towards a comprehensive manhunt mission to catch the top al Qaeda leaders, rather than deploy hundreds of thousands of troops and private contractors to conduct an occupation. Many observers have argued that America would have looked weak by taking such a targeted response, but time, effort and ingenuity would have vindicated American power, just as it was vindicated with the bin Laden raid.

Some foreign policy experts contend that applying the COIN lessons of Vietnam to Afghanistan makes for a false comparison. They are right. The human terrain in Afghanistan is far more challenging. As Lang puts it:

"Even though [COIN] was a very hard thing to do in South Vietnam, we actually didn't do badly. But the cost is just enormous. I mean you just go on forever in all these little villages, and this was a relatively benign environment. I mean, I lived for a year in a village on the border with Cambodia that was completely surrounded by enemy troops, and I used to walk around at night in the village and go to see people at their homes and go to barber shops and have the guy shave me, and things like that. And nobody ever made a hostile move at me. This was deep in Indian country. And you can just imagine doing something like that in Afghanistan. I mean, you'd be dead in about 10 minutes."

Of course, there are no guarantees with JSOC missions—just as there are no guarantees in war. "They can take time," Lang said. "Sometimes they take no time. Sometimes they can never get done.

Because [in the case of bin Laden] you are trying to find someone who is hiding from you with considerable ingenuity and is conscious of security. And as I say, this is very skill dependent, and you have to have the right people working on it at the right time. And if you do, bang, there it is."

The United States can recruit foreign allies in its intelligence operations, but it does not necessarily have to do so. It can also rely on managed deception. "You get somebody who will have access to another person who's a little closer, and then you work your way down a chain," said Lang. "It's a little like peeling an onion. And sometimes the people in that chain don't know who the actual recipient of the information that they pass on actually is," he said.

All the same, America must keep a sharp, discerning focus in regards to JSOC. That focus must be squarely directed towards any plotters that might be left associated with 9/11, or those currently planning to attack the United States. The JSOC community should not, under any circumstances, be put in the business of assassinating Islamists because they say they hate America, or some Pashtun warlord because he says he so admired bin Laden, or some Talib because he says he dreams of building a caliphate.

In short, JSOC should be squarely focused on meting out justice and protecting Americans from active plots to kill them. It is not a global police force. It should not be engaged in missions that are hoped to yield speculative gains or amorphous policy goals.

Afghanistan may or may not be better off with the execution of some of its warlords, but such a pursuit should not be a function of the U.S. government. Rather, such endeavors are the responsibility of the Afghan people and their state. And at any rate, the execution of warlords and jihadi leaders often does not yield the security bonanza so often hoped for, since they are swiftly replaced by capable, and often more brutal, successors. What's more, JSOC must operate within America's legal parameters. If units that are allowed to operate in secrecy are not held to legal or operational standards, they are liable to unwittingly injure U.S. interests to a degree that a captured jihadist might not justify.

And as JSOC flexes its impressive muscles, America must not forget the difficult reality that the physical perpetrators of the 9/11 attacks are now dead—and have been dead for over a decade. Some of their remains disintegrated into the air of Ground Zero, NY, which city authorities insisted for a long time was just fine for workers and residents to inhale. The phenomenon of suicide bombers poses a psychological hardship to a society, in denying it the ability to punish the physical perpetrators.

The government is left, then, with the only response left—pursing their handlers. That is, after all, how law enforcement is pursued in America and in most of the rest of the world. Officers pursue not only hit men but also their bosses. Regardless of the consequences, Washington would remain justified in penetrating foreign territory to mete out justice—if it had solid evidence to act.

What remains so striking in the aftermath of the bin Laden raid is how pathetic a figure bin Laden had become: how forgotten he was by the Islamic world, how circumscribed his movements were, and how limited his human interactions had grown. The massive military mobilization of the world's only superpower catapulted Osama bin Laden to jihadi superstardom. After hearing Washington's rhetoric on bin Laden for so long, America in May 2011 awakened to the killing of a diminished man.

Many Europeans may have scoffed at the bin Laden operation, but the rest of the world appears to have understood it—in contrast to other errant U.S. foreign policy. Washington had identified Osama bin Laden as the highest value fugitive in connection to 9/11—and it took action to address a crime against U.S. citizens. Unlike other U.S. policy gyrations, if the integrity of the bin Laden mission is borne out over time, then it will assert the credibility of America's special-force prowess—and inspire the attendant respect.

CHAPTER 25
TOWARDS A MID-EAST PEACE

Israel has nuclear weapons. It has a cutting edge military. And while the Iranian regime will remain an enemy of Israel (to varying degrees and for various reasons) for the foreseeable future, Tehran will never attack a nuclear-armed Israel—unless it is attacked first. So America should not infantilize Israel. Israel can and has been taking care of itself.

Undoubtedly, Israel faces some tough challenges, by way of geography and ethnography. And there is nothing the world's superpower can ever do to change that physical and human terrain. All the same, none of those challenges pose existential dangers for Israel. And the Israeli people are militarily and creatively capable of dealing with them by their own right.

Washington has undermined both Israeli and American interests by altering the cost-benefit ratio of war and peace in both political and real terms. In skewing that ratio, it has minimized Israel's natural cost of warring with the Palestinians and, by extension, the Muslim world. The benefits of peace appear, therefore, less convincing in comparison.

The Israeli people do not need to be schooled by the United States one way or another on the costs of war and the dividends of peace. The Israelis can do the math. But Washington has altered the equation.

So how could America now reckon with the challenge of fashioning a U.S. policy towards Israel that does not skew the cost-benefit calculus of war and peace? Undoubtedly, that is easier said than done. But some policy prescriptions are easily implemented and require nothing more than common sense. For starters, U.S. policymakers must cut out the apocalyptic rhetoric regarding Israel. America's dire, fantastical warnings regarding threats to Israel benefit the fear-mongering of Israeli ultra-nationalists and clearly sabotage prospects for peace.

U.S. officials (particularly legislators) routinely and dishonestly overstate the external threats Israel faces—further undermining the Israeli peace movement. It is true that Washington has tended to echo the claims of an incorrigibly hawkish Israeli lobbying group, which has tirelessly and aggressively advocated for U.S. foreign policy in its ideological image. But that is no excuse. Washington has aided and abetted those trumped up claims. And it bears its own responsibility for doing so. While it is important for a country to level with itself in recognizing threats to the homeland, an exaggeration of the dangers can also lead to policy errors of great consequence. Indeed, America is facing those very consequences now.

In political terms, America has forcefully blunted global condemnation of Israeli policies in the Palestinian territories. And that condemnation is a natural cost of conflict. It can serve as a force multiplier for peace. America's unvarying support not only of Israel but disproportionate Israeli actions has given invaluable credence to the cause of conflict—and forcefully castrated Israel's political movement for peace and restraint.

But America has to change more than the way it talks. U.S. security aid to Israel underwrites conflict—as it does in other countries around the world. Indeed, America should begin dismantling security aid to all foreign governments, since it introduces perverse incentives. Washington in part justifies security aid on the precept that Israel, as a country under siege, must be given that support. If Israel were to come to terms with the Palestinians and the neighboring countries, then the scale of U.S. aid might be reduced—and therein lies the "moral hazard" of U.S. security aid.

America's policies toward Israel have extended the reach of the U.S. military-industrial complex. (Sadly, the peace-racket doesn't pay well.) And so that complex becomes another vested interest for conflict. Exhibit A of that dynamic is the 20 F-35 Stealth fighters the United States sold to Israel.

It may seem to some Israelis that they are getting something for nothing with those Stealth fighters that the U.S. subsidizes—not such a bad deal. But, again, the arms sales from the world's only superpower legitimizes the cause of war; strengthens the hand of hawkish Israeli (not to mention American) politicians at the expense of those favoring peace; and gives greater credence to the logic of war. Because when Israeli politicians are weighing what tack to take with their neighbors, Israel's possession of new, gleaming stealth fighters do not aid the argument for peace. And so those arms sales come at a cost—of a financial nature for the U.S. taxpayer, and in more profound terms for Israeli citizens.

Again, none of this is to suggest that the Israelis are not capable of recognizing the benefits of a peace deal with their neighbors. But the United States has materially changed the peace calculus, making the benefits of peace less attractive in relative terms. And the actions of all parties in the conflict reflect that calculus.

America should inject some strategic ambiguity on the conditionality of all other types of U.S. aid to all countries, including Israel—except humanitarian aid that is delivered in wake of a disaster. All U.S. aid to all countries must have some strings attached. The love between a mother and child is unconditional, relations between countries is not. Reaching a peace should be part of the U.S. aid equation. If U.S. aid remains on autopilot, a regional peace might become part of its cost—a twisted irony, to be sure.

This is not to say that the United States should hastily pull the rug out if Israel does not make progress towards a regional peace agreement. Such a deal is not only Israel's to make. It remains to be seen if the region is serious about peace. And the idea is not to make conflict costlier for Israel, but merely for Israel to bear the organic cost of conflict, and to therefore be more inclined to opt for the natural dividends of a peace deal. At any rate, it seems unlikely that Israel would step off the brink, endangering its fruitful relationship with the United States if Washington had come to decide that conditions for a peace deal were favorable.

If the Jewish Diaspora and Israelis that favor peace with their neighbors want to advance their cause, they must be explicit in describing bluntly the impact of U.S. policy. Because the only way a change in U.S. policy could ever gain an iota of credence is if prominent American Jews and Israelis begin to publicly support reforms.

Interestingly, this is beginning to happen. Already, Jewish Americans with accrued influence are calling for a more discerning U.S. policy towards Israel. Walter Pincus, an award-winning journalist for The Washington Post, did just that on Oct. 17, 2011, in a piece titled "United States needs to reevaluate its assistance to Israel."

Such a reevaluation may seem to suggest that U.S. and Israeli interests are divergent. Indeed, that seems a popular idea these days—with many U.S. policy experts pushing for a Palestinian state, and their Israeli counterparts seeing the creation of such a state as a zero-sum proposition. But in the long term, America and Israel do not have conflicting interests. Indeed, the interests of both converge fundamentally. It is in both Israeli and American interests for Mid-East peace and security to prevail. Both the United States and Israel do not want Iran to develop nuclear weapons. And both nations ultimately incubate an appreciation for the spread of democracy and civil liberties deeply in the national psyche. Indeed, it is in the interests of both countries for sustainable democracy—perhaps with some Islamic "flavor"—to take root in the Greater Middle East.

But the stakes are quite different for each country. If Israel should give up land and ultimately not get peace in return, it risks losing terrain and water resources under its control, and all the demographic implications that go with it. And while it is true that America would stand to lose geopolitical clout if that were to occur, the consequences would be much less material.

And in regards to Iran, needless to say that country is much closer to Israel than America. True, neither the United States nor Israel seems to be primarily concerned with nuclear conflagration. Rather, both fear the ascendance of a nuclear-armed Tehran that would be almost impossible to intimidate and would be emboldened to act in a region that produces America's most dangerous enemies and the world's most coveted resources.

Still, for the United States, the Iranian threat remains somewhat abstract. For Israel, an Iran armed with nuclear weapons could entail an uptick in offensive or retaliatory proxy attacks, via Hezbollah. And yet even without such weapons, Iran is fulfilling some dreaded expectations. It is apparently continuing its proxy battles with Israel, in the understanding that Israeli retaliation could maim and enrage Iran, but never decisively cripple it.

And finally, while both countries would be gratified to see democracy spread, the cost of social upheaval in the Greater Middle East is quite different for each. Egypt is on Israel's border. And it remains a world apart from America, even with all the connectivity of globalization.

So while Israeli and U.S. interests converge, the stakes for each vary. It doesn't make sense for Washington to try to downplay what Israel's risks are—they are evident. But Washington need not enhance the logic of war, which already gets enough support in the Mid-East. If Washington calibrates its actions and rhetoric, Israel may well decide that it is willing to take the necessary risks to secure its fundamental, long-term interests—which America shares.

Nations craft policy based on perceived interests. Interests are usually calculated on a cost-benefit basis and, unfortunately, with short-term prerogatives at the fore. Washington, at the urging of interested but myopic parties, has distorted that calculation, to the detriment of U.S. and Israeli long-term interests. Hopefully, it will change course while opportunities still exist.

There is no question that helping to foster a peace deal would lift U.S. soft power around the world overnight. Generally speaking, American credibility must be recovered through plodding progress. But there is one potential policy coup, and a Mid-East pact holds that elusive but powerful promise.

POWER TO THE PEOPLE

In the end, policy recommendations often come down to so much ink and paper, even when they make sense. Reason is no match for entrenched power and well-established, political quid-pro-quo. And while interested parties should never stop forwarding their creative policy ideas, they must also think about alternative actions that circumvent officialdom.

Indeed, the range of such action is limited, but there are many grass root movements that begin small, and eventually take out-sized influence. The idea that American Jews and Israelis seriously focused on peace could form a new nucleus of influence is perhaps not so far-fetched. Such a global movement would bypass incorrigibly compromised governments in its efforts to bridge global gaps. Indeed, the much celebrated J Street lobbying firm is a step in that direction, but its economic prospects are too tied to governments that appear too compromised to make meaningful changes. A movement that is more divorced from the corridors of power could be driven by ordinary individuals who have their own day jobs and are not staking their professional advancement on tabling tepid proposals in fruitless meetings with impaired politicians.

Does dialogue have to be government-centric? Hasn't even the U.S. government demonstrated on a bipartisan level that it is too compromised by entrenched interests to make any substantive progress? And how productive, for example, could any discussion with the Saudi government be anyway?

Prior to 9/11, the W. Bush administration declined to address the ad hoc threat that terrorists could pose. They had such grander, bigger ticket items in mind. They favored government-to-government confrontations. The focus was on North Korea, Iran, Iraq: memorialized as the axis of evil in the run-up to the Iraq War.

But the 9/11 terrorists demonstrated the economic, cultural and military impact that unofficial groups can have on citizens around the world. True, they achieved it through insidious violence. But doesn't that precedent demonstrate the incremental influence that global groups in general could have—potentially to positive effect? Haven't peaceful demonstrations and people power across Muslim countries captured the attention, sympathy and imagination of the world? To many, such a proposition verges on Pollyanna, but what are the alternatives? Government to government dialogue would be the most direct and efficient route to deal making. But unfortunately, there is little momentum in that direction.

Although it may seem nothing more than a quaint and modest concept, dialogue between civilizations and nations does not always have to focus on sweeping geopolitics or peace. It can also proceed on a more functional basis: organization to organization, trade union to trade union, business group to business group.

Journalistic organizations, pediatric groups, chambers of commerce, scientific institutions could engage their counterparts in other countries, and involve Israelis and Palestinians. They could swap ideas on journalistic and business practices, scientific advances—in short, issues that pertain to their trade. In that way, individuals with something in common could open channels of communication. Cumulatively, that could come to have an effect.

Power to the people seems such a well-worn, trite slogan. But its reputation for naivety is perhaps ill deserved. Through the ages, the power of the people has paved the way for profound global shifts and progress. Unleashed in earnest, it could energize the region, and the era.

CHAPTER 26
ALL FACILE COMPARISONS LEAD TO ROME
Why the Imperial Analogy Has No Clothes

The decline of America has been reflexively compared to the fall of the world's greatest empires. And it is a romantic, cinematic analogy, with an air of inevitability and glamorous decadence. But it is also deceiving comparison.

For starters, America is not only overspending its way out of global superpowerdom. America's war-related, financial troubles are serious, but are just one aspect of the malaise. Indeed, our country's root affliction appears to be cultural and not uniquely imperial in nature.

America's downfall is intricately connected to the rise of a NCE focus on honor. And that is not an imperial phenomenon. Indeed, societies since time immemorial have been driven by and structured around male honor. And the industrialized world has made its strides thanks, in part, to its triumph over that obsession. The countries that have not made that cultural leap are often in the Third World.

Closely linked to concerns about male honor is the cultural conviction that problems can be resolved through the use of force. That conviction infects a society. It weakens economic and political institutions.

Of course, the devolution of America and the decline of Rome do have some symptoms in common—such as the hoarding of power by the executive and the ascendance of sordid and escapist entertainment. But reality shows are considerably more benign than gladiator fights. And the U.S. president still is no emperor. So that comparison also goes only so far.

Structurally, too, the comparison is limited. Because America has come nowhere close to wielding imperial-style control over Iraq and Afghanistan even during its most intense deployments—despite enormous military, civil and financial investment. America has no appetite for the methods, or the cost, of that level of control.

This is not to sugar coat American history. Our nation is engaged in some half-baked, foolish, brutal military adventures. But America still has too many structures, checks and balances and engrained antipathy to full-fledged, imperial subjugation to allow for such unmitigated penetration of foreign lands. And America was specifically constructed to withstand the imperial trap and overextension. The Founders were vigorously aware of the cyclical nature of imperial power, and sought to shore up checks and balances to prevent such threats to the nation's health and longevity.

But perhaps people really mean the British, and not Roman, Empire when they make allusions to America's imperial decline. The comparison there is even more flawed, and for much more worrisome reasons. America's devolution is more severe than the fall of that power. The British Empire undoubtedly was a victim of its own global overreach and myopic use of brutal, blunt force—like America. But even in its darkest hour, in its post-WWII penury, it did not backpedal on its political reforms and progress at home. This is not to excuse the imperialist atrocities the British committed abroad in its vain attempts to maintain its global dominion, but rather to point out that the subjugation did not spill over and corrupt domestic policy—as it has in America.

And today, Great Britain may be suffering economically (and it is no longer an empire or even a hegemon) but it is still firmly in the First World, safeguarded by First World institutions, scrutinized by a feisty, independent media. Furthermore, it was much quicker to exit Afghanistan and Iraq.

Also, under the British Empire, the zeal for expansion was mostly limited to the elite. In America, a shocked and injured citizenry helped drive a military, religious revenge. Much of the public has attached a vehement, religious rationale to the use of force. Undoubtedly, America's governing class and power brokers may have gleefully exploited those impulses, but that would not have been possible without the attacks and the rage and indignation they spawned.

And so America's degradation is not really an example of neo-imperial decline. In the Roman case, it is too extreme. In the British, it isn't extreme enough. And the comparisons often become a self-aggrandizing exercise that in part justifies American devolution. The analogy is often offered as if to suggest that all great powers wane. What goes up must come down.

Some observers have also compared current U.S. trends to neo-fascism. But that is also off the mark. Fascism revolves around the most coordinated, unrelenting and, it must be acknowledged, competent showcasing of the power and authority of the machinery of the state. Along with all its brute coercion, fascist states offer their people a trains-run-on-time tradeoff, along with some populist extras. Most reasonable people would rather wait for the train, but that is fascism's promise, offered in exchange for all its savagery.

The United States in the NCE has never come close to showcasing such coordinated machinery. It has bungled its foreign campaigns and has permitted an inexorable collapse of its domestic infrastructure. What's more, a fascist state would never have allowed the failures surrounding the Katrina disaster to occur.

So the fascist and imperial comparisons, while colorful, often seem facile. And the analogy that really makes sense is less grand and mythologized. It is found today in those swaths of the Third World that have developed democratically and economically to some degree, but continue to be undermined by way of culture and still struggling institutions. And that is no accident of development. Culture drives institutional and economic fortitude. And so as America regresses, it resembles those Third World countries that do have an executive, and a legislature, and a Central Bank—but remain institutionally immature. Indeed, America's government bodies are behaving the way those countries' institutions often do. And increasingly, the American people are giving up hope, the way people all around the Third World have done for so long.

The imperial analogy hints at the slow-paced, dramatic fall of a giant. But America's degradation appears swift footed. U.S. power is not only waning, it is also becoming a hazard in and of itself, creating multiple sources of weakness. Our country's decay is an encroaching, putrid and avoidable affair. And its legacy will not leave behind marble columns in far-flung parts of the world.

CHAPTER 27
A NEW COMMON ERA
A Clarification

The transition from one era to another does not entail an abrupt shift in the tectonic plates of time. There is usually a sense of continuity. Even in the nano-second world of today, events, ideas, actions tend to build on each other. Trends seem to wane, only to become recognizable again. The NCE is no different. It has occurred on a time continuum. And yet it also constitutes a dramatic break.

The NCE began with an unprecedented event in American history: an attack on America soil, broadly inconceivable in its brutality towards civilians. The visual drama of planes' impact, people jumping out of towering infernos to their deaths and the avalanche of collapsing buildings catalyzed the beginning of the era. The unprecedented attack on 9/11 goaded America into instituting a number of "firsts" in a range of areas.

America's current militarism fits into a pattern of conquest, but it is also breaks out from it. It is distinct in some crucial respects. America's current military struggles have no borders and engage a stateless enemy with diverse controlling authorities. It is fighting not by proxy, as it has challenged stateless groups in the past, but rather with its direct involvement—and credibility on the line. And unlike other direct U.S. military confrontations since WWII, these endeavors are widely seen, domestically and abroad, as a reflection of America's ability to dole out justice and retribution in wake of a ferocious attack on civilians. And importantly, any subsequent attack on Americans is likely to be interpreted as the result of insufficient military resolve and competency by a great many citizens. For those reasons, the current context is unique on a psychological level.

Unlike previous wars, America faces no head of state on the enemy side that could decide his people have suffered enough, or that the odds are too sharply against his favor, or that his supply of able-bodied conscripts has simply been exhausted. There are no figures to hold politically accountable. Indeed, the leaders of the eclectic jihadi groups certainly appear to believe that they benefit when U.S. military maneuvers take a high civilian toll. And when they do, those groups move quickly to capitalize on that human destruction. And so America's conventional and technological advantages, such as the use of drones, can become PR assets to the enemy.

This contest cannot be won through technological prowess or through brutality. As long as America is willing to wage the war, there seems to be a supply of combatants that are willing to fight on and expose their innocent Muslim brethren to U.S. retaliation. The combatant conscripts sign up voluntarily, from a variety of countries, to fight the perceived American barbarism and encroachment onto Muslim lands.

And there is another factor that distinguishes the NCE—in cultural terms. America is facing an enemy that cites religion as justification for attacking U.S. citizens in their homeland. The religion cited, Islam, is not widely represented in the United States. The growth of anti-Islamic feeling in America since 9/11 has had inestimable political, social and strategic consequences and will probably continue to manifest in unpredictable ways.

Another crucial difference is the degree to which private contractors are engaged militarily. Although mercenaries have appeared intermittently throughout U.S. and revolutionary history, the scale and deleterious impact of contractors in the NCE is unprecedented and difficult to exaggerate. Some contractors have been shown to bribe the very enemies fighting U.S. soldiers in Afghanistan. They do not follow the protocol or uphold the standards of the U.S. military. What's more, they have reared their head in almost every damaging event of the past few years, from "enhanced," brutal interrogations of detainees to the Abu Ghraib catastrophe.

Importantly, the extraordinary reliance on contractors has intruded on American democracy, establishing an extensive military force that is financed by the U.S. taxpayer but largely outside the purview of the American justice system and even U.S. military authority. Mercenaries are hired by, but not entirely subordinate to, the Pentagon—due to the details of the contracts. What's more, the contractors have exported their challenge to democratic systems around the world, particularly to those countries that supply recruits.

In addition, the particularly insipid role of the press, judging by the standards established in the past half century or so, has distinguished the NCE. Although there has long been legitimate criticism of the US. media, the failures of the recent past have been especially worrisome. In terms of war coverage, the U.S. media seems to have lowered, rather than heightened, standards and independence in comparison to the Vietnam War era. The media's forfeited vigilance has had a broad impact, permitting a host of other problems to continue obliquely.

In terms of modern information technologies, the U.S. government has behaved in ways that resemble the actions of repellant tyrants. The American government in the NCE has become an adversary—sometimes by way of corporate proxy—of information freedom, as evidenced by the government's dramatic and underhanded attacks on Wikileaks. And under the Obama administration, the U.S. government set a new record in pursuing whistleblowers—unmatched during the Nixon years or any other era.

It is true that, in terms of civil liberties, America has been shocked and awed before. To some degree, the NCE fits into a historical pattern, by which the government transgresses against civil liberties in times of war. But in this regard as well, the NCE is also a seam in time. Because when the executive in 1798 passed the Alien and Sedition Act (when the U.S. appeared to be on the verge of war with France), the American people punished President Adams by voting against him in the 1800 election. The laws that in effect curbed speech rights during the world wars had more popular support, but those laws were short lived in comparison to the foreseeable life span of the Patriot Act provisions limiting speech rights in the NCE.

A U.S. president had never authorized the summary execution of a U.S. citizen before by way of a hit list before the NCE. Or at least, not out in the open, as Obama did with Anwar al-Awlaki in Yemen in September 2011. Never before had U.S. presidents imprisoned America's foes on the battlefield as enemy combatants. Unlike prisoners of war, America's detainees in the NCE face the maddening fear of indefinite detention. Even U.S. citizens are subjected to de facto torment in the NCE, as the forced nudity, exposure and solitary confinement of Army Pfc. Bradley Manning indicates.

Throughout its history, the United States has faced off with enemies that observed norms dramatically below what America applied. And presidents past have not used those norms to justify a degradation of U.S. practices. George Washington, for example, issued this order regarding prisoners taken in the Battle of Princeton:

"Treat them with humanity, and let them have no reason to Complain of our Copying the brutal example of the British Army in their treatment of our unfortunate brethren…. Provide every-thing necessary for them on the road." As a matter of policy, America during its revolutionary struggle gave captured British sol-diers quarter, granting them the right to surrender and be kept alive. While some captured British soldiers may have indeed been executed, the killings were not a matter of policy. The British respected no such right of quarter, and took it upon themselves to either capture, or (as was often the case) murder U.S. revolutionaries.

And while Americans knew their fellow citizens were enslaved and languishing at the hands of corrupt Barbary pashas in Northern Africa, acting Secretary of the Navy Samuel Smith cautioned the legendary Commodore Richard Dale in 1801:

"Any prisoners you may take you will treat with humanity and attention, and land them on any part of the Barbary Shore most convenient to you…But you will be careful to select from such Christians as may be on board, whom you will treat kindly and land, when convenient, on some Christian shore."

Also, Smith warned Dale to keep a close eye on his young, spirited subordinates, lest they make the kind of mistakes that U.S. merce-naries have made in the NCE. Indeed, honor here takes a very different meaning here:

"In all cases of clashing with vessels, officers or subjects of other powers, we enjoin on you the most rigorous moderation, conformity to right and reason and suppression of all passions, which might lead to the commitment of our peace or our honor."

Before the NCE, the most egregious violation of civil rights also occurred after America was attacked on its home soil, in response to the Dec. 7, 1941 Japanese attack on Pearl Harbor. And subsequently, America also faced an enemy willing to execute suicide attacks. The number of individuals victimized by WWII-era internment far outstrips the foreigners abused in the NCE. But consider that those of Japanese descent were not brutalized in the way NCE detainees have been. They also did not bear the stigma of being accused of violent, murderous crime, often based on flimsy evidence. What's more, the suffering associated with WWII had a beginning and an end.

It is true that during the final months of the American civil war after the North decided to halt prison exchanges, prisoners of war from both sides suffered de facto abuse amid acute shortages and filthy, overcrowded conditions. Prisoners died in large percentages due to disease, starvation and exposure. But those deaths were caused by privation and force majeure.

Also, there are instances of torture in U.S. prisons even today and there were horrific experimentations on Guatemalan and other prisoners in the '40s, '50s and '60s in America. There is no minimizing the cruelty of those events. But in the early years of the NCE, torture and abuse became a matter of U.S. policy, by way of enhanced interrogation techniques, willful blindness to abuse and selective accountability. Never before has torture been inflicted in a chillingly premeditated, officially sanctioned manner and approved by the U.S. president. In committing such abuse, America violated not only its signed treaties but also its oldest traditions.

What's more, before 9/11, the U.S. Treasury, along with the Federal Reserve, had never underwritten the reckless bets of private U.S. banks with taxpayer money. Nor had the Federal Reserve relaxed monetary policy to such a degree that financial institutions were, in effect, hit with a tsunami of free liquidity.

Much has been written about the waning of America's superpower preeminence. But in the NCE, there is perhaps something broader, more alarming, to wring our hands over in America—a trend more worrisome than a potential sharing of our #1 status. America may well remain the alpha power far into the future—vis a vis other countries. But it is the wellbeing of its own citizens that could collapse.

The cultural and political currents of the NCE have an undertow. But if this analysis seems grim, there is also a hopeful subtext here. If the United States has self-inflicted most of its harm, it can reassess and recover. It holds the power to change course.

CHAPTER 28
ABOUT MULTICULTURALISM

In the Third World, people often have a sense of time that projects far into the past and the future. There is a patience and forbearance for the amount of effort that long-term efforts require. Individuals often have a rooted sense of belonging, in terms of ancestry and geography. They have always known the members of their extended families, spanning many generations. They have an understanding of where they fit into the world and the continuum of the time. They also have an intimate familiarity with infancy and old age. Often, they have a connection to the soil and the food they eat.

Many individuals in the Third World have a sense of their own significance by virtue of the fact that they are alive and belong to a transcendental maker. Their spiritual life arises organically from their everyday existence. There is a balance and seamlessness between private, political, social and religious spheres. Often, an organized religion is the direct and implicit driver of everyday life, from morning until night.

It is clear that those aspects of life can be inherently fulfilling to human beings. And for a multitude of people around the globe, those realities form their identity and existence. Those of us in the First world can only peer into that world with a sense of wonder.

No society can offer every conceivable form of satisfaction to its individuals. The rigors of the industrialized world often negate much of the human fulfillment that arises so spontaneously in the Third World. Many of us, especially in America—still a great melting pot—are the children of immigrants. And so we are separated by our ancestry by an ocean or land mass. Many of us must reckon with the practical requirements that come with competing in a modern, relentless economy. Few of us have any idea of where the food we eat comes from or have any direct participation in growing it.

Many Americans are religious and are involved in a religious institution. And those spiritual endeavors are often cordoned off from the rest of everyday life. Those of us Americans that live in cities interact with an enormous amount of people professionally and socially and often have only the most superficial understanding of them. In order to keep up with the pace of life, it is necessary to keep many natural questions and misgivings compartmentalized in a mental corner.

And so the business of identifying one culture as more desirable to another has largely been called off in the modern world—a consensus known as multiculturalism. If the preceding pages seemed to imply that American culture and traditions are superior, than that is an impression that needs correcting. No culture is better than another. There are trade-offs in all forms of government and societal organization. What's more, the customs and traditions that thrive in some countries cannot always be transferred to another, due to the existing environment, climate, resources, etc.

But there is a cultural context for institutional progress in the sense that most Westerners understand and appreciate it. And America is orientated towards that kind of institutional modernity. And so specifically for Americans, a deterioration in the cultural environment that hosts institutional integrity is problematic.

Other inhabitants of the world might well chose otherwise—and have a dignified right to self-determination. Americans, meanwhile, have decided on what an evolved society looks like, by their own standards. They should be duly warned, therefore, if it is being threatened.

Statistically speaking, fewer Americans have to face the grief of losing a child in infancy or losing a wife in childbirth. Americans do not have to submit to any religious authority. In terms of skilled work, Americans have the widest array of options on the planet. And the breadth of political and personal freedoms remains, even in the NCE, to be remarkably vast and accommodating.

Many Americans also have access to technology that can dramatically facilitate important projects and feed curiosities. Americans enjoy a large amount of physical mobility, given the ease with which we can settle, and then move, from one place to another. We enjoy a unique ability to start a business and other types of life ambitions.

And so most Americans put all that on balance and decide that the trade-offs are pretty good. We seem to have a very good deal, in relation to the inhabitants of much of the rest of the world. Many of us take pride in the life we have carved out for our nuclear family and would not choose to reside under any other system.

Indeed, many of us enjoy so many benefits that it becomes extraordinarily difficult to understand why individuals in other parts of the world would not labor with abandon to create an identical system. We cannot understand why some societies would not uphold and respect women's rights, or freedom of the press, or democracy, or a variety of other aspects of modern democracies. All of those institutional building blocks are regarded by many Americans as universal rights that are unassailable.

But those rights are also a challenge to traditional mores, such as women's role in the home and in raising children. Freedom of the press and democracy can be seen as a threat to stability that has been hard for some societies to come by. For some people, having religion predominate in all aspects of life is more important than individual rights.

In other words, many human beings would opt for the political and social centrality of religion over economic development—if given a choice. Indeed, economic development itself can be viewed warily. The rights and practices that many Americans and other First Worlders view as universal are not universally embraced.

In relative terms, the United States has been a model of high conduct towards its own citizens, even if the standards have fallen in the NCE. But abroad, U.S. standards have long been far lower. And that U.S. behavior is therefore linked, in the minds of many foreigners, with the American model itself. Many foreigners associate U.S. military action and other policies with the U.S. system.

It seems extraordinarily arrogant to attempt to erect U.S.-style institutions and modalities in foreign lands. Countries in the Third World may come to surprise wealthy countries in reconciling modernity and the exigencies of a global economy with their mores. Even the most traditional societies might find a way to afford women the space and realm to develop life ambitions. Modern technologies, such as the Internet, may come to play a role in that reconciliation. And Third World countries can harness the tenderness and dignity of their religions to effectively safeguard the welfare children, women and ethnic and religious minorities.

The United States must always support those values that its citizens consider universal, but not by coercion. Individuals around the world may have very different ideas about their future and welfare. The United States and other wealthy country must respect the right of foreigners to self determination—another "universal" principle that is sometimes in competition with others.

The United States has more or less come to an end of history on how to keep its complex economic, social and political machinery running smoothly. Crucial to that machinery is the separation of church and state; the role of a vibrant and independent press; the balance of powers and due process. Most Americans have already decided on the importance of those foundations. And given the heterogeneity of American society, there is no turning back.

The Third World must find its own way forward. Americans may be struggling with some ambivalence towards capitalism and related issues, but they recognize the underpinnings of democratic integrity—which have held up well for so long. The American way of life depends on a distinction from the modalities that prevail in so much of the world. There is no alternative to keeping the American social and economic engine running apace.

www.ingramcontent.com/pod-product-compliance
Lightning Source LLC
Chambersburg PA
CBHW070627290526
45790CB00001B/17